THE
FLORIDA
KEYS

Also by Joy Williams

NOVELS

State of Grace
The Changeling
Breaking and Entering

SHORT STORIES

Taking Care
Escapes

THE FLORIDA KEYS

A History & Guide

Eighth Edition

Joy Williams

Illustrations by Robert Carawan

Random House • New York

LIBRARY OF CONGRESS CATALOGING-IN-PUBLICATION DATA

Williams, Joy.
The Florida Keys: a history & guide/by Joy Williams:
illustrations by Robert Carawan.
p.   cm.
Includes index
ISBN 0-679-76977-3 (pbk.)
1. Florida Keys (Fla.)—Description and travel—Guidebooks.
2. Florida Keys (Fla.)—History.   I. Title.
F317.M7W54   1991
917.59'410463—dc20   91-52658

Random House website address: http://www.randomhouse.com/

Printed in the United States of America on acid-free paper

2 4 6 8 9 7 5 3

Eighth Edition

For Caitlin, the one and only

CONTENTS

Introduction   ix

The Upper Keys   1
  Key Largo   8
  Diving   12
  John Pennecamp Coral Reef State Park   15
  Where to Stay   20
  Where to Eat   22

  Tavernier   25
  Plantation Key   28
  The Backcountry   32
  Windley Key   37
  Upper Matecumbe Key   41
  Islamorada   42
  Where to Stay   43
  Where to Eat   46

  Lignumvitae and Indian Keys   48
  Lower Matecumbe Key   53
  Long Key   57

The Middle Keys   61
  Key Vaca   71
  Marathon   74
  Where to Stay   76
  Where to Eat   77

  Fishing   78
  The Seven-Mile Bridge   85
  Bahia Honda Key   87

The Lower Keys   93
  Big Pine Key   98
  No Name Key   104
  The Torch Keys   106
  Ramrod Key   111

Cudjoe Key   113
Sugarloaf Key   117
Stock Island and Approaches to Key West   123

Key West   127
The Streets   131
Changes and Confusions   132
Mystery and History   134
Collapse and Resurrection, Collapse and Restoration   139
Tourist Town   143
A Walk Up Duval Street   174
Beaches and Salt Ponds   186
Art and Antiques   189
Newspapers   191
Writers   192
Forts, Towers, and Museums   205
Old Town   214
The Graveyard   223
Where to Stay   225
Where to Eat   241

Bars   252
Fishing, Diving, and the Waters Beyond   257
Fort Jefferson and the Dry Tortugas   261

Index   267

INTRODUCTION

The Florida Keys do not run due south. They drift southwest, Route 1 running more east–west than north–south. The Gulf side is actually Florida Bay, the upper reaches of which belong to the Everglades. The Bay side is called the "backcountry" or "outback." The Atlantic side is actually the Straits of Florida, where wide Hawk Channel runs out from shore to the reef, which stretches the length of the Keys. Beyond the reef is the Gulf Stream—"out front"—that great oceanic river whose demarcation is clearly seen, the water being a profound and fabulous blue. Beyond the Gulf Stream lies, then, the ocean.

The Keys run from Biscayne Bay to the Dry Tortugas, a distance of some 180 miles. No road runs to the keys north of Key Largo—Sands, Elliott, and Old Rhodes—and the Tortugas are 70 watery, wild miles from Key West. The distance accessible by car is some 106 miles—from Key Largo to Key West. That road, originally built in the 1930s, replaced Henry Flagler's Florida East Coast Extension railroad line, an amazing piece of engineering which had linked the Keys since 1912 and which was destroyed by a hurricane in 1935. The mile markers (MM #——) referred to in this guide—green signs with white numerals, posted on the right-hand shoulder—were first placed along the Keys by the railroad.

On a map the Keys look fairly improbable—and Route 1, the line that drops down their sprinkled length, improbable too. The possibilities are vast, but the road itself is simple, which explains why some travelers begin at Key Largo, hang on to the steering wheel, and don't stop until Key West, heeding the billboards' urging, GO ALL THE WAY, with all its attendant, randy implications of reckless fulfillment. Other travelers arrive in the Keys, love them, stick close to Islamorada, and wouldn't dream of going all the way, considering Key West weird if not bizarre, as though that singular and raffish place were at the bottom of an ever-darkening well.

But of course the Keys don't really go from light to dark. The Keys sparkle downward, warm and bright, full of light and air and a bit of intrigue. The Keys are relaxed, a little reckless. The

Keys are water and sky, horizon, daybreak, spectacular sunsets, the cup of night. The least interesting thing about them is the road, but the road, as is its nature, allows entrance. The road is the beginning.

There are some automobile guides, such as the old Sanborn Guides to Mexico, that are wonderfully jittery backseat companions, not pointing out cathedrals and markets (because the route in question is manifestly lacking in cathedrals and markets) but taking great pains to point out everything else. A child selling an iguana is *here;* half a kilometer down the road you will pass a most peculiarly shaped boulder; a bit beyond that there was once a Pemex station, though unfortunately a Pemex station is no longer there, only a tire dump; two kilometers away the road curves. . . . And so on.

The Keys once lent themselves to this sort of innocent treatment, and in a way they still do. There is the road, and there are the dutiful descending markers accompanying your every mile, suggesting that a trip is little more than coloring your own experience between provided lines. At MM #—— there is an egret; at MM #—— there's a pretty view between two violet jacaranda trees; at MM #——, if you can wait that long, is a bar where the bartender wears live snakes wrapped around her neck and wrists—her "pretties," she calls them. . . . And so on.

Time passes, of course. The snake lady is run over one night as she is crossing the road. Someone builds his dream house in front of the pretty view, cutting down the jacaranda trees in the process. But the Keys, though no longer the empty, silent stretches they once were, still markedly lack (you might as well be told) historical and cultural monuments. And the osprey still builds his nest larger each year at MM #——. And the tarpon still roll and flash each spring under the bridge at MM #——. And certainly at MM #—— the disreputable bar remains. The best way to enjoy the Keys is still to seek out their simplicity and their eccentricity.

The Keys had been largely ignored until the 1970s, the lack of fresh water being the real inhibitor to development. The Navy had built an 18-inch pipeline in 1942 that ran the 130 miles from the Everglades wells in Florida City to Key West. The water took a week to travel the route. In 1982 the old pipe was replaced with a 36-inch pipe, increasing the quantity fourfold, providing indeed an oversupply of water and accelerating building and population growth. Oddly, the pipeline, as well as the construction of new bridges and wider roads, took place seven years after the state had designated Monroe County, which is the Keys, an "area of critical state concern" in an attempt to slow development (a perfectly nice word that unfortunately has been stolen away—undoubtedly while we were not looking—by the developers). In the 1980s realtors dressed up in wood rat costumes and organized motorcades and rallies to protest new state guidelines that would restrict development in the Keys. It's true. People who felt themselves endangered by environmental laws dressed up like the cotton mouse and the wood rat—present inhabitants of mangrove swamp and hammock—and, aroused by lawyers and politicians, made a long, noisy trip down the highway to Key West, where the governor was speaking, picking up additional incensed rat- and mouse-garbed people along the way. This was typical oddball Keys, but in this case, peculiarity had a threateningly modern and consumptive edge, which is familiarly Floridian.

W. C. Barron, the founder of Wall Street's *Barron's,* said early in this century that the only values in the state of Florida are the values created by man. This was how the state was perceived by the wealthy who came from elsewhere to exploit it. Florida, that splendid, subtle, once fabulous state, has been exploited, miscomprehended and misused, drained and diked, filled in and paved over. The values of man have been imposed with a vengeance.

Half of the historic Everglades is now farms, groves, and cities, and this marvelous ecosystem isn't working anymore. Over the last 50 years, 90 percent of the 'Glades' wading-bird population has been lost. To read the roll of its endangered species is heartbreaking. The reef is becoming increasingly stressed by sewage that flows quickly through the porous rock of the Keys and into the ocean, as well as by agricultural runoff from the mainland that gets dumped into Florida Bay from the Everglades. The rat-garbed protestors of the '80s recrudesced in the '90s as noisy foes of the National Marine Sanctuary, a designation conceived in 1990 that would protect and preserve the waters around the Keys, which need every bit of protection and preservation that they can get.

In 1996, in a nonbinding referendum, Keys residents voted 55 percent to 45 percent against the final Sanctuary plan. The plan had been five years in the making, during which time it underwent extensive public review. There were fears of a federal takeover, fears that people's property rights would be stripped away, despite the fact that the Sanctuary was intended to protect water—specifically 2,800 square miles of water from Key Largo to the Dry Tortugas. It was not designed to protect a pristine ecosystem, but rather as an emergency measure to prolong the life of an already impaired environment. Because of local public concerns, only one half of 1 percent of the Sanctuary waters have their use restricted—such as "no take" zones—compared with the original proposal of 14 percent. Even a half percent was too much sanctuary for the opponents who urged voters through print and radio ads not to "surrender." The Sanctuary, despite the local vote, was endorsed by the state and implemented. Its one half of 1 percent of restricted use survived further cuts and will be monitored as a research and replenishment preserve.

The bill is coming. It's not like the bill from a wonderful restaurant, Louie's, for example. It's not the bill for the lovely fresh snapper, the lovely wines, the lovely brownie with bourbon ice cream and caramel sauce at the lovely table beside the lovely sea. It's the bill for all our environmental mistakes of the past. The big bill.

"Keys" comes from the Spanish word *cayos,* for "little islands." The Keys are little, and they are fragile. They cannot sustain any more "dream houses" or "dream resorts." The sustaining dream is in the natural world—the world that each of us should respect, enjoy, and protect so that it may be enjoyed again—the world to which one can return and be refreshed.

Time passes. There are more of the many, and they want too much. What the traveler wants, of course, is not development but adventure, and this is still possible in the Keys. The Keys have always been different. May they remain that way. Here's to them.

THE
UPPER KEYS
Key Largo
to Long Key

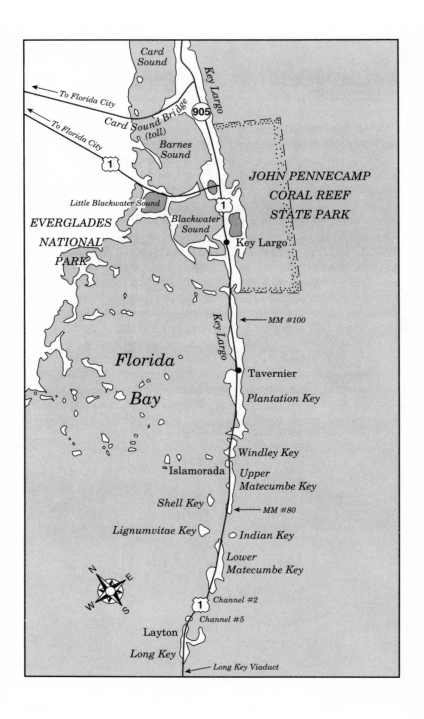

THE Spanish first found the Keys during Ponce de León's 1513 expedition and promptly called them, with inquisitional flair, Los Martires—the martyrs—because they seemed twisted and tortured. They logged out the mahogany that grew here early on, and probably enslaved the native Caloosa Indians, but they were indifferent to exploring or settling these stony islands. There was no gold, no fresh water, and many, many bugs. They mapped and named the Keys principally as an aid to their ships, which, laden with gold and silver, used the Florida Straits as their route from the New World back to the Old.

The first settlement in the Keys was at Cayo Hueso, or Key West, in 1822, more than two decades before Florida became a state. The other keys remained pretty much deserted until 1874, when the government surveyed them and plotted land for homesteading. The early homes were primitive, built from the local "coastal store"—the beach—with wood and materials washed up from shipwrecks. The biggest plague of the settlers was mosquitoes. The mosquito was king of the Keys. Mosquitoes blackened the sides of houses and obscured the shapes of animals. Mosquitoes blackened the cheesecloth which people swathed their heads in as they slept. If you swung a pint cup, the saying went, you'd come up with a quart full of mosquitoes. Smudge pots burned constantly inside and outside the driftwood houses. Burlap bags filled with wood chips soaked in old engine oil were hung to drip over stagnant water holes in an attempt to kill mosquito larvae. With mosquitoes gnawing on them day and night, a few pioneering families nevertheless managed to claw a living from what one writer of the time referred to as "worthless, chaotic fragments of coral reef, limestone and mangrove swamp."

The people who first made their homes in the Upper Keys were hardworking Methodist fishermen and farmers. They spoke with a Cockney accent, were closely interrelated, and bore the names Albury, Pinder, Johnson, Russell, and Lowe.

Their more flamboyant wrecking neighbors were in Key West, but life in the "outside keys" was earnestly drab, farming rock being somewhat Sisyphean in nature. But farm the rock they did, burning and clearing the land and planting coconuts, citrus, pineapple, and melons in the ashy interstices between the coral. They homesteaded on the Atlantic, and transportation between the scattered houses was by shallow-draft boat. These boats also took the produce out to deeper waters, where it was off-loaded onto schooners which sailed to Key West as well as to northern ports.

In 1905 Henry Flagler, a former partner of John D. Rockefeller in Standard Oil and president of the Florida East Coast Railroad, began extending the train track from Homestead, through the Everglades, to Key Largo. Flagler was always pushing southward, legend has it, because his wives were forever wanting to be warmer. (Flagler had three wives. The middle one, Ida Alice, went mad after finding too much solace in her Ouija board. The planchette kept telling her she was destined to marry the czar of Russia. The strict divorce laws of Florida were changed for Flagler. Sailing through the legislature and signed by the governor in a swift two and a half weeks, a new provision made incurable insanity grounds for divorce. Flagler disposed of Ida Alice and quickly wed a bubbly lady named Mary Lily who liked bourbon and laudanum but avoided the Ouija board.) Other railroad tycoons thought Flagler's interest in Florida absurd, considering it a worthless country, save for its climate. Flagler had the great field of Florida to himself. He pushed down from St. Augustine to Palm Beach, and then to Miami (then known as Fort Dallas), but shipping out from that point was limited by the 12-foot depth of Biscayne Bay. Key West, with its fine deepwater port, was the perfect terminus for the Florida East Coast Railway. With the Panama Canal being built, Flagler saw a rosy future for commerce, with rail and ferry lines extending to South America. Flagler was 75 years old when construction began on his oversea railway and died only a few months after the project was completed in 1912.

For seven years the track and train, freighted with peril and mishap, inched their way down the Keys to Key West. Settlers in the Upper Keys longed for the railroad to be completed, believing that it would put them in closer touch with their markets and make them wealthy. But eventually the railroad meant the end of their little coastal communities and their large fruit farms. Key West became a receiving center for produce from all over the Caribbean and South America, and cheaper fruit was introduced to the mainland. Too, the few inches of Keys topsoil that had supported such exotics as Porto Rico, Abbakka Queen, and Sugar Loaf pineapples was soon robbed of all nutrients, and the plantations failed. Towns like Planter, which once shipped out a million crates of limes, pineapples, tomatoes, and melons a year by schooner, simply disappeared, a victim of sporadic hurricanes and the railroad. Other communities that sprang up along the track vanished too, when the 1935 hurricane blew the train away.

It was this hurricane—*the* hurricane, the nameless one—that made the history of the Upper Keys. It swept across the Matecumbe Keys on September 2, 1935, with an 18-foot tidal wave and 200-mph winds. Matecumbe is a name of obscure origins, but it may be a corruption of the Spanish *mata hombre*—"kill man"—which was also the meaning of Cuchiyaga, the Indian name for the island. In any case, it was a fated place. More than 800 people died in the hurricane, many of them members of the second "Bonus Army" of World War I veterans who, seeking early military benefits, had been hired instead by the Federal Emergency Relief Administration for work projects across the country. In this instance they were building a road from Lower Matecumbe to Grassy Key so that the ferry route could be eliminated. Most of them died when the train sent down to rescue them was blown off the tracks in Islamorada. Of the 11 cars, only the 106-ton locomotive, *Old 447,* remained upright, saving the lives of the engineer and the fireman. Many of the dead were burned in funeral pyres overseen by the National Guard in the sunny days after the storm, while others were buried in a common crypt marked by a monument in Islamorada.

Besides winds, the history here is in the waters—in the wrecks and reefs. The waters off the Upper Keys conceal a remarkable number of wrecks, from Spanish galleons to British frigates to World War II freighters. Cannon from the HMS *Winchester,* a 60-gun British frigate which went down in a hurricane in 1695, are displayed on dry ground at Pennecamp Park, and the adventurous diver can frequently see less restored and

CONCHS

Englishmen, descendants of the adventurers who settled Eleuthera and the Great Abaco Islands in the Bahamas, explored the good fishing and turtling grounds off the Keys in the late 1700s but did not settle on the land, preferring instead to wait offshore for ships to founder on the reef. Particularly popular were the waters of the Upper Keys, where ships went down regularly. "Wrecking," which occasionally bordered on piracy, was much practiced by the Bahamians, who would salvage the cargo from sinking ships and sell the goods in the port of Nassau. Shortly after Spain ceded Florida to the United States in 1821, however, the Bahamians were forced to become residents of this country if they wanted to continue to engage in wrecking. They began to move their families to the new town of Key West, where an admiralty court had been established to legalize and regulate what had become a major industry. These Bahamians were called "Conchs" (pronounced *Konks*), after the large sea snails they ate in considerable amounts and perhaps because they used the conch shell as a trumpet. With a hole correctly placed at the tip, the shell could produce a plaintive wail heard for up to half a mile, a way of announcing, "Wreck ashore."

The strange collective nickname may have been used disparagingly at first, but today a Conch, a lifelong resident of the Keys, descendant of Conchs, is proud of the shrewd and stubborn individuality the name represents. Key West will maintain that the only true Conch is a person born on the "Rock" of Key West, where the birth of a baby was once announced by putting a conch shell on a stick in the front yard. It should be remembered, on the other hand, that until well into the 1900s *all* Keys babies went to Key West to be born, there being no doctors or midwives elsewhere.

The creature that began all this associative lore—the conch—has been mindlessly overharvested and, almost gone, is at last protected in Keys waters. Restaurant conch is not local. Even though conchs mate and lay eggs at the same time, they just can't keep up with our demands on them.

considerably wetter and blurrier artifacts. A wreck that is not present but that has left its contemporary and eternal mark is that of the *Wellwood,* a 400-foot Turkish freighter which ran aground within the park's boundaries in the fall of 1984. The *Wellwood,* filled with chicken feed and captained, it would certainly seem, with some incompetence by a C. H. Vickers, ignored the 45-foot flashing light that marks Molasses Reef on the southernmost boundary of the park and plowed into the reef, annihilating four acres of living coral. It made a portion of that fabulous tract—all the peaks and valleys and colorful caves bright with life—as flat and as gray as a parking lot.

The reef that runs along the Atlantic coast of the Keys, close to the great Gulf Stream, is fantastically fragile. All reefs are complex and highly particular life-forms, requiring lots of sunlight and clear, warm water. The Florida Keys tract (the only reef in the continental United States) exists at the northernmost limit of tropical reef development. It is threatened by this potentially chilly location. It is threatened by its own wonderful accessibility. It is threatened by development on land, by boat

---

THE 18-MILE STRETCH

People have been familiar with the 18-mile stretch between Florida City and Key Largo for many years. You're heading for the Keys! No development, the road narrow, unlit, burrowing through the sounds of Blackwater and Card, scruffy and wild. And twice you'd see the big string of signs: PATIENCE PAYS—PASSING LANE THREE MILES. It was challenging, different. You were in transition. It was a satisfying experience.

Now the state plans to four-lane the road. The existing roadbed is 34 feet wide; the proposed one will be 130 feet. It will take six years, cost $154 million, and fill in 150 acres of wetlands. One of the reasons given for the necessity of such extensive "improvement" is better hurricane evacuation, although the road, built at the same elevation, would not be impervious to flooding, and the official hurricane shelter for the Keys would continue to be Florida International University in Miami, 20 miles north of the beginning of the stretch.

bilge, by silt dredged up from marinas, by the effluent and rain-water runoff from condo complexes and parking lots. It is threatened by overuse and misuse. With all this close at hand, it seems cruel and unnecessary for fate to bring tons of chicken feed blundering out of the darkness for the singular purpose of extinguishing part of beautiful Molasses Reef, but blunder out of the darkness the chicken feed did. (More recently, a 147-foot freighter carrying candy and cigarettes deliberately grounded on Western Sambo Reef in the Lower Keys during a winter storm, demolishing that.) The Park Service has marked off the damaged tract with yellow cone-shaped buoys and they are monitoring it for signs of regeneration, which they do not expect to occur. The part of the reef visited by the wayward *Wellwood* has ceased to exist. It has become part of Keys history, as gone as the Caloosa Indians, the railroad, and the green turtle.

KEY LARGO

By car there are two approaches to the Keys. The most com-monly traveled is Route 1, the stretch that skirts the savannah of the Everglades, crosses Jewfish Creek (which is part of the Intracoastal Waterway) and broad Lake Surprise, so named by the first railroad survey party in 1902, who apparently had not anticipated its existence. The other, slightly longer way of entering the Keys is over the Card Sound Bridge—a toll that will deposit you farther up in the mangrove and hardwood ham-mock land of North Key Largo.

Sometimes it's nice to contemplate things that *aren't* there. The 11-mile strip between the wealthy and very private Ocean Reef Club (once considered by the FBI to be one of the most secure resorts in the country before it was battered by Hurri-cane Andrew in 1992) and Card Sound Road's convergence with Route 1 is empty, but grandiose projects have long been planned for this area. In 1955 speculators bought up 1,500 acres of virgin land here and incorporated it as the city of North Key Largo Beach. It was a phantom city with a phantom gov-ernment but with very large intentions. It would be a city of

100,000 people to begin with, which would have increased the population of the Keys by 150 percent. It would be a supercity, of course, with much modern gadgetry, like monorails. The land was rescued from this ghastly inspiration when the Nature Conservancy and the Fish and Wildlife Service purchased it for their Crocodile Lake National Wildlife Refuge. Construction of the notorious "Port Bougainvillea"—described by its developers as "an imitation Mediterranean coastal village" of almost 3,000 units, pocked with "baylets" and man-made lakes—was halted because the very enormity of the project bankrupted its backers. Many other condos and hotels have been planned for Card Sound Road, but so far three homely beasts have prevented them from being built—the alligator, the wood rat, and the cotton mouse. Modest and much maligned but all federally protected endangered species, these three have kept bulldozers from overrunning the Keys.

County Road 905 intersects Route 1 just as you begin to enter Key Largo. One half mile up 905, on the right, is the entrance to **Key Largo Hammocks State Botanical Site**. At 2,000 acres it is one of the largest contiguous tracts of subtropical West Indian hardwood hammock found in the United States. It is right where Port Bougainvillea was going to be built. There's a short nature trail (less than a mile) where you can marvel at the complexity and vegetative variety of a Keys "jungle." Off-limits and behind a tall fence is the ruin of the development's model villas. Some of Key Largo's youths like to access this ruin and practice spray-painting the symbol for anarchy on the rose-colored walls.

There used to be a sign just beyond the one welcoming travelers to the Florida Keys. It said, HELL IS TRUTH SEEN TOO LATE. But it was taken down, probably by a real estate developer.

Key Largo Key was once a series of barely connected keys with a few high ridges. Railroad construction filled in the channels between the islets, leaving us with what we now experience as a single long key which stretches all the way down to Tavernier. A four-lane road runs the length of the key, divided from MM #100 down to MM #92 by a wooded median.

The town of **Key Largo** was originally known as Rock Harbor. Real estate promoters sought to cash in on the publicity given the 1948 Bogart-Bacall movie and circulated a petition to have the name changed. The request was granted by postal authorities in 1952, and Rock Harbor became Key Largo.

The movie *Key Largo,* with the exception of a few interior set scenes shot inside the bar the Caribbean Club, was filmed entirely on a soundstage in Hollywood. The film itself may be drenched with Bogart charisma, but it certainly is counterfeit Keys; director John Huston ornamented the script with California touches such as fog and kelp. However, the fact that the actors never came to Key Largo, and that the film was not shot here, did not faze the town's boosters. Key West had Hemingway, why shouldn't Largo have Bogie? To compound matters, the owner of the Holiday Inn, maintaining that "Key Largo is laden with memories of the great actor," bought the riverboat used in the Bogart movie *The African Queen* (which was filmed mostly in England) and now offers "excursions" in it when it's working from his dock. As a random touch, he has the original Chris-Craft boat that was used in the movie *On Golden Pond* there as well—although there's a suspicion that it's really a double of the boat that was used in the movie, thereby rendering any experience you might have seeing it possibly doubly meaningless.

What Key Largo is far more justifiably known for is the reef, for here is the beautiful and unique **John Pennecamp Coral Reef State Park**. The coral reef is one of the world's most ancient and involved life-forms, and the easy availability of this

The queen conch

spectacular other world is what makes a trip to the Florida Keys so special. The reef, lying between four and seven miles offshore, runs parallel to the Keys from Largo to the Dry Tortugas. It protects the Keys from storms and is also the reason why there are no sandy beaches on these islands—the reef absorbs the roll of waves which, if they came ashore, would gradually wear away rock to sand. The depths at which the most variety of life and geological relief occur is between 15 and 35 feet of water. At greater depths there is not as much diversity, but the corals, sponges, and fish are larger.

The living animals that form and build the reef are coral polyps that feed on plankton—the tiny organisms that float past on ocean currents and become the food of great whales. There are both hard and soft corals. The hard ones have a flexible skeletal structure which undulates in the moving waters. These are the *gorgonians,* named for the snake-haired sisters of Greek myth; they come in shapes of tubes, plumes, whips, and fans and in a multitude of colors. One of the most beautiful and easily recognizable is the common sea fan, colored the most spectacular peacock blue. The hard corals are the castle builders: the brain, the staghorn and elkhorn, the pillar, the star, and the flower corals. Other hard corals have descriptive names like sheet, leaf, saucer, scroll, ribbon, tree, tube, and bush. Some colonies of polyps create massive spiraling structures that can rise as high as 35 feet from the ocean floor or spread out as boulders with deep, swirling convolutions. These coral polyps, building on the dead skeletons of former colonies, have a life span of centuries, but the reef grows with exceptional slowness. Staghorn and elkhorn corals grow only scant inches a year, and a good-sized brain coral may be hundreds of years old. According to Greek legend, coral grew out of the drops of blood of the Gorgon Medusa.

The reef is perhaps the most complicated of all ecosystems, for nowhere else in the animal kingdom do so many organisms live together and participate in such interdependent relationships. More than 500 species of fish live, feed, and are protected in its coraline caves. Some fish, like the dramatically streaked neon gobie, and crustaceans, like the banded coral shrimp, enjoy freedom from predation by grooming other fish of parasites. The gobie inhabits the deep grooves of brain corals, which other fish seem to regard as cleaning stations, while the coral shrimp actually lives within the jaws of the toothy moray eel.

Before marine sanctuaries were established and federal and state laws passed, commercial collectors were dynamiting the reef for coral, as well as removing it with crowbars and even cranes. It's remarkable that there's anything left of the living reef at all. But there is some left and it's enchanting. It's also irreplaceable and unrenewable.

Peculiarly enough, one of the first establishments that greets you as you enter Key Largo is **Shell Man** at MM #106, a "decor" emporium filled with corals yanked out of the peaceful and astounding depths and lined up on dusted shelves beneath fluorescent lights. Mystery has been transformed into mere novelty. (Does someone back home desire a toilet seat with seashells laminated deep within? This is the place to get it, perhaps the only place to get it.) The corals have been imported from the Philippines, since the taking of coral is prohibited in the Keys, but there are no signs posted to tell you of this fact. Instead the place is almost an invitation to the unaware to go diving, discover a pretty piece of coral, break it off, and take it home. *All* corals, including the "soft" sea fans and whips, are protected the entire length of the Keys' 150-mile reef tract. If you see anyone taking coral or harming or molesting other protected marine species—turtles, rays, and manatees—contact the Marine Patrol (743-6542) or, in Pennecamp, the park ranger. The area code for all the Keys, including Key West, is 305.

DIVING

The first of the many dive shops you will see on Key Largo is **Capt. Slate's Atlantis Dive Center** at MM #106.5 (451-3020). Those who dive with Capt. Slate, at least according to the pictures in his brochure, like to put largish dead fish in their mouths and feed them to larger alive fish. If this is not to your fancy, however, Capt. Slate offers the usual—snorkel and scuba charters, instruction, and night dives. Every Friday morning there is a "Creature Feature" extravaganza where you can witness a feeding frenzy among the fish. The Captain has had a relationship for some years now with a large barracuda he calls Psycho.

As well, there are **American Diving Headquarters**, MM #106 (451-0037); **Quiescence**, MM #103.2 (451-2440); **Sea Dwellers**, MM #100 (451-3640); **Ocean Divers**, MM #100 (451-1113); and **Divers' World**, MM #99.5 (451-3200).

Ocean Divers has two 50-foot boats: *Big Red,* which has a catamaran hull; and *Ocean Diver.* The problem with big boats, of course, is that they can carry a lot of people. The benefits are that they have showers and spacious decks and are more stable than smaller boats. The day may not be far off when a divemaster, asked once too often about the Christ of the Deep statue, goes berserk, but amazingly it hasn't happened yet. Ocean Divers will take you there. They also go as far north as the Elbow (see page 18).

Dive shops all along Key Largo Key down to Tavernier dive Pennecamp Park. There is an extensive dive concession within the park itself, but in general you have the potential of visiting a wider variety of reef sites with shops located on Route 1. Make sure you know how many will be aboard so you won't have the disappointment of ending up on a cattle boat. There are heavily dived reefs and there are areas that aren't even named, yet are beautiful and exciting. Many shops offer multi-day dive packages, and some will even arrange for motel or camping accommodations. (Conversely, most of the larger motels in the area offer dive packages.) Rates usually run around $35, with about one and a half hours of diving time. Gear is extra. Wet suits can be rented for $15; not a bad idea in the winter, when even first-felt-warm waters can turn chilly after an hour. Other equipment, such as underwater cameras, can also be rented.

For experienced scuba divers, a dive at night is an especially remarkable experience. The coral polyps open like flowers to feed on the plankton floating by, and the water is lit by luminescent organisms corkscrewing through the blackness. Some fish, like the triggerfish and the big blue-and-green parrotfish, snuggle into crevices and seem to sleep at night. Others, like the bizarrely beaked filefish, come out to eat their favorite foods, stinging fire-coral and black long-spined sea urchins. Many fish change or lose their colors at night, while sea fans seem veined in fire. Big-eyed squid appear—and octopuses, those boneless, enigmatic forms which, because of their highly developed nervous systems, are believed to be more intelligent than anything in the sea, except for mammals.

Contact **Reef Relief Environmental Education Center** in Key West for their brochure on the proper ways to see and protect the reef when snorkeling and diving. Call 294-3100. The Center, located at 210 William Street in Key West, has great videos and attitude, and a little shop with books and enviro gifts. Reef Relief is an important grassroots organization started in 1986. If you think everyone has been educated by now regarding the importance of preserving the Keys' water wildlife, think again. There are still some people out there hard to reach. A 4-ton, 30-foot minke whale stranded and died in the Lower Keys in the spring of '97. The whale had been shot five times with a variety of different-caliber weapons.

The new fad in Key Largo is **Jules' Undersea Lodge**, a two-room "hotel" at the bottom of the lagoon. "Through this wonderful experience of sub-surface habitation, we open to the public one of the planet's last frontiers," one of the owners says. This particular frontier is only 100 feet from shore and 30 feet below the surface; it has air-conditioning, television, a VCR, a microwave, telephones, and bathroom facilities. You can either stay from one in the afternoon to eleven the next morning for $325 or five in the afternoon to nine the next morning for $225. You're provided with hookah-type diving gear for when you venture outside. If you're not a certified diver, you can learn how to use this equipment in a resort course that costs another $50–$75. You can have lobster, steak, or chicken for dinner, and Belgian waffles for breakfast, but no alcohol is permitted unless you're on your honeymoon; then you're allowed some champagne. There are plans to create a six-acre undersea leisure park here—sort of a Snorkel World. Jules' is located at the Koblick Marine Center at MM #103.2 (451-2353).

Another fad is swimming with a dolphin. Some people just don't feel a Florida vacation is complete unless they do this. Embarrassed to go to a dolphin "show," they feel more comfortable taking part in a program supposedly designed for the greater good of all. Thus, **Dolphins Plus**, whose goal is to accli-

The coral reef

mate dolphins to humans so they (the dolphins) can advance the cause of animal-assisted therapy with the mentally and physically handicapped. (The **Dolphin Research Center** on Grassy Key [see pages 65–68] has a number of "therapy" dolphins as well.) Eighty dollars buys you some unstructured time with the dolphins. You should be a good swimmer and like to swim underwater. Still, you might not achieve direct contact. The dolphins might not be in the mood. The "structured" program, however, guarantees contact because the dolphins are being trained to assist people with problems (even though they may not be *your* problems). This costs $90. Call 451-1993 for reservations and directions to this facility, which is back oceanside at around MM #100.

JOHN PENNECAMP CORAL REEF STATE PARK

America's first underwater state park was established in 1960 and named for one of its most dedicated and determined advocates, John Pennecamp, a Miami newspaper editor who was also instrumental in creating Everglades National Park. Park waters stretch more than 21 miles, from Carysfort Reef to Molasses Reef and inshore to the coastline. With the additional protected waters of the Key Largo National Marine Sanctuary, the preserve extends more than eight miles into the ocean and encompasses 178 square miles. There are two small beaches on park grounds (in the shallow waters off one of them, the state has reconstructed a galleon wreck) and two nature trails, one winding by boardwalk through the mangroves. But the real meaning of the place is beneath the water's surface.

If this is your first time out to see the reef (remember, the reef lies several miles offshore—you can't just wade out, dip your face down, and see it), your first glimpse of the fanciful, lacy, undulating terrain and the beautiful bright fishes in the clear water will be startling. You will first be amazed. Then may follow—fleetingly—suspicion. Has the place been stocked? Have the fish been placed here by the concessionaire? Have these fish somehow, even, been *hired*? But your suspicions are unfounded. They fade away and wonder returns.

The entrance to Pennecamp is at MM #102.5. For camping reservations and information, call the park at 451-1202. For information on scuba tours and boat and equipment rental, call 451-6322. Entry fees at Pennecamp and all state recreation areas are $4 a car and 50¢ per person. Camping is $25 per night.

The park offers several types of diving trips and programs (for example, a one-day course in scuba diving costs $130 and a four-day certification course costs $350). A snorkeling tour leaves at 9 A.M., noon, and 3 P.M. and costs $25 per person. A snorkeling and sailing tour on a 38-foot catamaran costs $32 per person for a half day. Scuba trips cost $37 per person and leave at 9:30 A.M. and 1:30 P.M. The dive shop rents all equipment as well as a variety of boats. A 19-foot motorboat costs $95 for a half day, $160 for a full day. Other reef boats can be rented for about $25 an hour. High deposits are required on boat rentals. If you do decide to go out on your own, it's important that you be able to read charts well. The park service has white mooring buoys scattered around the most frequently dived sites. Tie up to these. If you must anchor, do so on a sandy spot.

Never anchor on the coral itself. Careless anchoring is highly destructive to the reef, for when coral is broken, the wound invites invasion by algae and other organisms which spread rapidly and can destroy an entire colony. When diving, always display the red-and-white "diver down" flag and stay within 100 feet of your boat. A lot of boats are cruising around these waters, and the flag speaks of your presence.

There are nine diving sites in the park, each distinguished by some fascinating peculiarity. Park-based dive boats usually go to White Bank Dry Rocks, French Reef, and Molasses Reef. The **Benwood** wreck, a mile and a half north of French Reef, is a popular scuba destination. The luckless freighter was first torpedoed by a German submarine during World War II and while limping home was then accidentally rammed by another boat. Her hull was used for bombing practice for a while, and then she was dynamited and sunk. Her battered and scattered remains are now host to large schools of fish and home to a secretive and commandingly repellent moray eel.

White Bank Dry Rocks is the largest of the snorkeling reefs. It is a shallow garden wealthy with staghorn and elkhorn beds and star and brain coral heads, and full of the brilliant flitting movement of small tropical fish of dots and stripes and bands and bars, tiny wrasses—fish so darkly purple their bones are blue—curious and fearless angelfish, rock beauties, triggerfish, and damselfish (these last being the most aggressive fish on the reef and the ones most likely to bite you—this dismaying prospect tempered, however, by the fact that they are no more than two inches long). This is a perfect reef for the novice diver to explore. **French Reef** is primarily a scuba site, noted for its caves, winding canyons, and large fish. **Molasses** is the biggest reef in the park and has what many divers consider the greatest variety of both terrain and fish. There are shipwrecks, and sandy channels winding through towering coral wells. It's very likely you'll see beautiful manta rays here.

Dive shops on Route 1 visit the middle and more northern areas of the park. If you have a particular site or wreck that you are interested in exploring, inquire, remembering that trips are dependent on visibility and weather and that visibility in winter can sometimes be disappointing. **Carysfort Reef** (named, with an inexplicable alteration of the last letter, for the HMS

Carysford, a frigate which ran aground there in 1770) is located at the extreme northern end of the park and is marked by a 100-foot lighthouse. This is a nice diving area and not a particularly busy one. There's a lot of staghorn coral at Carysfort. The main reef is at 35 feet, sloping down to a beautiful sandy floor at 72.

The **Elbow**, marked by a navigational light, is the closest of the reefs to the cleansing and swift Gulf Stream, making visibility almost always excellent. There are more shipwrecks located around here than almost anywhere else, and the fish have been fed so frequently by divers that they seem actually expectant of handouts.

Key Largo Dry Rocks is the site of the nine-foot **Christ of the Deep Statue**, a duplicate of the Christ of the Abysses Statue in the Mediterranean off Genoa. The bronze Christ with upraised arms placed here in 20 feet of water was donated to the park by an Italian industrialist and sports spearfisherman. Much flowery rhetoric swirls about it. A park bulletin, reprinting the original dedication of the Abysses statue, says, "The dead shall no longer be lonely. . . . Ships and phantoms of ships will crowd around Him; living men and dead men. The shadows of all those who lost their lives in the sea will be present, without discrimination of nationality, blood or color. With His liberal gesture of invitation, He will welcome everybody." And so on. The statue's liberal and equitable invitation is blurred frequently by algae. "It's real pretty when it's all scrubbed up," a park ranger says. "We've got to get out there more and scrub her up." What can't be scrubbed up is algae-smothered coral, and this is becoming an increasing problem throughout the park and sanctuary. A large area near the Dry Rocks is covered with green-brown coats of algae that look like fur, and stringy yellow strands of algae that look like hair. Wherever does this gross stuff come from? you might ask. (See Florida Bay, page 29.)

Not far from the Christ of the Deep is **Grecian Rocks**, a good reef for snorkelers because it has shallow waters and very little current. Close by is the intriguing **Cannon Patch**, where a number of cannon from unknown ships lie scattered about. Farther south, beyond the park's boundaries, is pretty **Conch Reef** and the site of three Spanish galleons; *Capitana, El Infante,* and *San Jose y las Animas,* all shipwrecked here in a

THE GLASS-BOTTOM BOAT

The **San Jose** leaves three times a day from the park, at 9:15 A.M., at 12:15 P.M., and at 3. The two-and-a-half-hour trip costs $13 for adults and $8.50 for children. *San Jose* trips are very popular, and reservations should be made in advance by calling 451-1621. The vessel winds through South Sound Creek and out 6 miles to Molasses Reef, which is the only reef it visits. Many people are disappointed that they do not see the Christ of the Deep Statue, but that is miles to the northeast. There is about a half hour of viewing time through the glass panels in the ship's hull while the *San Jose* wiggles and churns about.

The trip is most enjoyable if undertaken with a large group of children, who will be highly vocal in their enthusiasm for what they do and do not see. They will invariably spot the seasickness bags in the shelf above the panels and yell, "Look at the barf bags!" while the guide is pointing out a parrotfish. They will always insist that they have seen a shark, and they will have a very good time.

Actually, it is not likely that you will see a shark, a turtle, or any of the larger or shier inhabitants of the reef with all the bustling about the *San Jose* does, idling, then scooting sideways with a grand flourish of bubbles, leaving sea fans waving frantically in the propeller wash like shipwrecked maidens. What you will see are big basket sponges, a good variety of corals, and schools of porkfish and grunts. And you will frequently see barracuda wearing their customary peevish expressions.

The 'cuda is enjoying a period of revisionist thinking at present. He is no longer considered the aggressive man-mauler he was once believed to be. The new attitude is that if he does blunder into you with his razory teeth, it will be because of poor visibility or because you were wearing something shiny. In any case, it will be a mistake. Another mistake—this time one that people make—is eating barracuda. The fish shows his considerable resentment at being eaten by infecting the eater with ciguatera, a violent fish poisoning, although folk wisdom claims that if you cook a dime with a 'cuda and the dime stays shiny, it's safe to eat him. If the dime turns black, though, you'd better not.

A *San Jose* trip is undeniably the driest way to see the reef, but it is probably the least satisfying. If you're able to swim at all, it's far more enjoyable to take one of the dive boats out and snorkel. The reef is another world, and to be able to enter it with the rudiments of a glass mask and a plastic tube is almost miraculous. Besides having that silly name, snorkelers *look* silly to the nonsnorkeler, floating flatly around, making occasional rude noises through their tubes. But a snorkeler is not what he appears to others, he is what he *sees*. He has a magic glass wrapped around his eyes and he is in a world of beauty and color. Graceful movement. Silence.

1733 hurricane. Even the ballast stones—mere stones, after all—are fascinating here. Conch Reef drops off to a depth of 115 feet, but close to the surface is a large stand of elkhorn coral, and there are stumpy remnants of formerly large colonies of pillar coral. (It was the devastation of Conch Reef by collectors that prompted state legislators to prohibit the taking of coral.)

WHERE TO STAY

Exploring the reef and taking advantage of the different packages the dive shops offer take days at the very least. Many places to stay are completely booked in the winter season and on weekends. You are only 60 miles from the Miami International Airport here, after all. The motels are clustered in two areas—just south of the entrance to Pennecamp, and below MM #100, just beyond where the four-lane road divides. Most of them are on the Bay side.

There's a **Howard Johnson** at MM #102 beside the splendid monolith of Southern Bell, and the aforementioned **Holiday Inn** at MM #100. The Holiday Inn takes seriously the fact that it is close to Miami, and behaves accordingly: noisy, crowded complex, big marina, a gambling-casino boat named the *Sun Cruz* that is not the most skillfully skippered boat in the area, and a glass-bottom boat that goes out three times a day on two-hour trips to the reef. It takes 45 minutes to get to the reef, which allows you 30 minutes for viewing. Since the boat, the *Princess,* can take up to 125 passengers out, fighting for viewing position can be oftimes nasty.

Best of the chains is the **Sheraton** at MM #97 (Bay side), not far from the Wynken, Blynken and Nod Trailer Park, where ancient immobile homes reside on streets such as Tweety Pie Terrace, Thumper Thoroughfare, and Little Miss Muffet Lane. The Sheraton looks immense from the water but seems subtle because it isn't a high-rise. Built in a buttonwood grove, it gives the illusion of fitting in with nature, though its boardwalks run nonsensically here and there. There's a small fabricated beach and two pools, as well as a tennis court and a 20-slip marina. It's deluxe—far nicer than its new sister in Key West. Rooms start at $280 in season and mosey up to $500; from May to mid-December they're $220 to $360 (852-5553).

Although there are many more chains and deluxe resorts in the Keys than there used to be, small cottages and more eccentrically personalized lodgings can still be found. Many people stay in these places for weeks, bringing their own coffeepots, broiling up the fish they catch, eating from the mismatched plates stacked in the cupboard (ant motel tin discreetly tucked in the

Basket sponges and a barracuda

corner), shaking the scatter rugs out each day, and sitting outside on the dock at twilight with their compeers, sipping martinis they have mixed exactly to their taste. There's always a
little boat tied up that the kids can use, and the swimming pool
is usually part of the Bay itself, set off by flaking cement walls,
its depth dictated by the tides.

Largo Lodge, less than a mile south of the park at MM
#102, is a cool, jungly enclave—very refreshing after a day on
and under the bright water. The grounds, though not extensive,
are unique for their lushness. The palms are towering, the
orchids profuse, and every healthy leaf shines. The cottages are
large, with screened porches and separate kitchens, and can
sleep four. There is a boat ramp and a little dock on the Bay, on
what is here called Tarpon Basin. The place is very pleasant,
the landlady jolly, but the rule in this Eden is that no one under
the age of 16 is allowed. Prices are $105 a night for two in sea-
son, $10 for each additional person. There's a two-night mini-
mum on weekends. May through Thanksgiving it's $85 per
night. Telephone: 451-0424.

Rock Reef (852-2401) and **Kona Kai** (852-7200), side by
side at MM #98, both have cottages on tree-dotted grounds, little man-made beaches on the Bay, and dockage. Rock Reef has
comfy pine-paneled rooms good for vacationing families, with
kitchens and separate bedrooms. Rates range from $90 to $130.
Kona Kai has been lightly refurbished and has an art gallery.
Recently the stunning black-and-white photographs of Clyde
Butcher, South Florida's Ansel Adams, were shown here.
Popp's (852-5201) and **Stoneledge** (852-8114), farther down
at MM #96 and MM #95, are both small, valued classics. Efficiencies run about $80 in season and on holidays, $90 for a one-
room apartment; off-season, $60 and $70. Many people like to
come for longer and do the weekly rate.

WHERE TO EAT

Key Largo has many eating establishments that aren't worth
writing home about—perhaps more than most vacation desti-
nations—but there's no need to resign yourself to yet another
awesome blizzard from the Dairy Queen.

Tiny **Harriet's**, close to Popp's around MM #95, is good for breakfast, as is the **Hideout** at MM #103.5 on the water at the end of a street peculiarly named Transylvania Avenue. In a humble house very much unrestored (close to **Jules'**, "one of the planet's last frontiers") you can have fish and grits and biscuits for breakfast. It is common knowledge that nothing beats fish and grits and biscuits for breakfast. You can have it for lunch, too. Open 7–2 seven days a week. Telephone: 451-0128. **Mrs. Mac's Kitchen** (451-3722) has basic burgers and good chili as well as cold Key lime pie that will make your teeth sing. Authentic-license-plate decor. Open Monday–Saturday 7 A.M.– 9:30 P.M.

The **Italian Fisherman** at MM #104 is large and open with big white statues gleaming nakedly in the parking lot (some heavily lipsticked individual has been smacking the bum of the cement Italian fisherman himself of late) and outside dining on extended terraces. The place has a sprawling, free-form quality—it's been expanding now for more than 20 years. The bar is the place to watch Key Largo sunsets. The ambience here is better than the food, which is, however, reasonably priced. The portions are large. They seem to worry about the conch dishes somewhat. ("Have you ever had conch before?" the waitress asks. "Maybe you should have it parmigiana.") It is the beginning of the Keys up here, but if you're trying conch, try it the simplest way possible. The more elaborate the preparation sounds, the tougher it's going to be. Open from 11:30 A.M. until 11 P.M. (451-4471).

Snooks at MM #99.5, behind Largo Honda, is a clubby place with roast beef and white tablecloths. The catch of the day runs your usual $16.95. **Patricks** is its open-air counterpart, on the water, with a simpler menu.

Coconuts (follow the loud signs) is a big, casual place on a stuffed marina. Their specialty is a fish covered with a sauce of bananas, oranges, pineapple, and rum. Other dishes are gathered under peculiar headings. Meat and fish are under "For Real Estate Lovers," while salads can be found under "For Those Who Care" (453-9794).

Snapper's Waterfront Saloon at MM #94.5, the place with the mermaid sitting on the turtle, is far nicer and appreciated by many. Overlooking the waters of another marina, it has decks, three bars, a big and easy menu, and is open from 11 A.M. to 10 P.M. (852-5956).

A BAR

Right beside the Italian Fisherman is the **Caribbean Club Bar**, the bar of movie myth. A sign inside says ABSOLUTELY NO DOGS ALLOWED. Outside there's a bit of littered waterfront and some benches and beer bottles scattered about. Inside, in the morning, there are men drinking shots and playing pool and women sliding off their stools. It certainly doesn't look like the kind of place where a dog wouldn't be welcome.

But there is an explanation for the sign. Once dogs wandered in and out of here freely. They slept, snarled, scratched, and drank beer here. It was a democratic place. One man who frequented the Caribbean Club would often bring his pit bull bitch. One day he brought her in with a few of her puppies. While the man drank, the dogs went for a dip. One of the puppies, frightened of the water, climbed on the bitch's back and would not let go, and managed to drown its very own mother. The bitch was a champion who had been worth a great deal of money, and the owner, as well as being upset, was disbelieving. He gave the drowned dog mouth-to-mouth resuscitation and pounded on her heart, but the dog remained drowned. He was so mad at the puppy he kicked it to death. The management decided that dogs hanging out in the bar were a potential problem. Now dogs are not allowed. Absolutely.

Ballyhoo's Seafood Grill at MM #97.8, in the median, is open for breakfast, lunch, and dinner. Little place, full bar, lots of variety. You'd probably shoot right past it unless you were staying in Key Largo. Fairly new and not yet a hangout (852-0822).

The **Fish House**, at MM #102.4. Carved wooden parrots, carved wooden pirates, captain's chairs, netting with little lights and plastic lobsters and buoys enmeshed in it. Chummy Cape Cod fish-house feel. Big servings, corn on the cob sides, wine and beer. Lunch and dinner every day (451-4665).

TAVERNIER

At MM #93.5 is the **Florida Keys Wild Bird Rehabilitation Center**, back in the mangroves along the Bay, marked with a rickety wooden heron sign. The facility used to have a little corner of the Dolphin Research Center, but perhaps the sight of injured and mutilated birds is too depressing to be educational. In any case, the Center has been moved here and it rescues, rehabilitates, and releases ill, injured, and orphaned wild birds. It has a considerable number of residents, some of whom will never be able to return to their natural homes. This is not a fun experience, but it is a very moving one. The Center is staffed by volunteers and subsists entirely on donations. A wonderful boardwalk trail zigzags through a wedge of hammock, and there's a very informative pamphlet that tells about the distinctive trees that grow here and their importance, particularly to butterflies. Many of the birds at the Center are pelicans, Audubon's "reverend sirs"; and most of their injuries are the result of fishhooks and monofilament line. Never discard old fishing line for a bird to become entangled in. Don't toss away those eternal six-pack grippers, either: A pelican looks large but weighs only six pounds, and because their bones are hollow they usually can't be set. If you find an injured bird, call 852-4486.

At the end of Key Largo Key at MM #92.5, just north of the community of Tavernier, is the turn to the Keys' original settlement of **Planter**, which was homesteaded in 1866. **Harry Harris County Park** occupies the ocean site today. At the turn of the century, Planter had the only post office between Miami and Key West, but the town was abandoned when the railroad came through and people moved inland to be around the station, founding the new town of **Tavernier**, named for a small key offshore that the Spaniards had previously named Cayo Tabona, or Horsefly Key. If you want to go to the park, take a left on Burton Drive, wind your way past many streets filled with houses and trailers all festooned with Styrofoam lobster-pot markers, and you will eventually reach it. There is a sandy beach and many concrete picnic tables that look like small temples dedicated to hibachi gods. Before you advance to the beach, picnic temples, and playgrounds, a great many signs will place grave demands on your sense of freedom and delight. STOP, they say. NO DOGS, they say. NO PARKING. STOP. SLOW. NO SPORTS OR GAMES. Perhaps you will find it more congenial to turn back to Route 1 and drive down to **Harry's Place** at MM #91. Harry's Place (it's the same Harry Harris actually, an early restaurateur and county commissioner called Hi-Rise Harry for his lucrative friendships with developers) is inexpensive, with weekend buffets and breakfast served as early as 6 A.M. The bar stays open until 4 A.M.

The development of Tavernier was inhibited by the Depression of 1929 and the almost constant arrival of hurricanes, the most severe being the storm of September 1935, which devastated most of Tavernier's structures and erased all signs of habitation eight miles south on Matecumbe Key. A peculiar result of the hurricane for Tavernier was the subsequent construction of "Red Cross houses," built with the help of the Federal Emergency Relief Administration and the Red Cross. These were four-room houses built of reinforced concrete containing 80,000 pounds of steel, with steel rods anchoring the house to bedrock. The floors and roof were also made of concrete, and the walls were a foot thick. The window sashes were made of steel and contained double-strength glass. The houses were ugly as sin, of course, but built to withstand anything short of the Apocalypse. Unfortunately, seawater was used in the mixing of the cement, which rusted the steel reinforcing rods so that all the structures cracked.

But Tavernier is proud of these oddities, proud indeed of anything that dates at all, for the Keys, with the exception of Key West, are scant on old buildings. The town plans to establish a historical district that will include these hurricane houses as well as the simple wooden structures that remain from the days of the railroad, when Tavernier was the first station stop in the Keys. One of these historic homes is the one-story 1920s house with the coral-rock fireplace where Robert Porter Allen wrote *The Flame Birds* (see page 35). Another is the **Tavernier Hotel** at MM #91.8 (852-4131), very pink-and-white these days and open for business. The tiny rooms are $99 in season and during special events out of season. Since there are many spe-

CUCO BOBO

During the Depression, a round-trip ticket from Miami to Key West on the railroad cost a dollar. When the train stopped for water just south of Tavernier, passengers would dash into the lime groves and gather Key limes to liven up their rum drinks. In Key West, a Cuban called Cuco Bobo made a living in bars by imitating the railroad as it chugged down the Keys. Cuco was attired somewhat militarily, with a dazzling array of medals and ribbons. He would stand on the bar, move his arms like an engine gathering steam, shuffle his feet, and make toot-tooting noises. Several drinks were purchased for him during this process. He'd blow a whistle, eliciting further drinks. Then he'd start to call out the stops—"Tavernier! Islamorada! Matecumbe!" Oh, it was a long, dry trip. "Grassy Key!" Very seldom was Key West reached before Cuco Bobo fell off the bar.

cial events in the Keys, the diminutive grandmotherly proprietess indicated that rooms are very often $99. Next door is the **Copper Kettle**, a frilly restaurant that isn't so frilly as to deny itself a full bar (852-4113).

Tavernier was once considered an outpost—subdued, but an outpost nonetheless. No longer an outpost, the town remains subdued, hugging the road in a mannerly fashion. It has a shopping center, **Tavernier Towne** (complete with dignified *e*), at MM #91.5, and the only movie theater in the Upper Keys. It's a modest, rather dusty community and seems far removed from the water, although the water is there, of course. Along the ocean where the early settlers built their lonely little homes, situated to catch the breezes and keep the mosquitoes away, are the large weekend retreats of Miamians, each equipped with a slick car and a motorboat. Hurricane bunkers these houses are not.

PLANTATION KEY

Across Tavernier Creek at MM #90 and running down to Snake Creek at MM #87 is **Plantation Key**. Centuries ago it was inhabited by the Caloosa Indians. Remnants of a considerably large midden can be found Bayside on the northernmost end of the key. As you are probably aware, however, Indian mounds and middens can be very boring, consisting of dirt, small grimy shells, and once-useful stones—dumps of nonacquisition. These middens are of most interest to enterprising gardeners, who can be seen carting away buckets of the old, rich soil for their own flowery purposes. A marvelous nursery here that specializes in native plants is **Florida Keys Native Nursery** (852-2636). Even undeveloped lands and "natural" areas in Florida are being infested by invasive exotic species that don't support bird and animal populations. The natives lead fine supportive and interrelated lives. Learning to appreciate the right stuff is always satisfying.

At the turn of the century the first large schooner in the Upper Keys was built on Plantation Key by "Brush" Pinder. It was built "by the idea," without plans, the same way it was done in the Bahamas. Pinder named the 60-foot, 40-ton schooner, which was made of Everglades mahogany, *Island Home,* and she sailed Keys waters for 15 years, carrying ice, pineapples, passengers, and mail before the coming of the railroad.

A small group of mangrove islands off Plantation are called the **Cowpens**. Manatees were once so numerous that they were herded into these watery corrals to await their future as meat. The odd, gentle manatee is now almost extinct.

Plantation Key boasts the restaurant **Marker 88** (located helpfully at MM #88), often described as "a destination of gourmets." Open for dinner only, it is attractive, expensive, requires reservations, and is quietly placed among trees on the Bay. Inside, however, it is anything but quiet. The tables are set very close together and the noise is beyond discordance, beyond clamor, beyond din or hubbub. It is not that the waitresses scream at one another or drop trays—it is the shrieking, babbling, crowing uproar of the patrons themselves. The kitchen may create inspired bisques and sauces and stuffings, but it is difficult not to be more impressed by the surrounding cacophony. Marker 88 is open from 5 P.M. For reservations, call 852-9315. (The **Naughty and Nice Gag Shop** has appeared just across the highway, hoping to get some of the gourmet trade too.)

A mile away, at MM #87, is the **Plantation Yacht Harbor Resort**, with its big marina and its candlelit Commodore Room for those who regret ever having left Ft. Lauderdale. Reserva-

---

FLORIDA BAY

Florida Bay, the great nursery, is in the throes of environmental collapse, falling apart, as one researcher put it, "like a rotting piece of cloth." The dead zone, clearly visible from airplane and boat, sprawls farther each year—a spreading area of massive turtle grass die-off that has fueled an algae bloom in which marine life perishes or from which it flees. Many people will tell you how clear the Bay's waters used to be, that you could see 30 feet straight to the bottom in submarine canyons that wound through the shallow flats, that you felt as if you were flying, that looking into the water was like looking through the air. Now visibility is measured in inches. Once-crystal waters have turned murky and opaque, a milky green, a pea green, even a phosphorescent green. Loss of sea grasses has turned underwater acres into mud meadows. Where the algae passes, the die-off of sponges is 100 percent, and it is those sponges that had provided food and protection for young fish, shrimp, and spiny lobsters.

The nursery is shutting down: Florida Bay is becoming a hypersaline, superheated lagoon, a hot death soup for marine life. This is a direct result of the dying of the Everglades itself: years of flood control and government water-management practices there have promoted cities and farms and just about accomplished their original mandate of sucking the Everglades dry. The health of the Florida Keys is utterly dependent on the health of the Everglades. Books could be written about this, of course. Millions of words *have* been written, mostly assuring those who care that steps are being considered (if not yet taken) to bring the Everglades back from the brink of death, but "replumbing," as the engineers like to say, the ecosystem might be impossible.

Big Sugar has a stranglehold on much of the Everglades, and many of the problems of polluted, phosphorous-laden, nutrient-rich water can be traced directly to the special interests of Everglades sugar cane agriculture. More and more of the 'Glades' wading birds are dying or not breeding because of mercury poisoning from eating contaminated fish. Big Sugar's farming practices are suspected as the mercury source. Even the very water that falls from the heavens (a good two thirds of it in any case) is diverted into the Gulf or the Atlantic to keep growers' fields and suburbanite lawns from flooding. The bad water, that which is flushed into the Bay after being used by agriculture, flows eastward, affecting the Gulf-side reef, which is becoming increasingly stressed and diseased. The waters of the reef in winter are frequently silty and green now, offering zero visibility.

Another threat to the Everglades and Florida Bay is development pressure, which never goes away. In 1994 a new threat arrived in the person of Blockbuster Video sorcerer Wayne Huizenga, who had a brief desire to build the biggest tourist attraction in America. It was to be a gargantuan sports and entertainment complex covering 2,500 acres, only three miles from the parched lip of the Everglades. He swiftly, one might even say uncannily, collected all the permits and permissions he needed to do this, at which point the project was, for the moment, suspended. If it's ever built, it will include a vast virtual reality amusement center where you'll be able to pay a fee and enter the Keys that so recently were—see the bright and extraordinary worlds of water and sky where remarkable creatures, not of our kind, existed. Of course, it will really be make-believe.

tions: 852-2381. Open 6–11 P.M. Adjacent is the more casual El Capitan Room, open 8 A.M.–3 P.M., and 5–10 P.M., where the children are screaming for nachos or potato skins. There are many rooms here, most of them fairly run-down, separated from the highway by a vast green unlandscaped lawn. This expanse often hosts events like classic car rallies, so egalitarian that even the most rotted-out '67 Mustang can get a trophy. Rates run $95–$135 in season, higher on weekends. Telephone: 852-2381.

A bit of old Keys funk is a half mile away on your left, in the shape of a small and startling perma-stone castle—the former home of McKee's Museum of Sunken Treasure. When you toured the Keys in the 1950s, you'd do some fishing, eat some fish, and visit Art McKee's museum. McKee was a well-known local treasure diver of the 1940s and '50s who built his miniaturized version of a Spanish fort in 1949 and filled it with the things he'd found in nearby waters—cannon, muskets, swords, and gold coins. The museum closed in 1976, and the "castle," for sale for years, recently became **Treasure Village**, with lots of candles and crafts and dried flowers. The best thing about it now is the gigantic spiny lobster sculpture out front. Very inviting, but *no toque esta langosta*. Across the road at MM #86.5 is the **Rain Barrel**, with more craft shops. This is not the place to buy the armadillo pocketbook you've always wanted, or coconuts with spangled, painted faces. There are artful things back here, where printmakers, potters, jewelsmiths, sculptors, and wood and leather workers all exercise their talents. It's as though the entire graduating class of the Putney School in Vermont had come down to Plantation Key.

If you want to explore the reef off Plantation, local dive shops will take you to a variety of areas, usually visiting the reefs of **Inner and Outer Conch** and the ledges and drop-offs of **Davis Reef** and **Crocker Wall**. Outer Conch has a zigzag maze of ridges separated by long, winding valleys of sand, where huge rays can often be seen gracefully swimming. Sometimes captains bring bags of bread crumbs and chopped sea urchins to feed the fish. Other trips concentrate on spearfishing, or lobstering. Dive boats make morning and afternoon trips, and the costs usually run about $30 for a two-tank scuba trip, $35 for night dives, $20 for snorkelers. Make reservations, and inquire as to location and group intention; you don't want to be happily feeding a fish and have your dive companion nail it right before your eyes:

Lady Cyana, MM #86 (664-8717)
World Down Under, MM #81.5 (664-9312)
Holiday Isle, MM #84.5 (664-4145)

A popular wreck dive here for the experienced is the *Duane,* a 327-foot scuttled Coast Guard cutter that sits upright in 120 feet of water. Another cutter, *The Bibb,* rests on her starboard side at 130 feet. The county is looking into the possibility of getting, and sinking, surplus army tanks as well. It isn't yet known what kind of fish will favor a tank environment. An increasing number of big unwanted ships are being cleaned up and sunk for divers' entertainment.

An in-shore patch reef, easily accessible if you're just poking about in a rental boat, is **Hens and Chickens Reef**. This reef, originally named by the Spanish, lies three miles offshore and is marked by a navigational light. Large star-coral heads once grew here, but the reef was killed in 1970, when a particularly cold winter brought cold water laden with sediment out of the bay through Snake Creek into the Gulf. The living coral is gone but the structures remain and are being repopulated by soft corals. Fish and lobsters still live among the rocky remains, and many moray eels also lurk about here. As is often the case with reefs close to shore, visibility at Hens and Chickens is frequently nonexistent.

THE BACKCOUNTRY

To the west of Plantation Key are the waters of Florida Bay, the "backcountry" that—once you pass the Intracoastal Waterway, which roughly and rather closely parallels the Upper Keys—is the Everglades National Park. These uninhabited islands of the upper and central Bay have names like Caloosa, Buttonwood, Triplet, Tern, Eagle, Black Betsy, and Manatee. All are mangrove, red and black, the red the pioneer, its roots graceful as hooped skirts, clumping forward, building land. There are primitive campsites on some of the keys in the Bay, including Nest in the eastern portion and Rabbit and Man of War keys in the Dildo Key Bank (there is a modest explanation for this name, one is certain; there *is* a native cactus called the dildo, which has loping, three-angled thorny stems, but such information doesn't seem all that helpful). For the interest of etymologists, the grim name of Arsenic Bank nearby is a distortion of *Arsenicker,* in turn a mispronunciation of these keys' *real* name, Marsh Sneaker.

A Keys gator

The backcountry is unique and mysterious, both subtle and grand. It's a silent wilderness of extravagant rushing clouds, shallow waters brightened by sun and darkened by the shapes of fishes, green islands appearing as if by magic on the horizon, and 360-degree sunsets. The northwestern part of the bay is home to the secretive, slender-snouted crocodile, rarer than the freshwater alligator. Crocs are said to have five distinct calls, all to do with love and warning. Poachers say that their red eyes look just like dollar bills. In the warmer months the beleaguered manatee grazes on the succulent grasses of these flats. A docile, dallying creature, its biggest enemy is, of course, man, this time piloting the motorboat that churns thoughtlessly across its great, browsing bulk.

The grass beds of the backcountry support large numbers of redfish, trout, snook, mangrove snapper, tarpon, and the small, fast, hard-fighting gamefish jack crevalles, and provide a nursery for lobsters and crabs. And this is where the bird rookeries are, the nesting islands and feeding grounds, the resting areas for those who make long migrations. Brown pelicans nest in great numbers, favoring a new key each season. The American bald eagle, too, nests here, usually raising its young on one key and fishing and hunting on another, perhaps not liking to dispose of its most immediate neighbors. There are a multitude of herons who work these waters—Louisiana, little, green, white, and blue. And egrets, terns, turnstones, plovers, skimmers. Some stalk or spear. Some glide and scoop. Others sprint through shallow water, striking right and left. Others dabble and probe or are masters of the surprise attack. One of the most beautiful birds that live and breed here, though not in great numbers, is the roseate spoonbill. No one who sees the brilliant colors of this bird against the dark green mangroves and blue backcountry sky will ever forget it.

These are fabulous waters to explore in a small boat, although the backcountry takes years to know, and voyaging into its quiet wonders should not be undertaken lightly by the casual boater. Channels are complex, usually little more than a tortured winding through mangroves and hammocks which suddenly open out to basins and flats. Always stay in channels and do not stray into the shallows, where prop damage can wreak havoc on fragile seagrass meadows. The time of high and low tides can differ several hours between locations only a few miles apart. Basically, you can tell water depth by color. If it's brown, you're going to run aground. If it's white, you might.

In the winter the Bay can be whipped by winds into choppy foam. In the summer the waters can be flat as glass, with faraway boats seemingly floating in the air and the sticks that mark channels turning into long-legged herons that fly away. At any time of the year you should be prepared for very rapid

Roseate spoonbills

THE ROSEATE SPOONBILL

"It is as though an orchid had spread its lovely wings and flown," an enthusiast once described the spoonbill.

The spoonbill had almost been exterminated by plume hunters at the turn of the century. The feathers were not as popular as those of the egret for ladies' hats, but the wings were torn off and made into fans, though the buyer was often disappointed when the brilliant colors quickly faded. Knowledge of the horrors of avian carnage gives reading Edith Wharton a new dimension.

Julian Huxley once noted that the "bird mind is not yet complicated by reason." The roseate spoonbill is a simple and shy creature of many troubles, yet garbed in glory. The young are an immaculate white and only gradually become suffused with pink. Three years must pass and three moltings occur before the bird achieves its full brilliance of nuptial plumage—in rose and carmine and orange—and will mate. The drawing of the spoonbill in John Audubon's *Birds of America,* considered not to be by Audubon, does not reflect the true radiance of the bird's colors. It is not likely that Audubon saw many of them. In his remarks he noted that their flesh was oily and poor eating, and that they were difficult to kill. (Some years later, in 1874, a man named Frederick Tingley Jencks, realizing that the species was growing scarce, visited two nesting colonies in the Lake Okeechobee region of Florida. He found eradicating the birds time-consuming but not impossible. He returned day after day, shooting all the birds in both colonies until no spoonbill remained. He "collected" a total of 26 skins.)

By 1939 the only nesting site for the birds in the state of Florida was on Bottlepoint (now called Bottle) Key, off Tavernier in Florida Bay. Robert Porter Allen, an ornithologist working for the National Audubon Society, made an intensive study of the colony in 1939 and 1940, camping on the far end of the key away from the birds and on a skiff offshore, observing their courtship, breeding, and feeding habits and writing a charming book, *The Flame Birds.*

The spoonbill favors the little killifishes of the marly flats of shallow mangrove pools, grazing the opaque water, swinging their sensitive bills to and fro, feeling through the water

as "one might with the fingers of the hand." Mating between
the birds is decorous, the female showing her willingness by
isolating herself upon a pleasant bush and shaking conve-
nient twigs or branches with her bill. After a seemly amount
of bill-clashing and twig-rattling—which usually goes on
for two weeks—the male perches behind the female, reach-
ing across her back and grasping the twig she is fiddling
with in his bill. Together they grip the twig. Then the twig
is dropped, and the male grasps firmly the slender middle
portion of the female's bill with his own. Progression pro-
gresses . . . and so are baby spoonbills begun!

Roseate spoonbills now nest in April and May on several of
the islands in Florida Bay, including the keys named for
Allen himself and the Audubon sanctuary, Cowpens, through
which the Inland Waterway cuts a swath. They remain far
from common, so to see them is indeed an event—their bright
existence making the beautiful backcountry of the Keys even
more beautiful.

weather changes—waterspouts in the summer, brisk squalls,
sudden wind shifts.

Your boat should be equipped with binoculars, good charts, a
compass, and a push pole (a ten-foot pole with a spatulate end,
which you use to push yourself off mud banks, pole across the
flats, and anchor in the marl). The marly bottom of the Bay is
alarming to the uninitiated who, hopping over the side of the
boat, will promptly proceed to sink. Visions of Amazonian quicksand movies flash through one's head, but it is not quicksand
and it will not devour you, although it is sucky, sticky stuff.
Always wear sneakers when tramping around either Bay or
Gulf waters, for protection against coral, spiny sea urchins, and
other skittering, perhaps stinging, perhaps slimy things.

Duly informed, but not unduly alarmed about squalls and
slither, make an effort to get "out back." The experience of bird-
ing, fishing, and exploring in the Bay is something you should
not miss in the Keys.

Ambassador Boat Rentals (MM #90.5, oceanside at the light)
has a number of 16-foot runabouts and 20-foot center-console

boats for rent by the half and full day. All the boats have Bimini
tops. Telephone: 853-0222.

WINDLEY KEY

Eric's Floating Restaurant could once be found just across the
Snake Creek Bridge at MM #86.5. It was a houseboat ambigu-
ously decorated with animal skins and heads, and lace tablecloths. There was also a vague Viking ship motif; some
occasional nymph statuary as well. It was all . . . uncanny. But
it sank. No diners were reported having gone down with it.

Another celebrated event occurred in March of 1988 when the
bridge at Snake Creek got stuck during Spring Break. A gust of
wind misaligned the spans when they were in their highest
open position—a gust that bartenders for ten miles in each
direction considered "an act of God." People were stranded for
17 hours. Beer was delivered in iced-up wheelbarrows. It was
the wheelbarrows that made the moment "Conch."

Holiday Isle is one of the best-known pleasure and partying
meccas in the Keys, but if you want a smaller, quieter place to
lay your head, there is a cluster of little motels here on the
ocean. The **Drop Anchor** is pretty and relaxing, with a palm-
studded beach miraculously some feet higher than the water,
which is kept at a remove by a seawall. In season (December
15–mid-April), rooms are $70, two-room suites $160, kitchenettes $85. Summer and fall prices drop $15–$30. You can set-
tle down here nicely for a week for around $400 in a little
kitchen apartment with a screened patio. Telephone: 664-4863.

Windley Key was once two separate islands named the Umbrella Keys, but they were joined with fill by railroad construction. The key was quarried extensively for bridge and causeway
fill, and after the railroad was completed, various companies continued to quarry the beautifully patterned fossilized coral rock
for use as decorative veneer on buildings. The rock was known as
keystone. The living reef runs along the Keys. The dead reef is
the foundation of the Upper Keys. The exposed rock of the quarry
walls shows the patterns and borings of polyps, gorgonians, and

HURRICANES

Reading about hurricanes and having hurricane parties are, naturally, much more enjoyable than evacuating for a hurricane, preparing for a hurricane, or assessing the damage from a hurricane. The Keys haven't had a hurricane in a very long while. Awful Andrew barely grazed the islands. Most people have never experienced one, and many think that those who voice their fears about hurricanes are just trying to put their bad mouth around the Keys.

A hurricane is a monster whirlwind. It has a name and massive amounts of rain. It has winds of between 74 and 200 mph and stirs up giant waves and strong tides. It is born of blazing sun, still water, and warm, wet air in either the Atlantic Ocean, the Gulf of Mexico, or the Caribbean Sea any time between June and November, although it's most likely to occur in the autumn equinox between mid-August and mid-October. It begins life as a vacuum, a *beckoning* vacuum, attracting faraway breezes which approach it in a clockwise-twisting curve, only to reverse and swirl excitedly in ever-tightening counterclockwise gyres. Cool air arrives, is sucked up and made warm; everything climbs higher and faster, creating wind and rain, and then this thing starts to *move*, gorged with water power, fatally attracted to land (which will weaken and eventually extinguish it)—a real 3-D monster.

Conchs know that a hurricane is coming when the poinciana loses its leaves or doesn't blossom, or when land crabs move to higher ground or ants climb straight up the walls or dogs and birds start acting peculiar. Scientists know that a hurricane is coming by reading their satellites, radar, and computers. But no one can forecast with true accuracy where a hurricane's point of landfall will be. A computer's reliability for predicting where a hurricane will hit ranges from 10 percent at 72 hours to almost 75 percent within 12 hours. Even with a half day's notice, the margin of error on a hurricane with a breadth of 150 miles remains at 65 miles in either direction. If the Hurricane Center in Miami forecasts 12 hours in advance that a storm will hit Marathon, it could strike anywhere from Key West to Key Largo, requiring total evacuation of the Keys. But the feasibility of complete over-the-road evacuation is nil, and if it were possible it would take at least 35 hours. Besides, behavioral studies have shown that 25 percent of the population in a hurricane's path wouldn't leave their homes even if ordered to.

So, what to do! According to a NOAA (National Oceanic and Atmospheric Administration) Coastal Hazards Program booklet, if you're at home you should stock up on candles, masking tape, and radio batteries, fill your bathtub and washing machine with water, and throw your aluminum furniture in the swimming pool. You should secure your boat in a safe harbor or tie it up in the mangroves. You should keep your ear pasted to NOAA weather radio. If you go to a Red Cross shelter, you should bring food and bedding. You should not bring intoxicating beverages, pets, or firearms. You should probably not bring John D. MacDonald's *Condominium* for reading material, either.

Some people feel that the Florida coastline is a disaster waiting to happen, and project 20-foot tidal waves sweeping over the Keys. Others trust in the offshore reefs to break up any mass of water before it reaches land, or don't even trouble themselves to think of hurricanes at all, believing them to be obsolete, rather like kerosene lamps. Whatever, almost everyone would agree that trying to determine which direction the wind is going to blow is like trying to chart the course of a leaf on a giant river.

other inhabitants of the ancient reef. Three of the old quarries can be found on the Bay side of the highway shortly after the Snake Creek Bridge at MM #85. Saved from being built out as a condominium, the land was acquired by the state in 1985 and sturdily named Windley Key Fossil Reef State Geologic Site. Bring some paper and a soft pencil and you can make rubbings of stone-feathery ancient corals. As well as the fascinating quarries, there is a dense hardwood hammock running along the high land above the walls with large mahogany, torchwood, joewood, and white ironwood, all rare native trees of the Florida Keys. Occasionally there are guided tours of the site. Contact Long Key State Park at MM #67.5 for information or perhaps a key to the quarry gates. Lady Cyana Divers sometimes has a key.

Theater of the Sea at MM #84.5 was created from one of the old quarries the railroad crews dug in 1907. It was flooded with seawater and stocked with fish as a tourist attraction in the 1940s, which makes it one of the oldest marine parks in the world. There are some very amorous sea lions here, and a number of more locally grown cheerful and acrobatic dolphins. They put on a very nice show for children. Shows are continuous from 9:30 A.M. to 4 P.M. Admission is $15 for adults, $8 for children 5–12; under 5, free. There are also some gloomy sharks and a blind crocodile. They do not put on shows. Telephone: 664-2431.

Holiday Isle (MM #84.5) is big and brassy, with the mood of a speeded-up film. From the road it looks as though something tumultuous—even disastrous—involving a great many people has just occurred, and it usually has. On winter weekends 5,000–6,000 people ready to fish and rock out crowd this complex, which is said to include ten bars—even taking double-vision into account, a considerable number. (You will see a lot of pliers in these bars, and in fact in all the bars scattered along the intensive fishing grounds of Islamorada and Marathon—machismo being measured by the size of the pliers sticking in belts or jeans pockets, as pliers are used for wrenching the hooks from the mouths of huge fish.) The resort sponsors offshore powerboat races and windsurfing and fishing tournaments throughout the year. For these special events and all holidays, minimum stay requirements apply. Languid it's not. December 15 to May 1, economy rooms $105, oceanview $150, suites $220–$360. Rates drop $20 to $25 between May 2 and Labor Day and drop slightly again between September and mid-December. All rates, however, go up between $10 and $25 each year. Telephone: 664-2321.

Within dueling distance, at MM #83.5, is the **Whale Harbor Restaurant and Marina** with the adjacent **Chesapeake Motel**, marked by a shell-plastered toy lighthouse. Hurricane Donna struck here vigorously in 1960—the area seems a popular landfall for storms. There's a good upstairs tiki bar here over the charter boat docks, and an extensive seafood buffet served daily from 4:30 P.M. for $12.95. Sunday the buffet begins at noon and costs $9.95. The Chesapeake is quieter and less wildly sociable than Holiday Isle yet close enough to make one's indulgences and then retreat to roomy villas and nicely landscaped grounds. Again, there's a three-day minimum stay during holidays and special events. Motel rooms are $125 a night; a nice room on the water is $170–$195. Villas range from $130 to $350 in season, $10 or so less at other times. Telephone: 664-4662 or 664-4663. Reservations are important during the season.

UPPER MATECUMBE KEY

On the morning of September 2, 1935, large red-and-black hurricane warning flags were flying along the Keys. The foremen for the hundreds of workmen who were building a road here telephoned the Oversea Railroad headquarters in Miami and begged for an evacuation train to be sent down for them. A rescue train left Miami late in the afternoon, stopping at Homestead, the last mainland stop, to shift the locomotive from the front to the rear of the train, the engineer planning on pulling out of the storm rather than backing out of it. When the train stopped at Snake Creek at 7 P.M. to take on evacuees, a cable, torn loose by winds that were blowing over 150 mph, snagged on the engine cab, and more than an hour's effort was required to free it. By the time the train had backed down to Islamorada, winds had reached 200 mph. Hundreds of people were on board when a tidal wave engulfed the train and tore it from the tracks.

Hurricane!

After the hurricane, one could stand in the middle of the key and see from ocean to Bay and from one end of the island to the other. Nothing remained standing except the angel that marked a grave in a tiny cemetery on the beach in Islamorada. The angel can be seen today on the grounds of the Cheeca Lodge, of all places between the Cheeca's oceanfront villas and the golf driving range and heliport pad—a bit of memento mori in the midst of the good and fancy life.

> *This lovely bud so young so fair*
> *Called home to early doom*
> *Just called to show how sweet a flower*
> *In Paradise would bloom*

The angel is missing a hand and part of one wing, but she is still there, watching over the grave of Etta Dolores Pinder, who was born in 1899 and died in 1914, the only child of one of the early homesteading families of the Upper Keys.

Just beyond Cheeca, around MM #81.5, is a hurricane monument that marks the mass grave of many of those killed in the storm. The monument is constructed of locally quarried limestone and bears a striking art nouveau impression of palm trees bending in the wind.

ISLAMORADA

Most of the restaurants, resorts, and shops on Plantation, Windley, and Matecumbe Keys running from MM #88 down to MM #73 and Channel #2 use **Islamorada** as their address, for that is the community and post office which serves these keys.

For many people this area is easily comprehended by its attractions (**Theater of the Sea**), the concentration of restaurants (unnerving buffet excess is available at the **Whale Harbor Inn** at MM #83.5, and the **Coral Grille**), and its accommodations (which range from the calm and dignified **Cheeca Lodge** to the playful, disorderly **Holiday Isle**) and is their ultimate destination in the Keys. Here, within a few miles, are the big marinas at **Holiday Isle**, **Whale Harbor**, and **Bud 'n'**

Mary's, these three providing the largest concentration of charter fishing boats in the entire island chain, a fact which allows Islamorada to claim for itself the title Sport Fishing Capital of the World.

People come here to fish, eat, drink, fish, drink, and fish. From December to May there is the annual South Florida Fishing Tournament. In February there's the Ladies Sailfish Tournament. There's the Bonefish Fly Tournament in April, and the Ladies Invitational Tarpon Tournament. In the summer there are Shark Tournaments which allowed, until recently, the use of shotguns and baseball bats. There are Great Grunt Rodeos and Dolphin Scrambles. In the fall there are more bonefish tournaments and billfish tournaments and sailfish tournaments. Tournaments are usually sponsored by breweries and resorts, and there are cash prizes and trophies and patches and plaques and citations. Prizes are given for the biggest fish, the smallest fish, the weirdest fish, and the most fish.

For tournament and charter information, contact:

Whale Harbor Marina, MM #84 (664-4511)
Holiday Isle, MM #84.5 (664-2321)
Bud 'n' Mary's, MM #80 (664-2461)
Abel's Tackle Box, MM #84 (664-2521)

For a great day of fly-fishing on the flats, contact Mike Collins, an exceptionally able and articulate guide. It's $325 for a full day. Flats boats are too cool to have names. Call 852-5837. Remember: Catch. Pose. Release.

For a brochure containing the names, addresses, telephone numbers, and specialties of fishing guides, write to **Marathon Guides Association**, P.O. Box 500065, Marathon, FL 33050. Key West captains have finally admitted that there are really too many charter boats operating in the Keys, but you won't hear such heresy up here.

WHERE TO STAY

The **Cheeca Lodge** (MM #82). Cheeca sounds like something meaningfully Indian, but in fact it's just a preppy nickname for

Cynthia Twitchell, who with her husband ran the lodge as a private club in the 1950s. Known for years as one of the Keys' few resorts, it had an understated, clubby atmosphere, a forgiving nine-hole golf course, a white-sand beach, and a seemingly endless 525-foot fishing pier down which all guests were obliged to trek. Everything went on in a low-key way until new owners decided they wanted to spend $40 million. Everyone thought that was a lot, so an expensive study was commissioned to see if it was possible to spend that much. The study determined that it was possible. Cheeca now has 203 rooms, more than double the original number, two more tennis courts, another pool, a date palm–lined courtyard, parrots burbling in cages, and a series of meandering lagoons. Cheeca's elegance isn't so low-key anymore—the new majority-owner consortium also operates resorts in Palm Springs, Monterey, and Tucson—but it is still a friendly resort. Rooms run $225–$500 in season, suites $275 all the way up to $800. If you have $1,000, you're welcome to stay in the Presidential Suite, unless former president Bush is using it—then you can't. Cheeca has a dizzying number of ways to keep you occupied: fast Hobies, parasailing, water-skiing, endless water aerobics classes. Of course there are masseurs and masseuses, boutiques. There are also extensive activity programs for children. A baby-sitter will cost you $27 for three hours, and you might as well take the three hours off because it will cost you the same for an hour. Cheeca has become very much a place for families. The Ocean Terrace Grill ambience for lunch is small quaking children in wet bathing suits and towels knocking over drinks and demanding large hamburgers, so unless you are accompanied by one or two hungry children in wet bathing suits of your own, you might want to eschew a meal here. Cheeca has adopted an odd availability policy for their room rates, just like the airlines. If you arrange for your room far enough ahead of time, you get a better rate. But if you're the more carefree, spur-of-the-moment type, well, you suffer. Telephone: 664-4651.

The **Islander** (MM #82) occupies almost the same amount of land as the Cheeca Lodge—over 20 acres—and has an ample shorefront and two swimming pools, one saltwater and one fresh. It's nice; less cachet-burdened than Cheeca. Rooms are about $75 in season, but for another $20 you get your own roomy "villa" with a screened-in porch—definitely worth the extra money. Quiet, old-fashioned, lots of room to wander. The beach is not exactly a beach, that is, sand; it's more down-to-earth marl. It's sincere. Telephone: 664-2031.

The Moorings (Beach Road off the old highway). Hard to find. Everyone knows where it is but it's still hard to find. Stay on the old road that parallels Route 1 after Manny and Isa's heading south and turn down Beach Road toward the ocean. This is a wonderful spot, 17 palmy acres on a lovely beach. Old, comfy, carefully restored housekeeping cottages on the right, and newer, tasteful, but less interesting houses with suites on the left. The original fishing camp here was built after the '35 hurricane with Arm & Hammer money. It has become a very popular place to conduct fashion shoots, so you will see some unnervingly perfect people here in bathing suits. Quiet, classy, simple. Children and their parents are encouraged to stay over at Cheeca, where there would be "more for them to do." The old cottages have a two-night minimum stay and run between $115 and $145 a night. A two-bedroom cottage on the beach is $1,500 a week. Telephone: 664-4708.

Breezy Palms (MM #80). Small and pleasant. Nicely furnished rooms and efficiencies on the ocean. Little lime green cottages, a pool beneath the palms. No beach really, but small, busy piers and assorted sunning spots. Winter rates, $75. An apartment by the pool, $105. Telephone: 664-2361.

Oceanside Motel (MM #82.5). Most famous for the abduction of Bert, a peacock who blew in after Hurricane Andrew in 1992. Two carpenters from Miami snatched the bird but were arrested by alert sheriff's deputies who saw Bert's tail feathers sticking out the van's sliding doors. "No matter what their intentions, I think it was a real bad thing to do. The bird was happy here and all of a sudden he was kidnapped," the manager said. You can see Bert (one hopes) and even enjoy a great suite on the ocean with a wraparound balcony for $170 a night. Telephone: 664-3681.

Oceania Motel (MM #77.5). Very clean, reasonable, older motel a dip down from the highway. A saltwater pool. Lots of palms. A nice little operation directly on the water. Costs are $79–$99 in season, $59–$69 otherwise. Sometimes they charge $10 more on the weekends. Telephone: 664-2961.

WHERE TO EAT

Ziggie's Conch at MM #83 is small, crowded, and plain, with the exception of a wonderful painting of Flagler's train chugging across the Long Key Bridge. There's an extensive fish menu and a popular bar. A longtime eccentric favorite, it's tamed down a bit and now may be . . . just another restaurant. Open 6 P.M. Closed Wednesdays. Telephone: 664-3391.

Lorelei (MM #82 at the Islamorada Yacht Basin). The tiki bar outside is friendly, the gathering place at the end of the day for backcountry guides. The restaurant has lots of glass and lovely Bay views, although you may be seated by a large mermaid with a tail of glued-on tarpon scales which occupies one wall. Lorelei has many steak, lobster, and rich seafood casserole offerings. Their snapper stuffed with crabmeat is good, but expensive even by Key West standards. Open 11 A.M. to 3 P.M. for lunch, 5:30 to 9:30 P.M. for dinner; Saturdays 11 A.M. to 9:30 P.M. Telephone: 664-4656. Nearby is **Woody's** (664-4335), a popular place for pizza and pasta but most renowned for its lounge life after 10, when a band called Big Dick and the Extenders plays.

Grove Park Cafe (MM #81.7 old road) next to Manny and Isa's has overreacted to the manly watering holes of Islamorada in a big way. A fussy tearoom, it is peach and green and blue. Also lavender. After you dine sensibly you can buy a stuffed animal in the boutique at the cash register. Open for lunch and dinner (664-0116).

Green Turtle Inn (MM #81). Popular, crowded, and cluttered, the Green Turtle has been around since 1947, when patrons really tucked in the turtle steaks. In 1970, just before the government passed laws prohibiting the killing and selling of green turtle, the owner of Sid and Roxie's Cannery across the street was processing more than 1,000 pounds of turtle meat weekly. The turtle steaks and chowders you now get at the inn are from freshwater turtles raised in farms around Lake Okeechobee. Several old cottages have been joined to make up the restaurant, which is cozy and hearty, the walls covered with photographs of jolly, beaming patrons and framed newspaper headlines of puzzling relevance—ANOTHER JAP WARLORD KILLS SELF. At night there's a piano player who'll play anything you request. "I'm Back in Baby's Arms" seems to be popular with the diners. Maybe you'll be on hand for the "turtle wave," which everyone seems to know how to do. Open from noon until 10 P.M. Closed Mondays. Telephone: 664-4918.

Papa Joe's (MM #80). A nice old place at the end of Upper Matecumbe, overlooking Tea Table Channel. Italian dishes, fresh and inexpensive fish dinners. A tiki bar is cantilevered over a bait shop in back. Open from 11 A.M. until 10 P.M. Closed Tuesdays. Telephone: 664-8109. You can arrange for rental boats and backcountry charters here, too. The marina's number is 664-5005.

Manny and Isa's (MM #81.6). Manny has an orchard behind his tiny restaurant, and each summer he squeezes 9,000 Key limes for you. The pies are classic: $1.75 a slice, $10 for the whole statement. Open 11 A.M. to 9 P.M. Closed Tuesdays. Telephone: 664-5019. Don't expect ambience here, just good . . . pie.

Islamorada Fish Company (MM #81.6). There's a busy fish market here sandwiched between the picnic tables on the parking lot and the picnic tables back on the bayside waters. Very popular. Fritters, cracked conch, fried seafood baskets, and stone crab claws. Soft drinks only. Open from Monday to Saturday 11–9. Sunday 9–5 (664-9271).

LIGNUMVITAE AND INDIAN KEYS

Between Upper and Lower Matecumbe Keys lie two uncon-
nected, uninhabited keys of considerable historic and natural
interest: Lignumvitae and Indian.

Lignumvitae, a 345-acre island, along with Shell Key and
Indian Key, was purchased by the Nature Conservancy and the
state in 1970. Of all the Keys, Lignumvitae is the highest—16
feet above sea level—and is a true island. Although the giant
mahoganies were removed in the nineteenth century, and
although some building and introduction of exotic plants and
animals took place in the 1920s, Lignumvitae is considered to
be virgin hammock, the last untouched bit of tropical forest in
Florida. Botanists say that to enter Lignumvitae is to enter the
primeval past. Certainly it is to see a portion of the wonder that
Florida once was.

The history of the Keys is a harsh one of dynamiting, burning, collecting, and developing. Lignumvitae has miraculously
escaped all that. Its last owner, a Miami dentist, wanted to
build a bridge from Lower Matecumbe Key and develop a resort
there. He liked golf, so there would have been a golf course.
Restaurants. The works. Amazingly, this didn't happen.
Lignumvitae was saved. Perhaps it's blessed. It has never been
burned like the other keys; fire has never destroyed the organic
humus that takes centuries to form over the coral rock. Farmers never cleared and seared the land to get a year or two of
good fruit production. Snail collectors never discovered it and
burned the hammock when they left, as was their habit. (All of
Florida's tropical hammocks were home to varieties of tree
snails. The snails of each area evolved distinct color patterns on
their shells and were astonishingly popular with collectors
throughout the world. It was common for a collector to go to a
hammock, collect a few snails, then set the land on fire to
increase the rarity and value of the variety he had collected.
The snail peculiar to Lignumvitae has a shell neatly circled
with fine bands of red and green on a base of cream.)

Lignum vitae is a tree noted for the extreme density of its
wood. Because of the rich resins which keep it from drying out,

it has been used in boat outfitting, outlasting even steel and bronze. Lignum vitae was first described in *Ortus Sanitatis,* one of the major botanical works of the fifteenth century, as a tree in the Garden of Eden. Whoever consumed it was said to be strengthened with perpetual health, clothed in immortality, and protected from anxiety, weakness, and infirmity. It was described as being not only nonflammable, but purified by fire, and it was the wood from which the Holy Grail was created. In the Bahamas today, lignum vitae is called holywood or broke-iron tree and is used as a cure for impotence.

The Matheson family, which owned Lignumvitae from 1919 to 1953, built the large limestone house visible from the dock, as well as the windmill and cistern. They decorated the lawn with six cannon from the wrecked HMS *Winchester,* which ran aground on Carysfort Reef in 1695 and was discovered in 1939. They built an airstrip, brought in a bulldozer to maintain a trail, and imported burros, Galapagos tortoises, Angora goats, round-eared brown rabbits, Indian geese, ducks, and peafowl. They also made extensive plantings of exotics with the assistance of their friend, the famous botanist David Fairchild.

In the 1970s the Key Largo wood rat, Florida's endangered rodent, was introduced here, but after surviving for two decades it suddenly vanished. Biologists believe that the small population had an inadequate gene pool and that a damaging recessive gene eventually destroyed them.

All the strange species are gone now, along with the other disturbances. The house remains, the only interruption in the mangrove shoreline, facing east away from the sea, untouched by the 1935 hurricane that cut such a narrow and ferocious swath between Tavernier and Marathon. Around the house are huge mastics and banyans and sapodilla trees, and beyond is the forest of the hammock. There are 133 varieties of trees here, including the thorny plants of the low, hot woods on the western shore—prickly ash, cockspur, hog plum, and cat's claw. There is also an enigmatic half-mile-long, four-foot-high coral rock wall built no one knows when, or why, as well as a Caloosa burial ground.

For years before the state purchased the key, the caretakers of the property were the remarkable Russel and Charlotte

Niedhauk. *Charlotte's Story,* a 1930s diary of the Niedhauks' caretaking of Elliott Key, north of Key Largo, is available in local bookstores and is a charming and guileless account of risk, ingenuity, and adventure in a primitive Florida. Charlotte and her pet parrot are buried on Lignumvitae.

A boat leaves from Indian Key Fill to Indian Key at 9 and at 1 and to Lignumvitae at 10 and at 2, Thursday through Monday. The boat trip costs $7 for adults, $3 for children. A one-hour ranger-guided tour of Lignumvitae costs another $1. For reservations call 664-9814 or 664-4196. Or you can rent a boat from **Bud 'n' Mary's** (MM #79.5, 664-2461) or **Robbie's** (MM #77.5, opposite the motel Oceanina at the Lignum Vitae Bridge, 664-9814). Bud 'n' Mary's rents a 25-horsepower, 17-foot boat for $75 a half day, $100 for a full day; 50 hp runs $95 and $135; a 125-hp, 21-foot Divemaster costs $125 and $175. Robbie's boats range from 14-foot, 25-hp Boston Whalers to a 20-foot, 130-hp Seamaster. For half a day the Whalers run $60–$95 and $80–$145; the bigger boats go about $145 for half a day, $200 for a full one. There are good weekly rates. Be sure to have a chart, and take special care over the sea grass beds. A prop scar through a sea grass meadow is a terrible thing to make, and to see. Never operate your boat in less than three feet of water, and pole, don't motor, in brown water. The brown on the grass blades are tiny plants and animals known as epiphytes, which are important forage for fish. Robbie's also runs a tour boat to Lignumvitae. The cost is $15 per person. You can see Indian Key for an additional $10. The trips run twice a day, except for Tuesdays and Wednesdays, when no boat landings on the Keys are permitted.

A nice time to visit Lignumvitae is during the first two weeks in April, when the trees are in bloom. This is old-timey Keys out here, remember. Lots of mosquitoes.

The Spanish named **Indian Key** Matanzas, which means slaughter, purportedly because 400 shipwrecked Frenchmen were killed by the Caloosa Indians here. The slaughter seems more legend than fact and may just be another example of the Spaniard's gloomy penchant for bloody place names. Once again, however, the name proved historically fateful.

In the 1830s the 11-acre island was a flourishing town, the personal kingdom of a wrecker named Jacob Housman, who established a salvaging station here so that he would not have to obey the rules and pay the fees set by Key West courts. Indian Key had a post office, three streets, 20 houses, wharves, warehouses, and a resort hotel called the Tropical. There was even a bowling alley in this best of all possible worlds, the bowling balls probably made of lignum vitae wood.

Audubon anchored offshore on the revenue cutter *Marion* for a week in the spring of 1832 and discovered birds there which were entirely new to him, including the roseate tern, the double-breasted cormorant, and the reddish egret. He extensively used the services of one of Housman's pilots, a man named Egan. Egan took him along the channels and through the maze of mangrove unerringly to the objects of his desire. "Not a cormorant or pelican, a flamingo, an ibis, or heron, had ever in his days formed its nest without his having marked the spot," Audubon wrote. While George Lehman, his background artist, drew the key itself, Audubon sketched the birds.

Audubon was not a precociously gifted draftsman. Even after he had perfected his method, in which freshly killed specimens were run through with wires and arranged in lifelike positions, he still had to keep shooting the same species over and over, so that he could sketch them in different positions. In *The Birds of America* he wrote of the brown pelican, "This superb male whose portrait is before you . . . was selected from a great number." In his writings he also shares with us a disappointment he suffered:

Lo, I came in sight of several pelicans, perched on the branches of the mangrove trees, seated in comfortable harmony, as near each other as the strength of the boughs would allow. I ordered to back water gently. I waded to the shore under cover of the rushes along it, saw the pelicans fast asleep, examined their countenances and deportment well and leisurely, and after all, levelled, fired my piece and dropped two of the finest specimens I ever saw. I really believe I would have shot one hundred of these reverend sirs, had not a mistake taken place in the reloading of my gun. A mistake, however, did take place, and to my utmost disappointment, I saw each pelican, young and old, leave his perch and take to wing.

Audubon loved the singular plants, the gorgeous flowers, and the "salubrious" air of Indian Key. He gives an account of a raucous party the islanders threw, complete with fiddles and diluted claret for the ladies.

Jacob Housman was a wealthy man and a law unto himself, but he still had to worry about the Indians. He arranged to have the Navy's Florida Squadron, a fleet of seven ships based on nearby Tea Table Key, to protect his holdings, but the squadron, known for spending more money on "medicines," primarily rum, than all the other units of the Navy combined, were to be of little use to the townspeople of Indian Key.

By 1840 Housman's town had 55 inhabitants, including a physician-botanist, Dr. Henry Perrine, and his family. Perrine established a nursery on the northeast end of Lower Matecumbe and did plant research on Indian Key. All in all he introduced more than 200 plants to tropical Florida. He had many interests, including silkworms and stingless bees, but his true obsession was *agave*—a plant cultivated for its sturdy sisal, a durable fiber, and also, less prosaically, as a source of hashish. Dr. Perrine also treated the sick, including Seminole Indians. Housman, on the other hand, ever enterprising, was trying to negotiate a contract with the government which would permit him to hunt and kill the Indians at $200 a head.

On August 7, 1840, with the Naval squadron away, the Seminoles, no doubt having heard of Housman's income-producing scheme, attacked the island, burning every building except the home of the postman, Charles Howe. Howe was a Mason, and his Masonic apron with its all-seeing eye and other mystic symbols was found spread upon the table. The eye may have given the Indians pause, but they went on anyway to kill 16 people, one of whom was Dr. Perrine. Those who escaped the massacre hid in turtle kraals near the houses or in the cisterns beneath them, although gruesome popular history claims that some who sought safety there were boiled alive. Housman and his family survived, but he never reestablished his empire. He returned to Key West and worked on a former rival's salvage vessel, dying in a ship accident six months later. His body was buried on Indian Key, and there is a historical plaque identifying the site. Someone has stolen the skeleton, to say nothing of the tombstone, although fragments of the stone were recovered and taken to Lignumvitae for safekeeping. Other markers identify the house site, the hotel cistern, and so on.

A new community was formed on the island in the 1870s, when the key became a site for building schooners and sloops. It was also on this tiny key that the construction workers for the Alligator Reef lighthouse, built in 1873, lived, and where the iron pile structure, built and dismantled in a northern foundry, then shipped to Florida, was stored before being transported to the reef.

Indian Key is certainly not the unblemished paradise that Lignumvitae is. It seems ironic that it ended up as a historic site rather than a botanical one when one considers Dr. Perrine's extensive introduction of exotic plants here. Damage was done in the 1930s and 1940s when treasure hunters dynamited it to search for valuables they thought were buried there. Tourists were even brought over at $5 a day and furnished with shovels so that they could dig. Today the landscape seems almost Mexican, with its sisal plants and prickly pear, descendants of the doctor's plants, but there is also a restful wild tamarind grove, the delicate, feathery foliage softening the glare of the sun.

As with Lignumvitae, you must acquire or hire a boat to get over to Indian Key, but then you're on your own. You may explore from 8 A.M. to sunset.

A mile south of Indian Key is the wreck of the *San Pedro*, a ship that went down in 1733. It lies in 18 feet of water and consists mostly of ballast stones, although it has recently been enhanced by replicas of timbers, anchors, and cannon.

LOWER MATECUMBE KEY

Judging from the amount of tangled monofilament around the power lines, some of the worst fishermen in the Keys frequent the catwalks over Indian Key and Lignumvitae channels. Fishing here and along the bridges that span Channel #2 and Channel #5 between Lower Matecumbe and Long Key is very good, offering catches of snapper, grouper, and, in the spring and early summer, snook. In the winter, after a cold snap and the ensuing nor'wester, shrimp leave the cooler waters of the Bay and can be netted from the bridges at night.

Alligator Lighthouse, the most beautiful on the reef, white and stately, is visible off the Matecumbe keys. More than 500 species of fish have been found on the reef the light marks.

Lower Matecumbe has a number of troubled time-shares, most of which would be thrilled if you rented a room for the night. Developers went into a greed frenzy in the early 1980s, when they came up with the idea of selling both space *and* time. The new structures are circular, erected on pedestals, with an ambience of early space station. The old ones are old motels. **Caloosa Cove** at MM #73.8 covers all bases—it's a time-share condominium resort with a full marina, charters, room and boat rentals, tennis courts, and a bar which is inexplicably called the Safari and filled with African "artifacts." The establishment leaps into the void of hyperbole with its billboard slogan, PARADISE AT YOUR COMMAND. Telephone: 664-8811. Just south of here is **Anne's Beach**, public, tiny, and very, very crowded. From the road it merely looks like a used-car lot. In the water, the owners of the cars stand shin-deep, museful.

A far lovelier sight is the watery stretch between Lower Matecumbe and tiny Craig Key at MM #72. This area has some very pretty picnicking spots and some of the most beautiful views to be had from the highway in the Keys. You will see many birds feeding here—little blue herons, which when young are pure white; white ibis, with their bright orange curved bills; white egrets, with their black legs and beautiful long breeding feathers, which are called *aigrettes;* and great white herons, the largest of the herons—over four feet in height, with a wingspan of seven feet—readily distinguished from the egrets by their much greater size and their light-colored legs. The great white is rare except in the Keys, where it is frequently seen. This very limited range, however, indicates low total numbers, and their small population is devastated by storms and hurricanes.

Craig Key once had several fishing shacks built out over the water and even a post office, established in the late 1920s because President Herbert Hoover had once anchored his yacht close by and it was thought that he might want to mail some-

PELICANS: COLORS AND A LEGEND

Brown pelicans can be seen everywhere, all year long, in the Keys. The white pelican breeds in the summer near the mountain lakes of Montana and Utah and is only a winter visitor to the islands in Florida Bay. (Unlike brown pelicans, white pelicans don't dive for fish. Instead their fishing is a communal effort, with ten to fifteen birds forming a semicircle and herding the fish to shore, where they can then scoop them up with their bills.) Many of the brown pelicans you see begging for fish off docks and bridges are young birds. A pelican in his first year has a brown neck and wings and a very white belly. In the second year his body is more gray than brown. By the third year his belly is quite dark. In the summertime the adult pelican's head is white with a dark brown stripe on the back of the neck. In early fall the brown stripe molts to white, and yellow courting plumage appears.

The pelican is a bird of myth as well as droll actuality. His image is common on ecclesiastical heraldry and was often engraved on chalices. Many medieval bestiaries include a story in which the mother pelican caresses her offspring with such devotion that she kills them. When the father returns to the nest, he so despairs over the death of his young that he tears at his breast with his bill, and the blood from his wounds revives the dead birds. Dante, in the *Paradiso* (canto XXV, line 113), calls Jesus Christ *nostro Pellicano*—mankind's pelican.

Pelicans feeding

thing. Storms blew everything away, but in the 1960s a concrete-block mansion was built on the Bay side by the Twitchell
family, the original owners of the Cheeca Lodge. Concealed
behind a stone wall and a grove of pine, the manse has five bedrooms, two full kitchens, eight baths, and a mirrored bar mod-
eled after Cheeca's. Mrs. Twitchell was an A&P heiress who
was known for her sense of humor. Mrs. Twitchell's sense of
humor is responsible, it is said, for the air jets in the front door
jamb that would blast up ladies' dresses.

The road curves sharply after Craig, crossing Channel #5 and
the Intracoastal Waterway, which links the ocean and the Bay
at MM #70. The next key, **Fiesta**, is a fill, as is Craig. Fiesta
was originally called Jewfish Key, then Greyhound when the
Greyhound Corporation built a post house there for its bus passengers, shortly after the highway was pushed down to Grassy
Key in 1937. Now it's the site of a KOA (Kampgrounds of America) campground.

Layton is a city, incorporated in 1963, but certainly a modest
one. Once, two locked black-and-white police cars (actually, one
of them was only painted to *look* like a police car) were parked
on either side of the highway near MM #68 and people thought
they were somewhere and slowed down, but these were recently

Reddish egret

hauled away, one of Layton's biggest events in years. At MM #69 there is yet another Keys marine laboratory, this one actually called the **Keys Marine Laboratory**, closed to the public but offering a number of programs to students of the marine sciences. Lots of research goes on back here, and many papers are written as a result. There's a large book in the office which lists the titles of these papers and the intent of the studies, and it makes for pretty heavy browsing.

Tennessee Reef is one of the few areas in the National Marine Sanctuary Plan designated for research only. It is a beautiful reef, with lots of variety and unique deepwater slow-growth corals and sponges, but its location in the path of waters from the ailing Florida Bay has resulted in poor water quality. The health of this reef will be monitored and compared with another research-only site which has very good water quality, the Spur and Grove Bank Reef of the Eastern Sambos some distance south.

Lime Tree Bay Resort (MM #68.5, 664-4740). The rooms used to be more intriguing here, with varied motifs, but they've been redone and homogenized. Now each bed has the standardized polyester bright hibiscus-patterned quilt. There's a collection of rooms and efficiencies, even a few cottages, and a swimming pool you have to climb up a few steps to address. Rooms are $120 in season. The two-bedroom treehouse apartment, complete with a tree growing through the porch, is $200. Close by there are lots of different types of boats to rent. Layton is quiet, and the waters are beautiful here.

LONG KEY

Long Key State Recreation Area at MM #67.5 is one of the three state parks on the Keys. The swimming here is poor—you see people far, far from shore and they're still only up to their knees—and the beach is narrow, squeezed close to the park road and the speeding parade of humanity on Route 1. There is a nature walk through the mangroves on a recently constructed boardwalk, complete with interpretive signs that urge you to reflect, ponder, and mull. One invites you to imagine a Caloosa Indian poking about the mangroves doing his inscrutable Caloosa Indian thing. "Life must have been so different then . . . ," it trails off wistfully.

The walkway is called the Golden Orb trail after the spectacular spiders that weave their webs here. The webs are heavy and huge, the female spider a royal red and gold. The males are tiny little things crouched in the corner or are not around at all. They spend so much time searching for females, courting them, and mating with them that they neglect eating and often drop dead from exhaustion.

You can rent a canoe and explore a winding tidal lagoon. Very pretty. Watch out for the "skinny water," where the coral cap rock lies close to the surface.

Off the beach the snorkeling is a great deal of fun—you'll see lobsters and octopuses—and the beachcombing can be interesting if you're able to block out the astonishing amount of discarded plastic. Always there seem to be dolls' heads on remote beaches, and Long Key is no exception. Here, too, scattered amid the plastic, can be found the rubbery, flattened egg cases of turtles.

There's quite a bit of bird activity on the flats. The best show is put on by the reddish egret as he attempts to acquire lunch. This is a gangly, charming bird—a two-toned heron, the head and neck reddish brown, the body slate gray. He also goes through a white phase, when you could easily confuse him with a variety of herons and egrets, including even the immature little blue. But what distinguishes the reddish egret is his peculiar eating habits. Other wading birds have dignity. They stalk. They stand motionless. They are patient and aloof. The red selects the minnow he wants and chases it until he gets it, in a frenzy of running, lurching, splashing, and zigzagging, flapping his wings and clacking his bill until the minnow, exhausted, surrenders in a blur of foam.

Campgrounds in the Keys are very popular places, in both the winter and summer months. The state parks have an ingenious system of reserving 50 percent of the campsites, leaving the other half available on a first-come, first-served basis. You have to make reservations early, though not *too* early—not more than 60 days in advance, and by telephone, not mail. Checkout time is 2 P.M. and there's a two-week maximum stay for $23.50 a night, $25.75 with electric hookup.

The seaweed that coats the beach here is a kitchen cupboard for the birds, jumping and crawling with tasty amphipods. But for you, the adventurous camper, the seaweed after the sun goes down becomes a jumping, crawling hell. You cannot imagine how many bugs creep, crawl, and fly on a Keys beach after dark. So don't undertake your overnighters lightly, with a beach towel and a can of Coke. Bring lots of insect repellent and cover-ups, so that you can enjoy the enormous sky and the glittering ocean phosphorescent with life.

By 1906 construction of the railroad had come as far as Long Key. Henry Flagler built screened cottages for his workers while they labored on the Long Key Viaduct. Other workers were housed on large covered barges called quarterboats. When a hurricane struck Long Key in the fall of 1906, one of these quarterboats broke its moorings and was swept out to sea, drowning more than a hundred men.

After the viaduct was completed, Flagler turned the construction camp into a fishing camp, the Long Key Fishing Club, for the wealthy who arrived by yacht and rail. He supplemented the bungalows with a luxury lodge on a white-sand beach on the ocean side, and even built a narrow-gauge railroad that ran through a tunnel beneath the tracks for the convenience of his guests.

Zane Grey (Was he really christened Pearl Grey?) was one of the camp's most famous guests. The well-known writer of west-

---

BUGS

Mosquitoes are big here. They have been called the most reliable defenders of wilderness in the state. Sandflies are big. They're called "flying teeth." Palmetto bugs, the Southern cockroach, are very big, and shiny too. You'll see them in the best of places as well as in the wilds. At a pool party at an elegant home, a guest was heard to exclaim, "Oh, look at the little turtles!" as a family of these creepies lumbered across the patio. If you crush them, there is a terrible smell of almonds.

erns first visited here in 1913 and organized the club's fishing contests, established "to develop the best and finest traits of sport, to restrict the killing of fish, to educate the inexperienced angler by helping him and to promote good fellowship." Grey brought sailfishing into vogue. At that time sailfish were considered pests and were called spikefish or "boohoo" because of the disappointment they often caused by slicing through lines intended for more popular quarry, such as kingfish. Grey introduced light-tackle methods, and taking sailfish became an art. He found the fish the gamest and most beautiful fish to catch on light tackle, with its pirouetting leaps and its great sail spread.

Grey visited the fishing camp frequently over the years, in January and February, adhering to a schedule of rising early, writing for one hour, fishing for ten, then writing for another hour or two in the evenings. He worked on books such as *Code of the West* and *The Light of Western Stars* here, as well as doing a great deal of exploring and photography. "So much beauty and wildlife," he wrote, "so wild it was tame." Grey was also known for releasing trophy-sized catches and not mourning the ones that got away. He wrote of a lost tarpon, "Into my memory had been burned indelibly a picture of a sunlit, cloud-mirroring, green and gold bordered cove, above the center of which shone a glorious fish-creature in the air."

The Long Key Fishing Club was completely destroyed in the 1935 hurricane. Just south of the boat rentals in Layton there is a historical tablet commemorating the site, if not accurately marking it.

THE MIDDLE KEYS
Long Key Viaduct to Bahia Honda

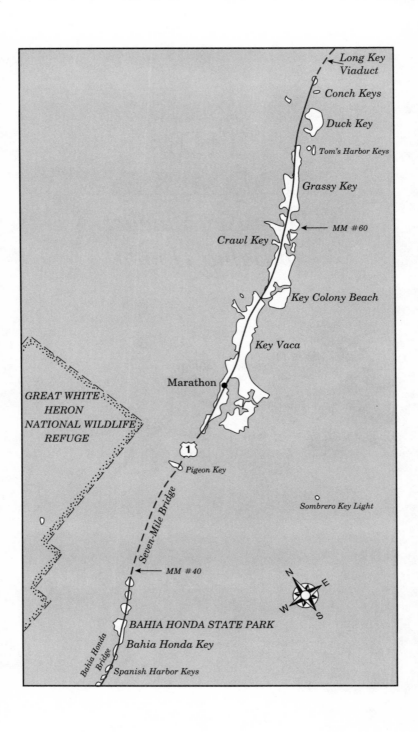

Long Key
Viaduct

Conch Keys

Duck Key

Tom's Harbor Keys

Grassy Key

MM #60

Crawl Key

Key Colony Beach

Key Vaca

Marathon

GREAT WHITE
HERON
NATIONAL WILDLIFE
REFUGE

1

Pigeon Key

Sombrero Key Light

Seven-Mile Bridge

MM #40

N

E

W

S

BAHIA HONDA STATE PARK

Bahia Honda Key

Bahia Honda
Bridge

Spanish Harbor Keys

F ORTY-TWO bridges link the Keys, but it is in the Middle Keys where the three longest and most impressive ones stand. Beside them are their shadows, the bridges recently built. The road now traverses these shadows—the strong old bridges run emptily alongside. Everywhere there is water, water that becomes sky, the shadows of rays like clouds moving across the blue. Water loves light. The light changes. Dawn and sunset break. Thunderclouds mass. The water is black, emerald, azure, sheer, and the vault of sky becomes the vault of water. Flocks of egrets fly bone-white across that impossible interstice. The Keys are lovely litanies of colors and creatures, fishes and birds.

If one were to know the Keys only by car, this passage over the bridges of the Middle Keys is the most impressive. The trip by train must have been astonishing. John Dos Passos in a letter to Hemingway called it a "dreamlike journey." The trains crept across the bridges no faster than 15 miles an hour and seldom exceeded 40 miles an hour over the mostly deserted Keys. The dreamlike journey made possible by the railroad was created with swarms of vessels, workboats, dredges, seagoing cranes, pile drivers, quarterboats, and floating cement mixers. At one point Flagler's general manager, Joseph Parrott, had every freight steamer on the Atlantic coast that flew the American flag under charter to bring in materials.

Before the railroad there were few people on any of these keys. There were saltworks on Duck Key in the early 1800s, but they were abandoned by 1837. A few Bahamian families had lived along Key Vaca, but they had deserted it by 1860. In 1926 the population of Marathon was only 17. It was not until the 1940s that sportfishing created a reason for the town's existence. Other, now highly populated areas are of even more recent invention. In the 1950s causeways were built to islands such as Duck Key, and even islands that weren't, such as Key Colony Beach. One best perceives the beauty of this area—its remaining wilderness—from the great bridges, even though, as in the case of the newly installed utility poles which run the distance of the Seven-Mile Bridge, modernization has reduced the awesome effect.

People remember traveling on the old bridges with fondness, even though delays were common. Accidents and breakdowns would jam up the narrow lanes. The drawspan on the Seven-Mile Bridge would stick. Small airplanes would sometimes make emergency landings. These were usually occasions for a party. People would abandon their cars, throw out a fishing line, set up the cooler and the radio, become tight friends with complete strangers, and socialize in the sunshine, beneath the merging seas and the sky.

The beautiful **Long Key Viaduct** at MM #65.5 was Flagler's favorite bridge, and the one he used in photographs advertising the railroad. One hundred eighty arches span two and one half miles of water, making it the second largest span in the Keys. Be sure to pull off the road to the left just before crossing the new Long Key Bridge built close alongside. Walk down the embankment, where in spring there will be a profusion of flowering vines and stacked crayfish traps, and look at the graceful old arches, darkly Roman against the green tropical waters and far nobler than the sensible modern piers.

Stacked crayfish traps are once again in evidence on the other side of the bridge during the closed season, April 1 to July 25. Here at MM #63 is **Conch Key**. Conch Key consists of 16 acres, every inch of which is covered with houses and crayfish traps. The crayfish, or "bug," or Florida spiny lobster has long antennae, many legs, and no claws. All the meat is in the muscles of the tail, which is used for backward propulsion. Fishermen, lobstermen, and retirees inhabit Conch Key, along with hundreds of crayfish traps.

Crossing the bridge over Tom's Harbor Cut at MM #61, you will see on your left **Duck Key**, dominated by the striking green-and-pink **Hawk's Cay Resort**. The colors, according to the designer, are actually seafoam green, salmon, cabbage green, and paper-bag brown. This is no place to bag your lunch, however. For luxury, this is *the* place in the Middle Keys—

awash in Jacuzzis, chefs in white hats, chaise lounges, linen tablecloths, and fresh cans of tennis balls. Hawk's Cay used to be the Indies Inn before the Indies became ramshackle and slipped into receivership. Fifteen million dollars' worth of renovations later, it is now ready to receive you. It is very tasteful, very comfortable, very elegant, with lots of French doors, wicker furniture, and gleaming tiles, but there is the flavor of the boardroom in some of its larger pavilions and terraces. One ambitious journalist wrote that the property "glowed with a lovely patina," then went on to add, rather alarmingly, "with a Vaseline-on-the-lens sort of softness to it." The clay tennis courts are called gardens here, for they are set amid some sea grape and palm, and there is a marina a short distance away that offers fishing charters, and a nightclub with a dance floor. As well, Hawk's Cay has somehow acquired dolphins as part of their on-site resort amenities.

Many are the planned activities at Hawk's Cay, and adult guests are treated rather like shy campers who must gently be introduced to fishing rods and tiny sailboats and even, behind and beyond the mannered affluence of the place, Nature. A bizarrely named Scratch 'n' Sniff tour will take you by rubber raft past the canals and expensive stuccoed homes of Duck Key and encourage you to observe starfish bumbling across the flats or herons clinging to a bit of undisturbed mangrove. And it will bring you back to the resort in time for lunch.

In season (mid-December to mid-April), large suites are $500 a night, smaller suites are around $400. Water-view rooms are $325; land-view rooms (which might give you a glimpse of the parking area) are $250. Prices hurtle downward by $50 to $100 in summer and spring. A three-nights' deposit is required at Christmas, New Year's, and Easter. A lavish breakfast buffet is complimentary daily. Telephone: 743-7000.

Below elaborate Duck Key lies **Grassy Key**, where Flipper's Sea School used to be the big attraction: Flipper, the film star, whose real name was Mitzi, is buried here, and a 30-foot-tall monument to a dolphin mother and baby still stands on the Bay side of the highway at MM #59. Flipper's moved to a new and more elaborate site in Key West, invested a fortune in advertising, and promptly went out of business. The facility on Grassy Key became the **Dolphin Research Center** and is open to the public.

Dolphins are curious, playful, social, and very sexy. They're bisexual. They have complex brains even larger than man's. They have several stomachs and no sense of smell. They have an incredibly refined capacity to form auditory images and "hear" the texture of objects around them, suggesting that they can look into each other in eerie ways and read emotional states. They once lived on land, and gradually, for unknown reasons, took to the seas. One story, and why not believe it, is that they approached man around the time of Plato and Aristotle but philosophers and religious men rebuffed them, so they retreated into the depths of the sea to await a better time for communication and understanding. They have remarkable memories and can comprehend simple sonic sentences. They become bored easily. When they give birth there is frequently another female close by acting as midwife, assisting the new mother in bringing the baby to the surface for his first breath of air. Dolphins breathe through their blowholes, emitting occasional whiffs of sweet-smelling air, almost like chlorophyll. (Some Japanese fishermen, complaining that dolphins compete with them in catching cuttlefish and yellowtail, herd them ashore and club them to death.)

Dolphins have their own legend. It is said they believe that one day a few humans will break through to a new, transhuman level of consciousness and make contact with them. There are several versions of this legend. One is that these humans, true philosophers who comprehend the whole in all its parts, will join the dolphins and never return. Another is that they will return to the world of men and be locked up as lunatics. A third has them join forces with the dolphins, stage a bloodless coup d'état, and establish a peaceful and paradisiacal rule over all man- and animalkind. And, of course, the last version is that the dolphins, totally fed up with even the philosophers, will lead an insurrection of all the beasts and eliminate the human race because of its grave threat to the planet.

The Dolphin Research Center has about 15 dolphins and three sea lions and puts on what seem awfully similar to dolphin-show shows: tail walks, aerial acrobatics, rollovers, dorsal shakes. They are constantly being trained to perform new routines. They even go through "body examination husbandry training" or "medical behaviors" schooling to facilitate their constant physical monitoring. Dolphin births are not unusual at the Center, and there is a newsletter keeping dolphin "parents" ($200 a year) or "dolfriends" ($20 donation) apprised of Center activities: "Rainbow is still working on his new behavior, the vertical spin. He's progressing well. Aleta, Santini, and Merina were recently involved in a photo shoot for *Seventeen* magazine, and, loving the attention, they were very excited. The dolphins have distinctive personalities, of course, which are interpreted in detail. A.J. is a little guy with a subtle charisma that sweeps people right off their feet. Delphi is the suave father of many of our dolphin babies."

You can swim with the dolphins here, although you don't just swim with them, you "encounter" and "interact" with them. This "ultimate experience" is very popular, and reservations have to be made the first day of the month prior to the month of your encounter. It costs $90. Call 289-0002 between 9 and 5. For the more serious devotee of the divine dolphin there is Dolphinlab, a seven-day course of seminars, films, and field trips to the backcountry. It will cost you $1,100 to get involved and be brought up to date on dolphin psychology, language research, and behavior modification. Write to P.O. Box 522875, Marathon Shores, FL 33052, or call 289-1121.

The Center is the only facility in the Keys licensed to rescue and treat injured manatees. We might all be swimming with

The difference between dolphins and dolphins

THE DIFFERENCE BETWEEN DOLPHINS AND DOLPHINS

Dolphins are spiny-finned gamefish of flamboyant colors, the brilliance of which fades instantly with death. They are of the genus *Coryphaena,* family Coryphaenidae. People catch them and eat them because they taste very good.

Dolphins are also the smart and friendly mammals who nurse their young, speak in "clicks," and like to play around boats. They have little teeth and big smiles. Hemingway once remarked that he would shoot his own mother "if she flew in coveys and had a good strong flight," but most people would feel that dining on these individuals was rude, if not cannibalistic. These dolphins are small-toothed whales, genus *Delphinus,* family Delphinidae, and have a distinct and easily recognizable snout. The name *porpoise* can be applied only to a few species of Phocoenidae that lack this pronounced beak and have spade-shaped rather than conical teeth. However, most fishermen, restaurant owners, and even some scientists call mammalian dolphins porpoises, to distinguish them from the gamefish dolphins. The best-known of these mammals is the bottle-nose dolphin—the one seen in "shows"— which you can refer to as a porpoise if it will make you feel more comfortable while you're chowing down the dolphin fish, which perhaps should be called what it is in other parts of the world—*dorado* or *mahi-mahi. Dolphin* sounds so pretty, though. Most fish have such goofy epithets—jewfish, mullet, turbot, snapper. Bonefish. Permit. Grunt.

the manatees soon, though manatees are vegetarians and less show-offy as a rule. Plus they're shy and might not lend themselves so readily to vivid character analysis.

The main number at the Dolphin Research Center is 289-1121. It is open from 9 to 4 seven days a week. Admission is $7.50.

For eating out, the **Grassy Key Dairy Bar** at MM #58.5 is *the* place to go. The name is strange, but the food is the best for miles. There are two squat cement ice-cream cones in front. Seafood and beef dinners, with wine and beer, are served from 5 to 10 P.M. Closed Sundays and Mondays. Telephone: 743-3816.

Rainbow Bend Fishing Resort at MM #58 is a relaxing alternative to the hustle and sprawl of Marathon, eight miles farther down the road. A tiny place, hardly a resort but with a tidy beach, pier, and pool. Most of the units are suites and efficiencies and run around $200 a night. The management at times can be a bit cool, and draconian deposit/cancellation reservation rules are in effect, but as their guest you get the free use of a Boston Whaler—great for exploring the reef at Coffins Patch or fishing the flats off Duck Key. Coffins Patch was once called "Atlantis" because of the tall pillar coral that made exotic fishy cities there, before collectors and shell shops hauled off the larger specimens. (Pillar coral grows approximately one inch every 40 years, so it's unlikely you will ever see what the "collectors" did.) The airy second-story restaurant here is called the **Hideaway**, and the food is so fancy that they say people come down all the way from Miami to eat it. (That is, they don't do anything else here. They eat it and go back.) Prime rib, filet medallions, seafood Delmonico. Cognacs and creams and special sauces. Amaretto frequently figures. There's a good wine list. Call the Rainbow Bend at 289-1505.

Just beyond, on Crawl Key at MM #56.5, is a road to the left that leads to **Valhalla Beach Motel**. On the road maps a town named Ecstasy is mentioned, but Ecstasy is hard to find. You might, in fact, spend a very long time hunting around for Ecstasy. Valhalla Beach Motel, however, can be attained, and it's a nice little place with a sand beach on a tidal creek and bird-busy mangroves all around. You should make reservations (289-0616), for there are only a dozen rooms. Most of these are efficiencies that run about $75 a night. No credit cards. It's a return to a simpler, sweeter Keys back here, a sleepy exception to the wired development of so much of the area. The beautiful views seem almost illusory, a scrim before the pumped-up, pumped-out communities of Coco Plum Beach and Tennis Club, and Key Colony Beach beyond.

The next several miles are empty of all but mangroves. The water pipe that runs the length of the Keys is clearly visible here on the right. Activity begins just beyond the old Pull-and-Be-Damned Creek—the scourge of railroad workers who had to row supplies across its strong currents—a part of Vaca Cut now filled in. Here is **Adventure Island**, a feverish dream for the highly active, where there are sailboat, catamaran, sunfish, and jet-ski rentals. You can also have the thrilling, rackety fun of a helicopter ride. There was ambition here once—there are 27 picnic tables behind the tiki bar—but excited intentions have given way to exhausted somnolence. A bored Rottweiler is tied beneath a broken barbecue stand by the helicopter pad, and parrotfish with toothy smiles graze in the waters off the dock.

Beyond Adventure Island and to your left at the traffic light and over the causeway is the city of **Key Colony Beach**, created in 1959 by dredging up bay bottom and adding it to low-lying offshore Shelter Key. It has houses, condos, time-shares, boatels, tennis courts, a golf course, a marina, three miles of canals, and earnestly cared-for lawns. And there it is. Key Colony Beach is notorious for sponsoring, in 1969, a sail-fish tournament in which 553 sailfish were caught in four days of fish horror. The tournament continues to be held each November.

A bit farther south on Route 1 is the **Diving Site**, a dive shop behind which is **Coral Lagoon**, a nicely landscaped motel with bright, spacious efficiencies on a canal. It's a bit Florida-subur-ban but quiet and sunny (289-0121). The rooms are $70 a night in the fall, $100 in the summer (when the "green" water arrives with its calmness and clarity), $115 in the season. There are tennis courts and a pool, the good pool close to the bad pool, a deep, dark, unappetizing thing which seems to be connected to the dive shop. Whatever was this for? you might ask. Practice? Uhhh, I think they kept turtles in it or something, someone will say, . . . but there's nothing in there now. You peer at the slick, sad water and can't imagine . . . turtles.

Diving in the Marathon area is generally based more on the grimmer activities of spearfishing than on reef exploration. Spearfishing is not allowed closer than three miles from shore in the Upper Keys. Below Long Key it is permitted at distances of more than one mile from Route 1. Thus because of the config-uration of the Keys, speargunning often takes place close to shore here. The fish in Pennecamp are practically tame, plump with cracker crumbs and popcorn and used to having divers swim among them. There are giant grouper in the reefs off

Largo that are routinely petted and hand-fed by divers. The reefs off Marathon, however, are combat zones, and the dumb fish that expects to be pampered here will end up skewered.

Divers hunt fish around **Delta Shoal** and **East and West Turtle Shoals** and search the coral heads of the **Content Keys** for lobsters and stone crabs. The shallow Content Keys are on the Gulf side, southwest of Marathon—a good snorkeling area for windy days. The areas most dived are **East Washerwoman Shoal** and the lighthouse at **Sombrero Reef**. Sombrero has nice coral formations and impressively gaudy colonies of tiny fish safe from everything but aquarium collectors, for all tiny tropicals are poisonous if eaten.

The only wreck dive in the Marathon area is the *Thunderbolt*, an old Army cable-laying vessel intentionally sunk for divers, five miles south of Key Colony Beach.

The bridge over Vaca Cut brings you into the Marathon area. **Captain Hook's Marina**, on your left at MM #53, is worth a stop. There are live-fish pools and a complete and helpful tackle shop. Both a party boat, *Marathon Lady,* and a charter boat operate from here. The charter is a 25-foot open boat with Bimini top which offers a variety of fishing trips, including night expeditions and Everglades trips.

KEY VACA

The Spaniards might have originally called this key Cayos de Bacas, which means "berries," or Cayos de Vaccas, which means "cows." If it was cows, they were referring to the manatees that once thickly browsed on the vegetation offshore. Or they may have named it for one of their own conquistadores, named de Vaca. The name's obscure, to be sure. Key Vaca runs from Vaca Cut at MM #53 to Knight's Key at MM #47, the terminus of Henry Flagler's railroad from 1908 to 1911, while workers constructed the Seven-Mile Bridge.

Marathon and its remoralike subdivision, Marathon Shores, have consumed Key Vaca. There is simply nothing of Key Vaca which is not Marathon.

Optimistic travelers have for years harbored the hope that there is more to Marathon than what they see, but unremarkably this is not the case. Marathon is exactly what they see and what you will see as well—a careless, unrespectable town who presents her homely face to you without a bit of a blush. Under more demanding perusal she will turn a bit defensive, for she lacks panache, although she can show you a good time. Old football stars love her.

Sunset and a Beach

Marathon offers a very nice sunset, you'll be relieved to know, and watching it from the old Seven-Mile Bridge is relaxing, with none of the accompanying hysteria of the Key West production. There's a parking area at MM #46.8 and across the road at the Pigeon Key Visitors Center. The walk to Pigeon Key is just a little over two miles, giving you plenty of room to enjoy the sunset personally.

All down the Keys at that uncanny hour, drivers swerve their cars off the road to pause and pay their respects to the sun as it squashes down on the horizon.

The beach is **Sombrero Beach**, two miles down Sombrero Road at MM #50 (at the traffic light). You'll go through a subdivision of oftimes absurdly ornate houses, many of which are for sale. Man-made canals run behind them all. The swimming is good, for the water is not shallow, the beach is immaculate, and the carefully mowed grass of the adjacent park offers not one single sandspur. The park, which is on Hawk Channel and the Atlantic, also has a little playground and a softball diamond, though the gates are shut and put under lock and chain the instant darkness falls. The island off the southwest boundary of the park is Boot Key, joined in 1959 by a costly bridge to the highway. The bridge, complete with drawspan and bridge tender, is maintained by the county, and in the finest tradition of mystery bridges leads absolutely nowhere, a developer's scam having failed to produce anything on the key except access to it. There is a radio tower and a road that wanders neurotically about until it vanishes.

Curry Hammocks

Between MM #56 and MM #53 on the Bay side of the highway is the green and wild run of Fat Deer Key, which was recently acquired by the Florida Park Service. They plan to lay a trail and in some areas a boardwalk so that visitors can glimpse the dense palm hammock that comprises the largest uninhabited terrestrial tract (600 acres) between Key Largo and Big Pine Key. On the ocean side of the highway at MM #56, just past the road to Valhalla on Little Crawl Key, is another area of acquisition. There's peaceful endless horizon here, and great bonefishing flats. The state is planning campsites, though the final makeup of this park has not yet been determined. In 1997 it was pretty much beautifully undiscovered, although a quite chic stilt house had been erected as the ranger's station. There's also a "mercury monitoring" tower in place.

Crane Point Hammock

In the middle of Marathon, opposite the Gulfside Shopping Center, the typical paved wasteland that K mart and McDonald's like to dis-create from nature and call home, lies the lovely Crane Point Hammock, recently acquired by the Florida Keys Land and Sea Trust. This is a true tropical forest, a magnificent 64-acre hardwood and thatch palm hammock on the Gulf. It's a different world back here—a glimpse of the real Florida. But, too, there's a rather retro and overdesigned museum, the **Museum of the Florida Keys**. There are dioramas with stuffed birds, and one room depicts the reef as it might appear inside a very peculiar person's head—stuffed fish suspended from the ceiling and a clicking, whispering, gurgling sound track. The trail through the hammock, as it is now designed, is only a quarter of a mile loop. There is a brochure that informs you about the trees. Try to avoid the woman behind you reading from it. " '. . . Stop Five. If you are lucky and quiet you might encounter a raccoon or rosy rat snake.' *Ichhhh*, let's make noise." The museum is open 9–5, noon–5 on Sundays, and there's an entrance fee.

MARATHON

Marathon is a strip, heavily developed. Residents do live here happily, it is assumed, off the highway in subdivisions and along long canals that accommodate their boats. But to the traveler inching along the congested road, this community (for Marathon is not a town and has no form of local government, being more or less run by the Chamber of Commerce) appears a soiled servicing station for those enjoying the abstraction of "The Heart of the Keys." It's prettiest at night, when the neon lights, appearing after the blackness of Crawl Key, suggest a jackpot possibility.

Marathon's history is that of the railroad that virtually created it. It began as a base camp for thousands of railroad workers, the most reliable of them being men from the Caymans and from Spain. The rest were derelicts from Philadelphia and New York, shanghaied by railroad recruiters. After the 1906 hurricane, Flagler housed the men in wooden barracks on land rather than on quarterboats. The camp on Key Vaca consisted of not only tents and barracks but cottages, a hospital, a power plant, and repair shops for the locomotives. Railroad workers named their new settlement Marathon, legend has it, after their own endurance, and built gyms and basketball courts for themselves.

Eighty-six miles of the Oversea Railroad had been completed by 1906, and miles of open water remained. A long trestle and dock were built on the southernmost end of Key Vaca at **Knight's Key** so that steamships could meet the train. Nothing today remains of this port, where ships from Cuba unloaded pineapples, sugar, and oranges, and vacationers set off on the six-hour trip to Havana. Just before the bridge today, a railroad car painted in Flagler's favorite colors, yellow and brown, is on display. It is unlikely that this particular car ever made the journey, if you're a stickler for things like that. (Flagler's luxurious private car, *Rambler,* which he rode in elderly triumph into Key West, was discovered in the 1950s sitting in a field in Virginia, where it was being used by a tenant farmer. It is now at the Flagler Museum in Palm Beach.)

Flagler took soundings for a deepwater harbor at the tip of Key Vaca, and Key West feared that the railroad would go no farther, that Knight's Key would become the port of entry and Key West would remain remote and unlinked. But work began on "the great one"—the Seven-Mile Bridge—and was interrupted only by a 1909 hurricane that washed out 40 miles of embankment and track in the Upper Keys, convincing the engineers that more small bridges were needed, instead of filled embankments that dammed up hurricane tides. Eighteen miles of bridges replaced the originally planned six to provide a freer flow of water.

When the Seven-Mile Bridge was completed in 1911, the workers moved on. No more boats filled with girls and liquor (followed by other boats filled with preachers) plied the waters between Key West and Marathon. The population plummeted. The town became known to train passengers as a place where they were often sold colored water through the windows instead of whiskey.

Marathon remained a sprawling, wide-open outpost throughout the 1940s, when it was large enough to contain 13 bars and restaurants but still no churches or schools. During World War II an airstrip was installed as a training base for B-17s, or "Flying Fortresses." The 8,000-foot airstrip runs along the highway through Marathon Shores and is today home to a variety of private planes and charters. There are also regularly scheduled flights to Miami and elsewhere several times a day. It has a handsomely designed terminal.

During the 1950s a Detroit developer, Phil Sandowski, whose later gift to the planet was the city of Key Colony Beach, created the "instant" canals of Marathon and brought subdivisions to Key Vaca. The streets run from 126th Street down to 11th Street at MM #47.5, where the fishing and crayfish boat docks are.

Marathon has a breakfast hangout where an early-bird beer and big, bad biscuits are a favored combination (**Vernon's Iron Skillet** at MM #48); a big dance floor that rocks until 4 A.M. (the **Side Door Lounge** at MM #50); several liquor stores that are open all night long; and a hospital with a 24-hour emergency room. It *used* to have Fanny's, a strip joint whose sign read, WHATSA MATTER, YOU SCARED? Marathon is known for historical drinking. The first fatality of the completed Oversea Railroad was a local man, Tom Jones, who, when he saw Flagler's special

train pass through at 9 A.M. on January 22, 1912, began cele-
brating and didn't stop until seven days later, when he was pronounced dead of alcohol poisoning.

WHERE TO STAY

Marathon has an astonishing turnover in motel and resort own-
ership, with places going in and out of receivership. Mushroom-
like villas and stylized Singapore hat–like rooflines abound.
Most are time-shares. Coco Plum Beach and Tennis Club off the
highway at MM #54.5 is a giant example. Just beyond it is the
mousy little Coco Plum Beach (closes at dusk), a tiny little hold
on nature where the volunteers from Save-A-Turtle release
their collected hatchlings in the spring.

Particularly charming in the area is **Conch Key Cottages**,
off the road at MM #62.3 (289-1377). Pine walls, big porches,
hammocks on the secluded beach. You can actually hear the
birds back here. There are five two-bedroom cottages and three
one-bedroom ones, as well as more mundane apartments and
efficiencies. The price is the same in the summer as in the winter because people like to settle in here during the hot months.
It's cool. There's a dock and a boat ramp too. Prices for a one-
bedroom cottage truly evocative of the sweet old days run
around $185 a night, $1,100 a week.

The Bonefish Resort at MM #58 (743-7107) is situated
among a number of modest establishments catering to the bud-
get conscious. (Most peculiar is the Golden Grouper, whose
most engaging feature is the mannequin head and machete on
a palm stump.) The Bonefish is more collected, *troppo* shacky
and friendly. Tiny rooms with kitchen run from $35 to $60. If
you can diet your dog down to 30 pounds or less, he can stay
here with you. Be prepared for more seaweed than beach at
many of the smaller oceanfront motels much of the year.

In Marathon one of the oldest and most established resorts
is **Faro Blanco** at MM #48 (743-9018). Built in the 1940s, it
has a four-story lighthouse where rooms can be rented for
$185, $135 in summer. This is not a real lighthouse, of course.
It was built by a contractor as the resort's centerpiece. You can

buy a more than usually awful tchotchke of it for $25. You can also rent a houseboat here, though you can't set out to sea in it. They're permanently piered. This experience, whatever it is, costs from $100 to $185 a night. The pleasant cottages on the grounds cost $90–$145. The cottages take kids; the condos ($235 a night) do not. There's an Olympic-sized pool, a bar, and a big marina. **Hall's Diving Center** is also located here (743-5929).

People are fond of the restaurant, **Kelsey's**, which serves up expensive portions of chateaubriand, rack of lamb, and shrimp scampi. They'll also cook your catch for you for $10, but only if you fillet it yourself. Their more casual restaurants are **Crocodile's** down 15th Street on the oceanside, and the **Angler's Lounge**, which overlooks the anarchy of a swimming pool.

Hidden Harbor (MM #48.5) is a little motel sandwiched between Faro Blanco and the rather gross Buccaneer. It has a boat ramp and docking facilities as well as a small pool and a long rocky shoreline, but its real distinction is in its turtle "hospital," a clean and complex open-air aquarium where you can see these marvelous sea creatures and ponder their peculiar paradisical visages. The owner is kindly obsessed with turtles, and you'll learn how to appreciate them here, too—a bonus for staying in the comfortable rooms. You'll pay $75; $85 for an efficiency; and $10 less in summer. Telephone: 743-5376.

WHERE TO EAT

Most people drive up to the Grassy Key Dairy Bar (see page 68). If you're flush, try the **Hideaway** (see page 69). You don't have to drive as far as the people from Miami. It's open from 5 to 11 and requires reservations.

In Marathon, **Herbie's** at MM #50 is an eternal favorite. An old-time breezy place of screens and picnic tables. Lots of fish, draft beer, and badinage. Good desserts. Always crowded. It is so popular that you are often discomfited by the hordes waiting outside, balefully regarding you as you eat. Open 11 A.M.–10 P.M. Closed Sundays. Telephone: 743-6373.

The Quay at MM #54 is prettily lit and formal, with nice views of the water. The menu is elaborate and reaches for the extraordinary, like the alligator steak, which is seldom available to the chef. If it was made available to the chef it might be for reasons you would prefer not to know about—for example, the occasion of a marine patrol officer being recently called upon to dispose of a gator for swallowing yet another someone's dog. Open every day from 11 A.M. Telephone: 289-1810.

The **Cracked Conch Cafe** at MM #50 has a bar and serves lunch and dinner all day long, from 11 A.M. until midnight. Casual, with a little outside patio and reasonable, well-prepared soups and dinners. Telephone: 743-2233.

The **7-Mile Grille** at MM #47 is another favorite open-air restaurant, although it's not open early, it's not open late, and it's closed Wednesdays and Thursdays. Very authentic, it appears, set back on the dusty access strip a little below the highway. Beer, grouper chowder, and uncomplicated fish baskets. Open 11:30 A.M.–8:30 P.M. Telephone: 743-4481.

People seem to love **Castaway** because it's funky and a little foul. Otherwise, why try to find this joint (which is hard to find around MM #48 down 15th Street on the ocean side) in a dour jumble of trailers on an odorous canal? Nonetheless, this is the Keys lifestyle people think of as endangered. Crab cakes, peel-and-eat shrimp. Beer. Opens at 5, closes at 10 (743-6247).

Shucker's is down 11th Street just as the road narrows before the Seven-Mile Bridge. It's across from one of the last do-it-yourself boatyards at Marathon Marina. You can eat either inside or out on the dock with one of the nicest views in town. A very good selection of fresh seafood dishes. Lively bar. Food is served from 11 to 10 (743-8686).

FISHING

Marathon is obsessed with fish. It has been said that there are 450 species of fish in the waters off the Keys, and Marathon is desirous of every single one of them. Here, too, there are tournaments—tarpon tournaments, sailfish tournaments, dolphin tournaments, and bonefish tournaments. There are derbys and slams and roundups as well. There is no kingfish tournament, that variety having been virtually wiped out by commercial netters. Occasionally the severe depletion of a species is noted, and bureaucracy lumbers into action, but gross overfishing of certain varieties can go on for years with the only complaint being that there aren't as many fish as there used to be.

Stone crabs and Florida lobsters have diminished greatly in number—there are three million crayfish traps between Key Largo and the Dry Tortugas, according to *National Fisherman*—and there is also a decline in the once-abounding populations of grouper and snapper, fishes taken intensively commercially as well as being the staple of party boats.

Tournament fishing is now encouraging releases, but a visit to the charter-boat docks or a glance at local tabloids, particularly the monthly *Florida Keys Angler,* published in Islamorada, will show you that many visitors have a deep desire to be seen standing beside large dead fish hanging from hooks, touching possessively the thing they have hauled up from the deep—a thing of once-remarkable colors turned gray, a thing with poundage numbers scrawled in white paint upon its sides. Deep-sea hunters will say that the killing of a big fish after a long battle is an emotional necessity (although battle time has

A marlin

been shortened considerably by the handling capabilities of
modern sportsfishing boats, which can back up and maneuver
quickly). Otherwise, anglers kill gamefish apparently for two
reasons: photographic confirmation (although dead fish of a
given species tend to bear an uncanny resemblance to one
another) and possession of a mount or "trophy" (a trophy being
a painted replica of the caught fish that can be hung in the living room or wherever). It is now known, and even grudgingly
acknowledged by taxidermists themselves, that there is very
little fish in a mounted fish. The taxidermist is a colorist who
works with a little skin and a lot of plastic. But what is reality
after all? Reality is a funny business. In any case, memories are
bigger and prettier than a dead fish. Go out with the guides who
encourage trophy releases and, just as important, who know
how to do it so the fish will survive.

Tarpon fishing is popular here in the spring and through
July—a little too popular for the beleaguered tarpon—particularly under the bridges where schools of "silver king" congregate to run through the deep channels back into the shallow
flats, where they spawn and feed. You can't eat tarpon, but people love to catch them because of the fish's extraordinary per-
formance when hooked. They "crash" the bait and for the first
five minutes, before they sound and "dog it out," a hooked tarpon jumps, shakes, and tail-walks. He then, it is said, feels to
the fisherman like a falling piano.

The terms you will hear used to describe types of fishing are
Gulf Stream, backcountry, reef or *wreck,* and *flats* or *bonefishing.* For a brochure on local guides and a captains' list, write to
the Marathon Guides Association (see page 43).

Gulf Stream fishing is done by charter. The fighting chairs
are for marlin and sailfish, and the bait is constantly trolled.
Dolphin is also found in deep water in the summer. Usually
four or fewer people make up a charter, and the cost runs
around $300 a day. Cobia, shark, wahoo, and bonito are often
caught.

Backcountry fishing is done bayside and is for bottom fish:
trout, grouper, snapper, and jewfish. Grouper is the fish that
most unerringly finds his way into your fish sandwich or your
all-you-can-eat fish fry. A fish of fickle history, the grouper
begins life as an egg-producing female, then changes sex later
on. It also completely changes color when frightened. Jewfish

are its speckled, obese, large-mouthed cousins, a type of giant sea bass that can weigh up to 700 pounds. Shark and barracuda are also fished for in the backcountry.

Reef and wreck fishing are done most often by party boats. These large boats take out 50 to 75 people at a time and charge around $25 a day per person, usually less for children. All bait and tackle are provided. Again, grouper and snapper are called upon and frequently answer. Some boats take two- and three-day trips to the Tortugas for even more extensive catches of bottom-feeding fish, returning to port with ice chests full of fish, floorboards covered with fish, fish blood, fish slime, gaping fish mouths, and staring fish eyes. Fish lust is a definite requirement for these Tortuga trips. Prices from Marathon are around $150, slightly more with rod rental, and the coveted stern spots

---

LIGHTHOUSES

From the Seven-Mile Bridge, four miles south of Marathon, you will see **Sombrero light**, one of six spidery, graceful lighthouses that mark the reef off the Keys. All were built between 1852 and 1880 and have an iron-pile construction, the pilings of the foundations driven deep within the coral on which they stand. They are the **Fowey Rocks light**, the "Eyes of Miami," which replaced the ineffectual Cape Florida light on the mainland; the **Carysfort Reef lighthouse** off Key Largo; **Alligator Reef light** off Lower Matecumbe Key; **Sombrero** off Marathon and the tallest of the reef lights at 140 feet; **American Shoal light** off Cudjoe Key and six miles west of Looe Key; and **Sand Key light**, eight miles southwest of Key West.

Vessels once ran aground regularly on the reef—there was at least one "good" wreck a week—supporting a flourishing salvage industry that made Key West, where the admiralty court was located, a very wealthy little town. "Everything that the commerce of the world afforded reached Key West," Jefferson Browne wrote in his 1912 book, *Key West: The Old and the New.* "The wrecks not only threw on these shores rich cargoes, but many valuable citizens were thus furnished. . . . Several of our prominent families owe their residence here to the fact that their ancestors were wrecked on the Florida Reef."

Keys people relished their wrecks, certainly, but however beneficial wrecks were to Key West, they did not appeal to shipowners, who demanded that the government erect navigational aids along this treacherous and much-traveled route. It seemed impossible at first to build lighthouses on the reefs, so lightships were used. The lightships were a dismal failure. They were unseaworthy, they blew off course and were sometimes grounded on the very reefs they were supposed to warn about, and their lights were scarcely discernible, erratically lit, and badly placed, so that mariners were deceived more often than assisted. Open-skeleton wrought-iron lighthouses were originally designed by Alexander Mitchell in 1836. The Carysfort Reef light was designed by I.W.P. Lewis and was built in 1852, the first of its kind. The lighthouses were erected on as few pilings as possible, in order not to obstruct the free flow of water, and their webby, open construction offered less resistance to wind and water during hurricanes. Another benefit of the iron-pile design was that it could be manufactured, assembled to make sure that all the parts fit, then broken down again and shipped to open water. The Carysfort Reef light was manned until 1960, but now a solar panel charges the battery powering the flashing light.

The second light to be built on the Keys was Sand Key, off Key West. There was originally a 60-foot brick lighthouse here which was destroyed in an 1846 hurricane, killing the woman tender and her children. The new structure was the first of the reef lights to be installed with a Fresnel lens, named for its inventor, the French physicist Augustin Fresnel, a lens which increased by many times the ability of lamp light to be concentrated and magnified. Hurricanes and storms have rearranged the sandy beach here or made it disappear altogether, but the rust-red, square, pyramidal tower, screw-piled into the coral beneath, has been unharmed. The Fresnel lens was recently removed and replaced with a flash-tube array, the battery again powered by solar energy, which projects the light for 19 miles.

Sombrero reef was first charted and named by the Spanish; a light was placed here because it was midway between the Carysfort and Sand Key lights. Like the earlier lights, it was built under the direction of George Gordon Meade, who later became a major general during the Civil War, commanding the Army of the Potomac which defeated Robert E. Lee at Gettysburg. The octagonal, pyramidal skeleton tower of Sombrero was completed in 1858; its original Fresnel lens is displayed at the Lighthouse Museum in Key West.

Ships continued to run aground in the dark interstices between the lights, but the Civil War delayed further construction of lighthouses. It was not until 1873 that Alligator Reef light was constructed off the Matecumbe Keys, on what was considered the long reef's "elbow." This beautiful black-and-white structure, considered by lighthouse historians to be one of the finest iron lighthouses in the world, was named for the USS *Alligator,* one of the eight schooners of the West India Squadron, which hunted pirates off the coast of Florida and went aground on the reef in 1821. She was blown up by her own crew so that pirates wouldn't salvage her. Alligator Reef light survived the 1935 hurricane, undamaged by the 20-foot tidal wave that surged past the light on its way to annihilate the shore.

The northernmost of the reef lights was built in 1878 on Fowey Rocks off Key Biscayne. During its construction, workmen were often terrified by ships bearing down on them and wrecking on the reefs only yards away.

American Shoal lighthouse was the last to be built, completing the system of reef lights in July 1880. Again, it was a pyramidal skeleton tower enclosing a lightkeeper's dwelling. Looe Key and the Sambos were reefs upon which ships continued to wreck in the cavernous darkness between the Sombrero and Sand Key lights. American Shoal realized the Keys' "band of light" and brought to an end the days of the wreckers.

All the lighthouses are automated now, the lights powered by batteries that store solar energy. No keepers are needed to trim the wicks and keep the lamps clean and full of oil, or to draw curtains over the lens at sunrise to protect it from the glare of day. The structures are massively graceful, and through their skeletal forms, the reef waters glitter and dance. They seem abandoned and improbable by day, vaguely stirring the spirit, beneficent and speechless icons that at night send messages of warning and comfort.

are extra. Party boats can be found at the **Winner-Sombrero Docks** down Sombrero Road at MM #50 by bearing right at the golf course. Charter boats can be found farther down this road, or behind the big motels such as Faro Blanco and the **Buccaneer** on Route 1, as well as at the big marina at Key Colony Beach, where bareboat charters and sailing trips are also offered. Or, again, ask around. Some charter-boat captains work out of their backyards. The **World Class Angler** (743-6138) gives good advice.

Flats fishing for bonefish and permit has more mystique connected to it than any other type of fishing in the Keys. This is not a blood-riot of hauling up creatures from the black depths, but a ghostly stalking through crystal-clear sands and turtle-grass flats. Zane Grey called the bonefish "the wisest, shyest, strangest, wariest fish," possessing "baffling cunning." The bonefish comes into the flats when the tide is low to feed on clams buried in the bottom, at which time it is prone to sharks, barracuda, and clever bonefishermen. It is a slim, furtive fish built for speed. It never leaps when hooked, but makes a long and astonishingly powerful run. Three to five pounds is the average size, eight to nine pounds is a big one, and anything larger is a trophy catch. The world record is 23 pounds. Its Latin name is *Albula vulpes*—white fox. Permits are easier to see than bonefish. They are larger and more vertical—like large silver dimes with black fins. Their eyes are the most sentient of any fish, and their bodies are clean and silken.

Flats fishing for bonefish and permit is done in an outboard with the engine stilled, the guide standing on a spotting platform and poling across the flats. It is a silent sport of considerable skill and even delicacy. There are guides who specialize in the flats, and most of them are booked solid in the bonefish months—May is considered the best month; the season runs until November. Almost all guides require the release of these fish caught during a charter. When former president Bush comes to the Keys to fish, he stays at Cheeca and goes bonefishing with guide George Hommell, who runs the tackle shop **World Wide Sportsman** in Islamorada. George the guide describes hooking a bonefish as "happiness." He says the other George "often gets quiet when he fishes," and that when he catches a fish "he gets excited."

THE SEVEN-MILE BRIDGE

It is said that Henry Flagler loved concrete with a passion. He was 75 years old when his workmen began construction on the Seven-Mile Bridge (MM #47 to MM #40), which when finished was considered the Eighth Wonder of the world. His young construction engineer, J. C. Meredith, literally worked himself to death on the project, collapsing a year after work on the span began.

The bridge was built in four parts. The first three spans—Knights Key Bridge, Pigeon Key Bridge, and Moser Channel Bridge—were made of steel-girder sections laid on top of concrete foundation piers. The entire bridge had 546 of these piers, more than any other bridge in the world. The underwater part of the piers was made from a special cement imported from Germany. The cement used above the high-water line came from New York. The piers were secured to bedrock that in some cases was 28 feet under water. The Moser Channel swing span was 253 feet long and opened for any boat that required more than a 23-foot clearance. The last, westernmost part of the bridge, running eastward from Little Duck Key, consisted of 210 spandrel arches, similar to those used on the Long Key Viaduct. The spandrel arch was used where the water was shallow, the pier and deck plate construction where the water was deep and where storm-generated waves would be higher. The pier columns are solid concrete and steel, gracefully tapering upward to receive the steel spans. The old bridge is much more handsome than the new.

The Seven-Mile Bridge, like all the bridges of the Keys, withstood all hurricanes, even the 1935 one that meant the end of the railroad. A year after that disaster, work began on converting the railway into a highway, and the 14-foot width of the bridge was widened to 22 feet with I-beams. Much of the old track was used as guardrails for the road. This highway served travelers, often harrowingly, for more than 40 years, until a new bridge was constructed and completed in 1982. The new bridge is wider and higher than the old and has eliminated the need for a drawspan by rising 40 feet higher over Moser Channel at MM #43.5, providing a 65-foot clearance.

Pigeon Key is a four-acre island between the old and new bridge a little more than two miles from Marathon. It was used as a work camp for the construction of the original bridge, and hundreds of workers lived here for four years. There were dormitories and bunkhouses, wharves and a mess hall. Cement had a huge warehouse all to itself. The camp at Pigeon Key seemed to pop up overnight in 1908, probably because many of the buildings were prefabricated in St. Augustine and then shipped down to be reassembled. When the bridge was completed, the buildings were dismantled again. The structures you see today date from 1912 to 1920 and were built for the bridge tenders, painters, and maintenance men and their families. Later, the island became headquarters for the toll district operation when the highway was briefly a toll road in the 1930s. During World War II it was used as a tropic zone GI training center and later was leased by researchers from the University of Miami who conducted a number of experiments here, one of which involved raising a sewage-eating fish. An African freshwater species, the blue tilapia, a pushy exotic that has driven many species out of the Everglades, loves to graze and grow on pollutants and agricultural runoff. The researchers were excited about this protein-packed fish as a potential new industry for parts of South Florida. The university, which leased the island from the state for $1 a year for many years, didn't spend much of their time maintaining the buildings. Even the waters were allowed to run down, with Sea World using the place as a staging area for collecting tropical fish for their amusement parks.

Today the Pigeon Key Foundation (289-0025) out of Marathon is managing and restoring the structures on the island. They offer a number of environmental workshops for young people. You may run into dozens of kids out there earnestly snorkeling and exploring. There's a three-day, two-night program where students and teachers camp out on Pigeon Key and take various field trips in the area. (Call Dan Gallagher at 289-9632 or 289-0025.) You can stroll, bike, or Rollerblade out to Pigeon Key, but you can't drive your car. A shuttle leaves from the Knight's Key Visitor Center on the hour 10–4 every day but Monday. It costs $5. If you walk out it costs $2, but nobody seems particularly interested in taking your money. There's a video on Flagler that makes him appear as nice as Jesus, and a tour led by enthusiastic ladies who will point out, among other things, a butterfly house near a particularly unappetizing flower patch. It's a cute little house on a pole with slits in it where butterflies are supposed to slip in and rest, away from the winds on Pigeon Key, but the butterflies haven't found it yet. They may not even know it exists.

Researchers are still out here. The Mote Marine Laboratory from Sarasota is growing live coral in saltwater tanks from sea "cuttings." They're "breeding" coral, not so much to put back on the reef but for uses in human bone grafts and for artificial eyes. Apparently people feel a little self-conscious when they have a glass eye because it just lies there in their head, it doesn't move. If muscles can be attached to a ball of coral (with a cosmetic glass front), the eye can roll around just like the real one does. Of course, they're also looking into the possibility that coral can cure cancer.

Each April there's a seven-mile run on the new bridge. Beneath the waters, also in the spring, the tarpon make their far more elegant silent and silvery run, frequently followed by large sharks, including the bizarre and voracious hammerhead.

Beyond the Seven-Mile Bridge at MM #40 is **Little Duck Key**, a filled area with a public boat ramp and several cement picnic shelters. This little Duck is many, many miles away from the big Duck (once touted as a fairyland playground for million-aires) at MM #61. Then come **Missouri** and **Ohio** keys, named by homesick railroad workers one would imagine, but they are more filled causeway than island. An extremely large American flag flies on Ohio Key, as if to assure travelers, after all these watery miles, that they are still in the U.S. of A. An elaborately appointed campground follows Sunshine Key, for those campers who don't want to get away from it all, and then there is **Bahia Honda**, a state park which has the finest beach on the Keys.

BAHIA HONDA KEY

The Spanish name means "Deep Bay," and this marks the geo-logic transition from the Upper Keys, which are coral, to the

Lower, which are limestone. As it is transitional, it is unique in many ways, its coral skeleton supporting sand beaches, dunes, and a coastal strand hammock in which a number of rare plants grow, including the yellow satinwood, the only tree of its kind in the Keys, and the Jamaica morning glory. The seeds have all been brought here from the Caribbean and the West Indies by birds, wind, and water. There is a nature trail that winds around a lagoon at the northeastern end of the park where you can wander through this subdued exotica—you will see quite a number of the slender silver palm, pale as the silvery raccoons that forage here under the hot sky.

The beach sand is fine and the swimming excellent here. There is a boat ramp for trailered boats as well as a marina and small dive shop. You can also rent Windsurfers. Bahia Honda costs $4 for the driver of the car, 50¢ for passengers. Camping runs around $25 a night. The phone number at the park is 872-2353. As with other state parks, half the sites are unreserved on a first-come, first-served basis. Stop by in the morning and have your name put on a waiting list. Names are called at 3 in the afternoon. Some handsome rental cottages on stilts have been built by the Park Service on the Bay side which can be seen from the highway at MM #37. The access road is available only through the park. These cottages are $125 a night. Mid-September through mid-December they're $97 a night. There is boat access, and all dishes, cookware, and linen are provided.

The beach at Bahia Honda Key

A bull shark with pilot fish

Each of the six cabins has two double beds, two bunk beds, and two cots. There's a minimum two-night stay required. And even if you're having the time of your life, which you very well may be, you can't stay longer than a week.

According to the histories of the Oversea Railroad, engineers and workers were in a continual state of amazement. Here, it seemed, they did not realize the significance of the Spanish name for the channel. Bahia Honda was far more difficult to build than the Seven-Mile Bridge because the waters are so deep. When trying to locate bedrock for the foundation of the center span, workmen found only water, more and more water in a hole that seemed, for weeks, to be bottomless. Since the water was so deep, tide surges would be higher in a storm, so the bridge, as well as being the hardest to build, was the highest. When the Overseas Highway came in 1936 to remodel it as a road, they could not widen its enclosed structure, so they built their road over the top, and it resembles nothing less than a roller coaster. The four-lane bridge you travel on today is a recent construction, and, of course, not nearly as nice.

Diving is good near the bridge pilings, which provide mini-reefs replete with corals, lobsters, sponges, and fish. However, bridge diving can be dangerous because of rapid and abrupt tide changes, a superabundance of sea urchins, and stinging fire coral which seems to flourish in areas of swift currents. The current that flows through Bahia Honda Channel is the fastest in all the Keys.

A phenomenon occurs here each year around the last full moon of May. Small reddish palolo worms hatch from rocks and sponges, and the tarpon come in great schools to slurp them up at the surface. At this time, tarpon can be caught on a small fly instead of the large live mullet they prefer as bait.

After the Bahia Honda Bridge come the **Spanish Harbor Keys**, including **West Summerland** which is marked by a sign, a sign that may bewilder you as West Summerland is ten miles *east* of **Summerland Key**. Two coral rock storage sheds for dynamite from the time that the railroad was being pushed through were found on West Summerland years ago, but they have been misplaced again in the overgrowth.

There are several places to pull off the road during these few miles to rest or picnic or walk along the damp, curving shore. You can sometimes find old bottles along the swampy shoreline of both Summerlands, and farther down on Sugarloaf Key.

SHARKS

Men hate sharks. They hate them a lot, as they do any creature whose existence cannot truly be confronted. The shark is not in the Tarot. It is not in the signs of Heaven, nor certainly was it invited onto the Ark. Its strict reality remains beneath the waters of the world, but it also seems to inhabit some other, deeper, less comprehensible depths.

When men catch sharks they do not simply kill them, they mutilate them as though in the grip of an ancient rite. They hatchet fins, chop out jaws, pry out teeth, slit open bellies, and grind up claspers or ovaries beneath the heels of their boots. Scientists and fishermen alike seem to be always stomping and skidding around in the blood and viscera of a ruined shark.

Shark can be eaten, but most people don't bother, for acids build up in the flesh if it is not cleaned and iced immediately, and the meat spoils quickly. Those who go shark fishing usually go just for the ambience.

This is how you go shark fishing: You usually go out at night. You chum the waters heavily with garbage, offal, the bloody remains of fish. You fish with very heavy tackle, stout leaders, large hooks. When a shark hits the line, lights are struck, and when the shark is reeled in alongside the boat your companions blast at him with shotguns, taking care not to strike each other or the boat. Winched up, the shark is then battered with clubs for a time, for a prevalent belief is that dead sharks often come back to life. Hauled aboard, the belly is then cut open and the contents of the stomach examined and marveled at. It was particularly intriguing to see a mangled shark, when thrown overboard, have the temerity to try and swim away.

At least that's how you fished for shark in the 1970s and '80s, those innocent days of recreational "monster fishing." In the '90s, with its glum and continuing message of diminishment, things are different. When they throw a shark tournament, the sharks don't come. It seems that drift nets, fish finders, and 600-hook long lines have drastically reduced their numbers, as has the commercial fishing habit of "live-finning," where the fins are sliced off and the animal is left to die right at home.

There are hundreds of species of sharks, and until recently most of the big species—the great white, the tiger, the hammerhead—seemed pretty indomitable. But sharks are slow-growing and give birth to a relatively small number of young—pups—each year. Encouraged ruthless destruction has taken out huge numbers of adults.

The rules for shark fishing are different now. There are limits—one per person or two per vessel—and sloppy slaughter is frowned upon. Newspaper photos of toddlers at dockside crouched beside the gaping head of a shark that Daddy just bagged is no longer considered cute news, and when a tourist killed a well-known, often-spotted resident hammerhead off a Key West reef recently, there were cries of pretty much total disapproval.

THE
LOWER KEYS
Big Pine Key to Key West

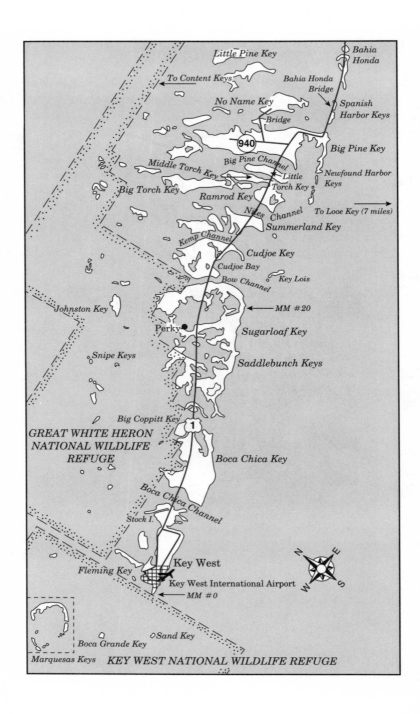

T HE Lower Keys are dark and wooded, and though settled, seem lonely. They are not fabulous, nor are they lush or exotic or breathtaking. They are too modest for superlatives. They are subdued, sometimes eccentric, even secretive. And some dirt roads that lead farther and farther back into the mangroves toward unnamed flats and channels are better left unexplored. It's said that when Fat Albert, the Naval surveillance blimp, is brought down for a checkup or because of bad weather, the air springs alive with the chatter of drug runners, and the sound of outboards popping into action is heard far and wide across this watery and muddy frontier. There are those who live simply here and those who live well, and those whose privacy is the best-known thing about them.

The land is scrub, cactus, slash pine. Big Pine has trees of uncommon size for the low-lying tropics, and Cudjoe even has a stand of cabbage palms. In the old days these keys seemed always to be burning. Settlers burned the trees to make charcoal and deliberately set other fires to flush out the tiny Key deer. Sparks from the passing railroad also set the Keys aflame. Even so, the land is low and wet, which makes great tracts of it uninhabitable. When the old iron water pipeline was laid alongside the road, it had to be raised on pilings so it wouldn't disappear into the muck. On a chart the area is sprinkled with bays, bights, harbors, lakes, and sounds. Offshore is **Looe Key**, a reef known for the clarity of its waters, which are cleansed constantly by the waters of the Gulf Stream.

The land moves back and forth upon itself, the woods rustle with palm warblers. Birds of prey like this landscape—eagles, falcons, red-tailed and red-shouldered hawks. A frequent sight along these keys is osprey nests on telephone poles on the south side of the highway. The osprey nests for life, and the nest grows larger and larger over the years, an indication of how long the couple have flown and hunted together. In March and April there's great activity around the nests and you'll

A nesting osprey

probably see an osprey returning, a fish hanging heavily from its talons, or perched hunched, carefully dissecting the meal for its young.

The Great White Heron National Wildlife Refuge, which encompasses the waters of the Lower Keys and Key West, was established in 1938 to give permanent protection to the largest of North America's wading birds. The great white heron is found only in the Florida Keys and the most southern part of the Florida mainland. The refuge covers over 264 square miles of open water in the Gulf of Mexico and 7,500 acres of isolated low-lying islands. To explore these waters is to realize the essence of the Keys.

For the safety and survival of wild things, don't anchor within 200 feet of islands, and keep speed and noise to a minimum when passing. The approach of a boat can frighten a bird from its nest, leaving the eggs or nestlings exposed to the frying sun. As well, avoid boat wakes around islands. Some ospreys nest low and a wake can wash right over the young. Jet skis have now been banned in the backcountry, and you should not support any business that promotes "a mangrove safari" on them. If you see a jet ski in the Refuge or see anyone behaving irresponsibly or harassing wildlife, don't ignore them, report them. Call the National Key Deer Refuge at 872-2239, or the marine patrol in Marathon at 289-2320.

You can rent your own boat from **Bud Boats**, off Watson Boulevard on Big Pine, near the Old Wooden Bridge Fishing Camp (which sounds much nicer than it appears) on the way to No Name. They have a variety of craft, from 13-foot Boston Whalers to Makos and Aquasports. A 17-foot Whaler with sunroof and VHF radio will cost $105 a day or $475 a week. If you have a dock where you're staying, they'll deliver. Telephone: 743-6316.

You can also rent from **Newfound Boat Rentals** (872-1204) at MM #28.5. You can see their boats coming off the bridge from Big Pine. A tri-hull with a 50-horsepower engine is $90 for a half day. A roomy 22-foot boat with a 120-horsepower engine is $155, $235 for a full fun day.

Coming off the Spanish Harbor Bridge, **Big Pine Fishing Lodge**, with tent and trailer camping and a few motel efficiencies (872-2351), is to your left, and the restaurant **Island Reef** is to your right at MM #31, behind several gigantic date palms. It's a harrowing turn-in from either direction, but once there you'll be happy. They have pot pies, steaks, and a few fish dishes, as well as a new expanded Spanish menu. On Sundays they have roast lamb and chicken and stuffing. They may be overly prideful of their homemade breads, but it's a nice place, casual, with the good Keys "feel." Wine and beer only. Open for lunch from 11 to 2:30 and for dinner at 5. But they close early— 9:30—and are shut on Mondays. On the weekends they're open for breakfast (872-2170).

Other good places to eat in the Lower Keys are the tiny **Big Pine Coffee Shop** at MM #30, open from 6 in the morning until 9 at night, **Mangrove Mama's** at MM #20, and the **Sugarloaf Club Restaurant** at MM #19.5, which has a pool, tennis, and groves of beautiful native silver palms. This place is open erratically. Sometimes they serve Sunday brunch, sometimes not. Sometimes they're open only until 5. Call them at 745-3276 for hours. For a small fee you can use all the facilities here, and many people like to arrange parties and cookouts on the palmy, unmanicured grounds. It has the feel of an old, comfy summer camp. It's down Crane Boulevard and Bad George Lane. Be sure to ask about *him*.

Best places to stay are the **Sugarloaf Lodge** (745-3211), the dive-oriented, canalside motel **Looe Key Reef Resort** (872-2215), and **Parmer's Place** (872-2157).

BIG PINE KEY

Big Pine, eight miles long and two miles wide, is second in size only to Key Largo. It is known primarily for its herd of tiny Key deer, a distinct subspecies of the Virginia white-tailed or a full species, *Dama clavia,* of its own, depending on which biologist you talk to. The deer stand only two and a half feet tall and weigh less than 75 pounds. Fawns weigh only two to four pounds at birth, and their tiny hoofprint is the size of a thumbnail. By the late 1940s hunting had almost exterminated them; there were less than 50 animals left. The publicized plight of the "toy" deer of Big Pine and that of the ivory-billed woodpecker in Louisiana sparked concern over endangered species and began the conservation movement in this country. The efforts to save the woodpecker were unsuccessful when one of the last nesting areas of the ivory-billed was bulldozed to plant the magnificent soybean, but the habitat of the deer was saved and, through rigorous law enforcement, their numbers increased.

"Rigorous law enforcement" was a pseudonym for Jack Watson, a former hunter turned militant environmentalist and the National Key Deer Refuge manager through the 1960s and '70s. Watson's war on poachers is legend. He is known to have burned the cars and sunk the boats of those in that gross fraternity. He even made house calls on those he heard were jacking deer. One famous incident concerned a poacher who was out and up repairing his roof when Watson confronted him. "Sure," the man bawled, "I've been shooting 'em, and I'll keep shooting 'em if I want until there ain't any left!" So Watson shot him, though unfatally, right off the roof.

Big Pine is a scrappy place whose residents seem always embattled, continually at odds with the Fish and Wildlife Service, which controls a third of the island and keeps it in the homely

Key deer

scrub-and-pine habitat the Key deer like. Many are the Big Pin-
ers who feel that if the tiny deer were managed properly, not by
the state but by private interests, and not allowed to roam at
all, there would be enough to cull and they would start appearing on restaurant menus as local venison, which would be a delicacy unique to Big Pine.

Big Pine Key doesn't look very Keys-like. It has pine trees
and subdivisions and shopping centers. An enormous flea market takes place every Saturday and Sunday from 8 to 2 at MM
#30.5 all year round and in the season it ties up traffic for miles.
A nice day on the beach at Bahia Honda can be ruined if you're
stuck in your car for an hour trying to get through Big Pine.
They love their Big Flea here and are hoping the Department of
Transportation will cure their bottleneck problem by building
another bridge around them.

The Key has scant human history. It was sparsely settled
even in the railroad days and though there were various
schemes to make use of the land—dairy farming for one (the
cows keeling over under the weight of mosquitoes), and a shark
processing plant—nothing was profitable and so the land was

inevitably bought up for development. The deer are forever frustrating Big Pine's dream of expansion.

Big Pine is formed of oolite, which means that the limestone cap rock is honeycombed with sinkholes. The sinkholes are caused by the underlying rock being dissolved by water, causing the surface rock to form pockets. Small, shallow sinkholes are called solution holes. Farmers called them "banana holes" and in them planted what they could. Ferns take advantage of the moist soil that accumulates and flourish in the rock. The larger sinkholes are dearly loved by gators, who move along the labyrinthian corridors beneath. If you see a largish snout poking from a medium-sized hole, you'll know that a considerably large gator resides below.

There are two basic biogeographic rules concerning plants and animals. One is that islands have fewer species than a comparably sized piece of mainland, and the other is that peninsulas support less and less diversity the farther they are from the landmass. These are perfectly good rules in general, as they apply to the rest of the state of Florida, which, of course, is a huge peninsula, but they have no relevance at all in the Keys. As well as being the only truly tropical area of the continental United States, the Keys have the most diverse terrestrial and marine ecosystems in the country. What this means on Big Pine is that you can enter the National Key Deer Refuge (passing churches, ball field, houses, and FOR SALE signs along the way, as well as many, many signs alerting you to the deer's presence—there appear to be more signs at this time than deer), walk through a pine-and-palm forest into a tropical hardwood hammock, and continue toward a tangled mangrove shoreline of small sandy beaches and coral outcroppings facing Big Pine Channel . . . which will lead you eventually into the deeper waters of the Straits of Florida, beyond which is the clear wild blue of the great Gulf Stream.

Fascinating to the biogeographer, and certainly interesting to anyone with a little time and some imagination or even just the luck to see the gators, little deer, hawks, herons, and orchids of this place.

To get to the Refuge, pass MM #31 and turn right at the light on Route 940, Key Deer Boulevard. Bear left toward the Big Pine Key Road Prison. Up a ways you'll see a sign to the Refuge.

About a mile and a half up the road, Watson Boulevard intersects. To the right is the road to No Name; to the left, Refuge headquarters. Continue on another mile and a half to the **Blue Hole**, a small freshwater sink which was blasted out to make it larger and provide fill for a parking lot where you can park your car and look at the Blue Hole. The pond ranges in depth from a half foot to 12 feet and has several resident alligators. Up until 1994 the biggest gator there was "Grandpa," who was 11 feet long and 400 pounds, but he was removed after he was seen eating a full-grown Rottweiler. (There are suspicions that the dog was deceased before Gramps came upon him, that the poor dog's body was used as a ploy to rid Blue Hole of its largest occupier.) People had been feeding Grandpa long before this incident, and he had taken to approaching them fearlessly and with increasingly disconcerting speed. Nonetheless, Grandpa had a lot of supporters on Big Pine, and they were sad when he was captured and carted off to Homosassa Springs State Wildlife Park near Tampa, where, it is said, he has become shy because there are gators there bigger than him.

To the immediate left here is Higgs Lane. Walk down this road until you see the Refuge sign, then bear to the left and go around a gate bar to take the trail that will go through pine lands to **Watson's Hammock**. The neatly constructed cement canals you see are mosquito ditches. These are connected to the Gulf and filled with tiny fish—gambusia—who do nothing but eat mosquito larvae night and day. This was the government-approved mosquito control for the Keys for decades, and a slippery concept to grasp. The backcountry is latticed with these ditches in which the mosquito lays its eggs and the mosquito fish eats them. Before the Navy built the water pipeline down the Keys in the 1940s, health authorities would come to individual homes and dump a handful of gambusia into private cisterns.

Watson's Hammock is a hardwood forest, dappled, lovely, cool, and quiet, with a 50-foot canopy. There's a huge gumbo-limbo tree here. With its peeling red bark, it is lightly called the "tourist tree" because the limbs look tortured with flaking sunburn. The tree is peculiar in a number of ways. Posts made of the stout limbs sprout roots and become living fences. The sap of the tree is very gummy and was once used to catch birds. The

BAD TREES

There are three trees that have really become pests in Florida—the punk, the pepper, and the Australian pine. Some people like all three because they're fast-growing and good screening material, and they like the punk (the melaleuca) because it reminds them of the eucalyptus, and the pepper (euphemistically called "Florida holly") because of its little red berries, and the pine (casuarina, not a true pine at all) because of the pretty sound the wind makes coursing through its branches.

But *you* should not like any of them and should never plant the punk, the pepper, or the Australian pine. All three, of course, are easily seeded and require no care whatsoever, and all grow like mad and crowd out indigenous trees. The melaleuca is ugly, with its thick, spongy, white, shredding bark. It was introduced into the Everglades *deliberately* by the Army Corps of Engineers more than half a century ago, to assist them in draining the River of Grass. The melaleuca, which is from Australia and a sort of vampirish member of the myrtle family, has been sucking the Everglades dry ever since. It flowers five times a year, and bees make lousy honey from its blossoms.

Unfortunately, bees make good honey from the blooms of the pepper, and beekeepers have been known to encourage the spread of this bad bush just to keep their bees busy. (Bees *are* terribly busy. Each lives but six weeks and works demonically all the while.) The casuarina is the nicest, with its susurrant voice—a pretty sight on a white-sand beach swaying green against a perfect sky—but it too is a pushy pest. Its needles and roots put a toxin in the soil that prevents other types of plants from growing around or beneath it. Also, with its shallow, spreading root system, it flops right over when a vigorous wind comes up.

Another bad tree is the poisonwood, which is the Keys' poison ivy except that it is a tropical hardwood which grows up to 30 feet tall. It has large, shiny, limp leaves. Its small, yellowish green flowers are arranged in sprays, and it bears an orange fruit in the fall. Its leaves and bark are often splotched with dried black sap. It has that *look* of being a no-good.

Caloosa Indians (of which little is known except that they were very tall and feared their dead), and later the white settlers, boiled down the sap and spread it on the tree limbs. The birds would alight and their little bird feet would *stick* to the branches. Even in the 1930s and '40s trapping wild birds on the Keys was a lucrative business.

You'll also see the Jamaican dogwood, or fish-fuddle tree, the branches of which those mysterious Indians scraped and laid on the water, causing fish to rise, insensate. There are also century plants, orchids, bromeliads, and the huge webs of the gigantic golden orb spiders.

Another nice walk is a few hundred yards beyond the Blue Hole. This is the **Jack Watson Nature Trail**, a well-marked loop trail less than a mile in length. There should be pamphlets available in a box at the beginning of the trail, but usually the box is empty. The numbers on the trail direct your attention to various palms, including the thatch and the elegant silver; poisonwood trees, highly toxic but with fruit prized by the white-crowned pigeon; and sinkholes, large and small. You can also make arrangements with the rangers for a hike in less traveled areas. Call 872-2239.

The best times to see the Key deer are at dusk or very early in the morning, in either the ferny parts of the forest or in the lower-lying buttonwood sloughs where there might be water. The deer also browse on the lawns of the burgeoning developments of Big Pine, their habitat being increasingly "shared" by humans. Now they're threatened by, of all things, schoolchildren. Since everywhere else has been built up, with no site for a school set aside, a big and raucous push is on to build the school right in the Refuge. A commensurate, commemorative statue in honor of the displaced animals will most surely be erected if this comes to pass. Perhaps the children themselves will be called the "Dearies." In May and June you might see fawns feeding with their mothers on the mowed shoulders of the roads, in terrifying proximity to traffic. Slow down, slow down, slow down—less than 300 deer remain, and they are a very condensed herd on a very developed island. A bad storm or widespread disease could wipe them out. They are not being assisted by a number of Cuban immigrant hunters who jacklight them at night, kill them with two-by-fours, and take them home to eat.

The most comfortable time to tramp around the backcountry is the dry, mosquito-free winter, but the trees are not in flower then and there is little bird activity. **Reflections Nature Tours** out of Parmer's Place on Little Torch offers kayaking trips in this area for $45 a person. Telephone: 872-2896.

NO NAME KEY

A Russian is said to have been No Name's first resident. He homesteaded almost 200 acres, setting trip-wired guns in the underbrush so that visitors were offered the opportunity of being shot. Little was known about him except that he grew very large sapodillas. (The sapodilla is a large shade tree that provides brown, baseball-sized fruit in the spring. The fruit of the "dilly" is coarse and pink and tastes rather like candy that fine sand has been sprinkled over.)

A small village with a school and post office sprang up in 1922, when a car ferry ran between Marathon and No Name. The railroad first bridged the gap in 1912, but there was no land route. Automobile travelers had to take two ferries to traverse the Keys, the other running between Lower Matecumbe Key and Grassy Key. The ferries—*The Florida Keys, The Pilgrim,* and *The Key West*—operated until 1938, when the Seven-Mile Bridge and the Bahia Honda Bridge were rebuilt to accommodate cars. The 15-mile trip to No Name took about two hours. At that time cars drove on a marl road to Big Pine, then south across Big Pine Channel to the north corner of Little Torch. Wooden bridges connected the Torches, Ramrod, and Summerland keys. Once the ferry service was disbanded, the village by the landing disappeared.

During 1962 a Key Wester sympathetic to the Cuban refugees allowed a group training to be guerrilla fighters to use his shack as headquarters on No Name. The key was fairly inaccessible, the bridge leading between it and Big Pine both rotted and burned. The revolutionary experiment ended when one guerrilla shot and killed another, mistaking him, he said, for a raccoon.

A new cement bridge crosses Bogie Channel and connects No

A REALLY BAD TREE

A really bad tree is the manchineel, one of the most poisonous trees in the world. It is not common but does grow wild on the Keys, particularly Big Pine. It is a small, sprawling tree with a spreading rounded crown and alternate oval leaves that narrow to a sharp point. It produces green and yellow flowers and a crab apple–sized fruit which is deadly when eaten. Some people confuse the tree with a guava, and it is said, although it's difficult to imagine by whom, that the fruit is sweet.

In more exotic locales, it is one of the means by which a zombie is made. One poisons the person with the little apple, then once he's buried simply calls him forth from the grave. Voodoo legend has it that the corpse must be spoken to by name and that it must answer the call; as a result, some corpses in Haiti are buried facedown, with the mouths filled with dirt and their lips sewn together.

Poisonous apple aside, the tree itself is vitriolic. The copious sap is caustic, and even rainwater runoff from the leaves can burn and sear the skin. Almost any kind of behavioral abnormality can be attributed to extinct tribes of Indians, which is why you should not be surprised when you hear that the Caloosas employed the manchineel as Grand Inquisitor, tying their luckless victims to the tree and letting the milky sap run where it wished over them, the sap pickling and flaying the flesh as it went.

Ponce de León was one visitor to the Keys who probably wished he'd never come. He was struck by a Caloosa arrow dipped in manchineel juice, and though he managed to escape to Havana, he found only his deathbed there.

Name to Big Pine today, used mostly by fishermen. The road runs straight to the vanished ferry landing and stops at some very impressive rocks. There is absolutely no way you can make the mistake of running off the road into the water without annihilating yourself on the boulders first. Deer appear at the end of the afternoon and congregate on the road. Don't feed them. A deer who is fed from a car will eventually be run over by one.

Right on Bogie Channel is the **Old Wooden Bridge Fishing**

Camp. Pleasantly funky old cottages somewhat compromised by newer drab funk environs. Kitchens and dockage. If you want a TV, you're welcome to bring one. One-bedroom cottages are $65 a night or $375 a week. Two-bedroom cottages are $90 and $500 (872-2241).

The **No Name Pub** is on Big Pine, though barely. Turn at the light on Watson Boulevard, then bear to the right to go down Wilder Road. The Pub is just before the humpback bridge to No Name. It's open until around 2 in the morning—scandalously late for Big Pine—and people love the pizza, but its real ambience is that it's hard to find.

THE TORCH KEYS

Big bad parties have been taking place on No Name and the Torches recently. Sometimes they get really bad and someone is found murdered after them. Three particularly gruesome murders remain unsolved. All that the police know is that the vultures didn't do it.

The Torches have always been a little strange. Just beyond the bridge crossing Big Pine Channel and linking Big Pine with Little Torch was once the Island Woman Bar, known principally for its owner's global economic views (the world's problems began with the invention of money). It is now out of business, perhaps because he gave free beer today rather than tomorrow. A succession of restaurants followed, but it would be chancy to stop by for a meal these days, as it has become a Jehovah's Witnesses meeting hall.

Down this road a half mile is **Parmer's Place**, a friendly complex of rooms, apartments, cottages, and trailers named after birds and fishes. You can stay in the Grunt, for example, for $75 a night, though you might prefer the more elegantly named Egret at $105. It's very quiet back here. Beautiful parrots and cockatoos live in splendid cages on cool, landscaped grounds. They all have names, too. July and August are in-season, but prices go down $25 in the fall. There's a pool and free breakfast, and boat basin and $10-per-night dockage; many people trailer their boat down and rent by the week. Or you can rent from Bud Boats on Big Pine and cruise around these unparalleled fishing and diving waters. Weekly rates at Parmer's are around $500. Telephone: 872-2157. A short walk back toward the highway is **Little Torch Sandbar**, a happy joint that serves wine and beer, lunch and dinner.

The Torches—Middle, Little, and Big—got their names unsurprisingly from the resinous torchwood trees that grow there. The wood burns when green, and was used for kindling by homesteaders. It may also have hallucinogenic properties. Woodcarvers who work with torchwood admit to getting a kick out of it. The rare Schaus swallowtail butterfly, which might know something, feeds exclusively on it. The butterfly was thought to be extinct at the turn of the century but was found on Matecumbe Key, only to disappear again after the 1940 hurricane. There are some on Lignumvitae.

Buttonwood trees, an upland mangrove, were also cut and burned to make charcoal for cooking fires. The habit in the Keys was to cut the hardwood and plant coconut palms, pineapples, and limes. None of these farming ventures was successful and all were abandoned. One can still find Key limes growing wild in the Torches. The trees, which are not indigenous but were introduced from the West Indies, are fiercely thorny and bear a small tart and juicy fruit which is yellow when ripe and falls into your hands nicely at a touch. One of the reasons Key limes were never successful commercially was because they were too thin-skinned and therefore too fragile to ship.

The Torches were most populated in the 1920s, when the old road ran down the western side of Little Torch. When the Overseas Highway was built after the 1935 hurricane, utilizing the railroad's bed and bridges, many of the old roads were abandoned along with the communities that had flourished beside them.

There is little here now, certainly—houses, trailers. There is a biologist on Middle Torch who keeps his six acres as a habitat for snakes, which sounds nice, or at least natural, until you realize that because his specialty is snakes and he wants to find snakes when he's looking for them, his six acres is a "Dixie farm" covered with trash. Old boats and flattened gasoline tanks, rotting boards and fabric, rusted metal of all sorts. All the kinds of snakes that exist in the Keys from the black racer and endemic

SNAKES

The Keys have all the varieties of snakes found in Florida.
Yes. All the harmless snakes, the *rat,* the *water,* the *indigo,*
the *black,* the *corn,* the *green,* and the *king*—as well as the
poisonous ones, the *cottonmouth,* the *rattlesnake,* and the
coral.

You may understandably be interested in the poisonous
snakes. The *cottonmouth* is rather difficult to identify because he changes color as he grows from a baby to an adult.
He can even resemble the gentle, huge indigo snake. But the
cottonmouth has a big thick triangular-shaped head which is
flat on top, and if you get very close he will probably show
you what he is by opening his mouth to display the whiteness
of his jaws. The *diamondback* is the heaviest poisonous
snake in the world, although at eight feet it is not the
longest. It is found in piney and palmetto woods, sandy
areas, and hammocks. *Coral snakes* are the most intriguing
because they're small and pretty as well as being the most
deadly. They grow only to a length of around two feet, and
their black bodies are brightly banded in orange and black.
The harmless *scarlet king snake* is often mistaken for the
coral snake, but the *scarlet king*'s nose is red, while the
coral's nose is black.

Proper snake identification depends upon considerable
calm.

Snake experts tend to have three maxims:

In identifying the coral snake, they say, "If his nose is
black, he's bad for Jack."

They say that all snakes are nonaggressive and will not go
out of their way to bite you.

They say that snakes are where you find them.

little ring-necked snake (weird in that it has no ring) to the huge
indigo and diamondback rattler can be found here. Except they
couldn't be found the hot winter morning we spent turning over
the trash. Perhaps they had been dined on too vigorously by
predators the previous fall. Or perhaps they were offended by
their littered home. Or worse, they were tired of the old funky

litter and wanted new funk! In any case, there were no snakes, in what had once been a lime grove.

A road that runs the length of Big Torch is called a Scenic Drive. Historically, Monroe County has been madly successful in using taxpayers' money to build roads and bridges that go nowhere. Condos, marinas, and golf courses are but a gleam in a speculator's beady eye when these projects are pushed through, and this "scenic drive" is no exception. There is nothing here but a few isolated houses showcasing basketball hoops and chained dogs. After about eight miles of zigzagging blacktop over swampy land, it ends in a showcase of mangrove—the red (not red, but identifiable by its arching aerial roots and long, pencil-shaped pods); the black (not black, but known by its numerous fingerlike projections—pneumatophores—rising from the muck); and the white (predictably, not white). The saintly mangrove is a splendid, hardworking, giving tree, nursery to nestlings and fishes, busily making land all the while it nourishes. Look upon it, this tangled swamp, and be both respectful and glad.

Off the humble Torches at the western end of the Newfound Harbor Keys is **Little Palm Island**, a five-acre sand-covered rock owned by a succession of millionaires and now run as a precious thatch-topped luxury resort. This place keeps getting extravagant awards and accolades. It has been named by some resort watchdog organization, for example, as "the second best resort in the world." This is all silly, of course, and the place is consistently disappointing to the truly rich, one of whom likened its ambience to a cross between Disney World and the Bahamas. "Thursday," she added (when they present the seven-course gourmet dinner), "must be the chef's night off." Someone else far less rich, the manicurist actually, noted that the biggest problem here is the no-see-ums.

Little Palm Island has a seaplane that will take you to their favorite unexplored islands, and of course they will arrange for any kind of personalized charter you can dream up. It all has been a boon to captains and guides from Summerland Key. A millionaire-style pool-lagoon conception runs through the place. Suites in the bungalows are $545 per couple per night (!). It's $775 per couple per night with meals. There are no telephones

Egrets in the mangroves

or televisions, but you do get a free newspaper. You can bring
your own watercraft, and yachts are welcome.

   If you feel you can't afford $545 for an evening at this time,
you can still go over to the restaurant for breakfast, lunch, or
dinner. There are certain regulations, however, involving lunch
that might make you think twice. The minimum for lunch is $25
per person and this does not include taxes, tips, and whatever
you would spend at the bar. Men must have "collars"—have to
leave your Hog's Breath shirt at home. If you want to go swimming, you have to have a beach club membership, which is extra
too. There are no children in your party, they hope. At night entrees are predictably pricey. The menu also offers *Les Desserts*—
(Desserts) they add helpfully. *Les Chocolats* (Chocolate) and *Les
Café et Thé* (Coffee and Tea). A launch called *The Escape* leaves
the **Dolpin Marina** at MM #28.5 every hour on the bottom of
the hour, 7:30–10:30. For dining reservations call 872-2551. Resort reservations: 872-2524. (You're really going to do this??)

RAMROD KEY

This key bears no resemblance whatsoever to a ramrod—it is shaped more like a helmet. In the days when the railroad passed through, Ramrod claimed a post office, although the train never stopped here. It merely slowed down while mail was tossed on and off.

The most interesting thing about Ramrod is **Looe Key**, which is seven miles offshore. Looe, named for a frigate that ran aground here in 1774, is a National Marine Sanctuary and perhaps the most beautiful reef in the Keys—certainly the most varied and interesting reef in the Lower Keys. The Sanctuary covers five square miles; the reef itself is roughly Y-shaped, 200 yards wide, and 800 yards long. Parts of the reef are awash. Other sections have gullies plunging down to 35 feet between the coral heads to a pristine sand base in what is called a spur-and-groove system. Looe is a lovely and lively community with exceptionally clear waters, so it is wonderful for the snorkeler as well as the diver. You'll see thousands of fish here, lobsters,

A brain coral gives lobsters shelter from a spotted eagle ray

octupuses, and rays. Long tongues of pillar coral rise within three feet of the surface, and there are massive brain corals as well as an array of "soft" corals—the undulating gorgonians, sea fans, and sea whips. Looe, with its winding coral corridors, its deeply carved caves, and diversity of life, is a spectacular reef, the jewel of the Keys. In the summer of 1994 a 170-foot University of Miami research ship carrying 21 marine scientists and practically every antenna known to man, cruising on autopilot at five knots, ran hard aground on the reef, causing ghastly damage. The Coast Guard charged the captain with negligence, but before a hearing could be held, he voluntarily surrendered his license, effectively closing the case against him. Many of the scientists were from NOAA, the federal agency that runs national marine sanctuaries. The vessel's name was the *Columbus Iselin,* though it might as well have been christened *The Ironic.* The scars left by the ship are quite distinct. The top of at least four of the reef's spurs have been stripped bald, leaving merely grayish rubble. Life in the untouched areas makes it appear even more barren. Scientists, ever plucky, are trying to develop "cures" for these disasters, such as installing precast concrete forms mimicking the reef's contours in the hope that desirable organisms will homestead them.

As for what you can do, any marine researcher would agree: Never anchor on coral, and when diving never touch it or stand on it. All life is protected in the Sanctuary. Spearfishing and collecting are not allowed. Dive shops offer full and half-day reef trips and night dives.

Underseas Inc., MM #31 on Big Pine, rents all equipment, including cameras. A half day is $25 per person. It's always a good idea to rent a wet suit for a few dollars more. Telephone: 872-2700.

Innerspace Dive Shop, MM #29.5 on Big Pine, makes trips on its 35-foot dive boat *Innerspace I.* Their snorkel package, which includes equipment, is $30. A scuba package, including two tanks, weights, and belt, costs $40. Telephone: 872-2319.

Reef Divers on Ramrod is located at the **Looe Key Reef Resort**, just past the Torch-Ramrod Channel at MM #27. The resort is a small motel on a canal with boat dockage. It's inexpensive and very popular. The rates change frequently, but a room runs around $65 throughout the fall, $85 in the spring, and $90 in February and March. Trips to the reef are $40 for divers, $25 for snorkelers. Dive packages are available whereby you save $15–$20. There's a pool, a crowded tiki bar, and an unhurried restaurant which serves an early bird special until two in the afternoon. Instruction, equipment, and two tank dives on Looe costs $75. Telephone: 872-2215.

Crossing pretty Niles Channel, where the generous sky allows you another opportunity to pick out a favorite cloud, you come to **Summerland Key**, where the outlines of some impressive housetops can be seen on the western shore. A road off to the right runs along the channel and ends at a dismantled dock leading to a small island with a familiar sign, KEEP OUT, with a perturbing twist—BE AWARE OF CARETAKER. Enigmatic Summerland is developed with a series of canals on the eastern end, and it has a dusty main strip of billboards which is a tiny, hopeful version of something larger and even more dusty.

Coco's Cantina at MM #22 is a good, no-frills restaurant where you can get a whole yellowtail for $11.95. Turkey dinner on Wednesday nights! Conch fritters. Plantains. And often just one waitress trying to provide it all. Closed Sunday. Telephone: 745-1564.

CUDJOE KEY

The best-tasting crayfish in the Keys are said to be found off Cudjoe. The second and last most interesting thing about Cudjoe is its name, about which there is much dispute. There is the slender "joewood" theory, the joewood being a common little tree with fragrant blossoms. There is the slenderer yet "Cousin Joe" theory—an early homesteader from Key West, Joe by name, cousin to someone, who first settled here. There is also the more thoughtful explanation that the name Cudjoe was a customary African name given to a male child born on the first

KEY LOIS

Off Cudjoe, in the Atlantic just before Hawk Channel, is Loggerhead Key, recently named Key Lois. Lois isn't visible from
the highway, although it is, clearly, from haute Little Palm.
Lois looks a little odd, as well it might since its only occupants are monkeys. One half of the key is gray, as though in
shadow; the other half is a healthy, mangrove-wooded green.
A narrow tidal river separates the two, a river which, it is
said by those who put the monkeys on the island in the first
place, they could cross but prefer not to. The monkeys, about
1,600 of them, inhabit the gray half, which they have de-
nuded with their climbing, scrambling, swinging, and clinging. They are 70-pound dog-faced rhesus monkeys, bred and
raised here for laboratory research. As with the cattle one
sees grazing in green pastures, they probably lead a very
happy life until they don't. There is no natural food for them
on the island and no fresh water, so someone arrives daily by
boat with water and hundreds of pounds of Purina Monkey
Chow. At other times a boat will arrive, collect some of them
to fill an order from a laboratory, and take them away. Boats
also arrive upon occasion to lug off the monkey feces accumu-
lating there. It's a very clean island, and the monkeys are
purportedly the biggest, blondest, and healthiest in the
world.

The original colony of 100 was captured in India in 1972.
The descendants are now a multimillion-dollar business
for the owners of the Massachusetts supplier of lab animals for the U.S. Food and Drug Administration. The veteri-
narian owner of the island, Dr. Henry Foster, wanted to
rename Loggerhead Key Key Lois, as a tribute to his wife, although why Lois would want an island full of yowling,
scratching, gibbering monkeys named after her is not known.
The state, however, apparently not liking to have places renamed willy-nilly for uxorious reasons, refused. The doctor
got his way nevertheless with the acronym Laboratory
Observing Island Simians, and Loggerhead Key became
Key Lois, even though it might be more accurately called
Mon Key.

NO TRESPASSING signs are posted around the island, but
there is no caretaker here, the monkeys apparently being

their own best protection. So one probably will not see them, but if one did, it would be across a great distance. And the monkeys would be watching from a great distance too— across that far distance that separates monkeys from men.

Key Lois, like the holy, ruined Indian city of Galta, but with nothing sacred here—no temples, no priests, no pilgrims. Just the monkeys, monkeys, monkeys.

In 1997 the state began formal proceedings to have the monkeys removed from Key Lois and from another, smaller island on the Gulf side, Raccoon Key, contending that they are destroying mangroves and polluting the waters with their waste. "It's inconsistent," a community affairs advocate argued, "to continue allowing the monkeys to pollute the island while the state requires treatment of human waste." Like, fair is fair. One monkey had the misfortune to escape to nearby Little Crane Key, which is a frigate bird nesting area and was shot by a U.S. Fish and Wildlife manager. Charles River Laboratory, a subsidiary of Bausch & Lomb, claimed that the monkeys can't escape because they "don't like salt water," but this poor voyaging primate was identified by his tattoo.

day of the week. The Africans, brought to Florida as slaves and then freed, often went to live among the Seminoles, by whom they were enslaved once more. It would not be unlikely for one of these men to leave the Everglades and migrate to an isolated key where he could lead an independent life. Nor would it be unusual for a freed black man to come up from Key West and, using the name he was born with, work one of the "outside" keys.

Be that as it may, Cudjoe is rather an orphan. Since it has no post office, it has no zip code, and since it has no zip, any person or establishment thereon is considered part of Summerland Key, which, as we recall, seems to the jaded eye to consist primarily of real estate offices.

Cudjoe is damp and low for the most part. Most of the development is on the eastern side, with tidy ranch-style homes and lots of lawns. People walk peppy small dogs along the well-man-

FAT ALBERT

Fat Albert is a 1,400-foot, ground-tethered blimp, a radar-stuffed aerostat that floats benignly over Cudjoe, keeping its eye and ear on everything, druggies mostly, with millions of dollars' worth of fancy electronics. Fat is a fine sight, but it crashes frequently, victim of storms and other mishaps. Once it even had to be shot down deliberately because it escaped. What you see today is Son of Fat. Perhaps even Son of the Son of Fat. Fat's twin, also known as Fat, beams TV Martí to Cuba, though there are few TV's there to receive the early morning transmissions.

It required millions of very heavy bricks to construct Fort Jefferson, which was built to oversee all activities in the Florida Straits, Havana, Pensacola, Mobile, the mouth of the Mississippi—in short, all of the Gulf of Mexico. Now the dainty Fat, lighter than the air it bobs in, does the job, although he may not float forever. Cute Fat is expensive to maintain.

icured streets. An Italian restaurant called **Raimondo's** offers ostrich as an occasional special. This is true. Also true is that this is not a restaurant you need to go out of your way for.

The most excitement people on Cudjoe Key have had for quite some time is pondering the possibility that the Air Force will launch missiles from land the military possesses on sleepy Blimp Road (see below).

Just over the bridge that crosses Bow Channel at MM #20 is **Mangrove Mama's** (745-3535), open 11:30–3 for lunch and 5:30–10 for dinner in the winter. When it's closed for the month of June, the place looks as though it's been shuttered for years. A fireplace, beer served in mason jars, and specials like veal curry. The food isn't that good, but it doesn't seem to matter. On seasonal Sundays there's barbecue and a band. You can run into anyone here, even a guy in an FBI cap on holiday. "Are you really in the FBI? I'd like to join the FBI," a girl says. "Oh, you should," he says, "it's a lot of fun."

THE BALLISTIC SANCTUARY

Down Blimp Road, where Fat lives, the Air Force, just before century's end, began making murmurs that they would like to put a missile site here. It was their desire to shoot off 44-foot, 26,000-pound Hera target missiles which would streak across the Gulf toward the Florida panhandle and be shot down by defense missiles from Elgin Air Force Base. They'd shoot off about a dozen a year for ten years; each launch would be "unique" and they'd learn a lot. If the missiles really worked (Elgin's, that is), they could perhaps be sold to South Korea, Taiwan, or even Israel. Of course, we'd keep a lot of them too. The Keys apparently are the ideal place to test missiles for the 1991 Military Ballistic Defense Theatre program, though in 1990 Congress mandated the Florida Keys National Marine Sanctuary and Protection Act. These two top-level decisions do not seem to dovetail nicely. The Pentagon says that they can never completely rule out some adverse effects to Sanctuary water quality and marine life but otherwise the launches will be perfectly safe. Most of the pollutants will be scattered about in the troposphere and the waters will be evacuated for about four hours during launch days. No one seriously believes that this will come to pass, but one never knows. The military has always enjoyed being in the Florida Keys.

SUGARLOAF KEY

Sugarloaf was settled at the turn of the century when a sponge raising station was built here. The farming venture consisted of cutting off bits of live, large sponges, attaching the bit to a piece of concrete, and allowing it to grow in a pen in the water. Charles Chase, an Englishman, created the Florida Sponge and Fruit Company in 1912 and built a town, which he named for himself, complete with watchtower and guard to chase off sponge poachers. The company went bankrupt on the eve of the First World War when Chase's assets were frozen in a London bank. He sold his holdings, which comprised almost all of Sugarloaf, to R. C. Perky, a Florida real estate salesman who quickly changed the town's name from Chase to Perky and set out to subdivide and develop it. Perky's town was never built, but the man is responsible for the key's weirdest and most winsome construction.

The Bat Tower

The bat tower, shingled, brown, and elegant, is about 35 feet tall and is to be found down a dirt road just past the Sugarloaf Lodge, to the right of the road that leads to the Sugarloaf Airport. People bounce down the road to view it, circle it warily in their cars, then look a little embarrassed because they've gone out of their way to see it. The bat tower, standing there quietly batless, suffers these visitations with dignity.

Dr. Charles Campbell, a former health officer for the city of San Antonio, Texas, wrote a book in the 1920s entitled *Bats, Mosquitoes and Dollars*. It was Campbell's belief that the bat was one of man's best friends, both because of its insatiable appetite for mosquitoes and its valuable excrement, which makes great fertilizer. The bat towers or "roosts" of cypress lath which he designed were condos for thousands of bats, and the chute in

The Perky bat tower as envisioned by Mr. Perky

the center of each structure collected guano, making each bat tower "a little gold mine."

It had not been that many years since malaria and yellow fever were found to be transmitted by the mosquito and that those diseases could be eliminated by mosquito eradication. Dr. Campbell's theories were well received. San Antonio, upon his urging, even passed an ordinance which made it illegal to hurt a bat. Sixteen bat towers were built according to his plans, which he did not charge for, charging only for the bait, which cost $175. This secret formula was said to be indispensable in attracting bats. Campbell never disclosed the formula, but it almost certainly consisted primarily of bat shit. One of the towers built in Texas was called the Asylum Bat Roost and was built on the grounds of the Southwestern Insane Asylum. Six of the towers were built in Italy and many were adorned with a crucifix.

Perky, frustrated in his attempts to develop his key into a huge resort—he had already built a gambling casino, restaurant, and cottages—because of a considerable mosquito problem, read *Bats, Mosquitoes and Dollars* and grew hopeful. He sent away for the plans and bait, built his bat tower, and dedicated it at a party on March 15, 1929, to "good health in Perky, Florida." The box of bait did not arrive in time for the party, but when it eventually did it was opened, water was sprinkled upon it, and it was installed in the recesses of the tower. It was noted by someone attending the event that "a smell like that ought to attract something," but sadly the bats never came. Never did a bat visit the bat tower. After a year, when it was believed that perhaps fresh bait was needed, Perky sent away for another box, but Campbell had died, and with him the formula for success. Perky shortly afterward went bankrupt. His fishing camp burned and he himself passed on. Only the bat tower remains, still pristine and expectant.

The **Sugarloaf Lodge** at MM #17 is a wonderful, relaxing old-time resort, the only lodging of note between Sugarloaf and Key West. It has tennis courts, an airstrip, a swimming pool, and a marina with fishing guides and boat charters available. The Lodge also has a pond in front of the glass-walled restaurant where until the early morning of Friday the 13th of June 1997, Sugar the dolphin had lived since 1968. Sugar was between 34 and 44 years of age when she died and was loved by thousands of people, most of all by the Good family, who run Sugarloaf Lodge. She was a beautiful lady, fond of her inner tube and palm frond, and it's difficult now to gaze into the empty lagoon that had been her home for so many years. There was nothing theatrical about Sugar—she was genuinely awesome. The week after her death, many of her admirers gathered and threw masses of flowers on her waters.

Sugar Good

In 1994, under the aegis of the Sugarloaf Dolphin Sanctuary, six other dolphins—three from the Ocean Reef Club north of Key Largo and three from a Navy facility in San Diego—were brought to the Lodge and kept in a large penned area in the Bay apart from Sugar, but the politics surrounding their care and their planned release to the wild became far murkier than their beautiful surroundings. There are diametrical views regarding captive dolphins and the feasibility of freeing them. The Dolphin Research Center on Grassy Key breeds dolphins and employs them as educational and therapeutic tools. The Sugarloaf Sanctuary was created only to eventually release the mammals, save for the elderly Sugar. In 1996 the Sanctuary was disbanded, the dolphins relocated to captivity elsewhere. Wild dolphins must have an attitude toward their suburbanized brothers, but for all the metacognition research being done, no one yet knows what it is.

The Sugarloaf Lodge restaurant is fine enough. Large cuts of roast beef are available, as is a variety of fish dishes, the entrees running around $18. The bar with its mounted fish and tiny dance floor remains a classic. So too are the wonderful rooms, with their individual murals, sleek '70s decor, and weird lamps. They all have a view of the water. Rates run about $110 in winter and drop to $75 during the summer. Efficiencies are $10 more. Telephone: 745-3211. The restaurant's number is 745-3741.

During the season, December to May, **Fantasy Dan's** at the Sugarloaf Airport gives sight-seeing airplane rides. A ten-minute trip costs $20, while a half-hour trip takes you around Key West for $40. Telephone: 745-2217. If you feel the need to jump from a plane, you can do that too. For only $200 you can get truly terrified. Call **SkyDive Key West**: 745-4386.

One of the last vestiges of the old road is on Sugarloaf. The new road is built on the former railroad bed, but before the hurricane of 1935, automobiles traveled a meandering westerly route along the Atlantic. The road is overgrown and quiet, good for bicycling and bird-watching.

Take Sugarloaf Boulevard, directly across from the Lodge, and follow it through a subdivision until it dead-ends. To the left are the "nude canals," an abandoned development which has been taken over by three rather distinct groups of sunbathers. There appears to be a rather overweight, if not obese, heterosexual section; a more comely heterosexual section; and a homosexual section. The water in the canal is an unusual robin's-egg blue and is dotted with rafts and inner tubes. Pickups and vans are parked on the barren, platted lots beside it. The road used to curve northward up to the famous old fishing camp Pirate's Cove, a rich man's retreat which was wiped out by a hurricane in 1945, continuing to a wooden bridge which paralleled the railroad bridge to Cudjoe. This road is unpassable now, a small bridge which once crossed Tarpon Channel having been destroyed.

If you choose to avoid the nude canals (and who could blame you) but still want to explore, take the right fork off 939. This, however, will only lead you, after three miles, to the wooden remains of another missing wooden bridge and a rusted Ford Landau with a GO GATORS sticker that has toppled grille-forward into the warm, quiet waters, bringing to mind the words of one of Thomas McGuane's characters: "I didn't know what I was, not a Southerner certainly. A Floridian. Drugs, alligators, macadam, the sea, sticky sex, laughter and sudden death."

It is customary to say good-bye to the bat tower before resuming the plunge to Key West, for now the pace picks up, the land crouches flatter. The **Saddlebunch Keys** are low and pale, the mangrove, growing on just a few inches of mud above coral rock, stunted. This is the "heavy dew" of the Keys, not quite land and not quite water.

Big Coppitt is the suburb for the Navy air base on **Boca**

Chica Key. It has one sterling attraction: **Geiger Key Marina**. Turn at the Circle K at MM #10.5. As the manager says, "All the folks who find this place are pretty pleased with themselves." Nestled in the mangroves, it's certainly no marina in the modern sense, and the grub is simple, but you feel like an old Keys hand here. Outdoor picnic tables, a beer bar, live music on the weekends, and a big barbecue on Sunday. Open until 11 (296-3553). Boca Chica used to be Key West's favorite beach, and there were fishing camps and restaurants here in the 1930s. The military condemned the property during World War II, the Army built airstrips here, and the Navy later took it over to train pilots. The Navy has gradually closed off much of the area over the years (there's still a bit of abandoned beach road you can walk at the end of State Road 941), and now the glum sight of old missile silos (the *new* missile silos are on Fleming Key), complete with buzzards brooding on top, is affordable only by boat. Our own American vultures congregate on Boca Chica bunkers. It is a sight that certainly can be missed, but it wouldn't hurt to remember it.

In March of 1991 the Navy was most surprised when a Cuban major landed his Soviet MiG on the airstrip. They never saw him up there. Another MiG slipped in two years later. NORAD (North American Defense Command) admits that by the time anything from Cuba appears on their radar, it's already "here." Joint military and civilian use is being planned for Boca Chica; 737s could be landing here by 1998, several flights a day, five days a week, direct from the cold hinterlands, their passengers continuing by bus to the Key West airport, which can't accept such large aircraft.

At MM #10 is **Sea Cloud Orchids**, a nice stop for a house present should you be fortunate enough to be staying with friends, thereby avoiding room-rate shock, but you will probably be driving faster now, past the low shimmering watery terrain. Everyone is driving faster. Even the cormorants, those worried birds with the piercing blue eyes, fly hurriedly across the flats, or, appearing more worried still, stand on pilings or wires, drying their sodden wings. **Shark Key** is a brand-new creation for the rich, with a gate and big new palms for the instant "look," but **Rockland Key** is industrial, little more than a borrow pit, the mangroves all gone, steam shovels moving the marl around, a concrete factory—Flagler would have been smitten.

STOCK ISLAND AND APPROACHES TO KEY WEST

Stock Island has always been a service island. Originally cattle were penned here to fulfill the dietary desires of those sick of fish in Key West. Today on Stock Island there is the new jail, which for some reason has a petting zoo, and the dump—popularly called Mount Trashmore (now "capped," as they say), looming over the Key West Resort Golf Course. The Florida Keys Hospital is here, as is the Tennessee Williams Fine Arts Center, which puts on a variety of plays and musicals and brings classical music and jazz ensembles to town. Call 294-6232 for their schedule.

On the other side of Stock, to the south of Route 1, at Junction 941, are trailer parks (which even the police prefer to avoid after dark); most of the remaining shrimp fleet; **Oceanside Marina**, where some excellent charter boat captains can be found (the marinas on Stock were previously best known for the "mother ships" of cocaine that found safe harbor here); and the infamous, recently closed dog track. Many people in the Keys have adopted greyhounds, well aware that otherwise these intelligent, elegant dogs would end up in the Gulf Stream or the landfill after their last race. Greyhounds make great pets and come in every color but gray . . . and why should that pose a problem?

Stock Islanders enjoy their sunsets, as capable of staring in crazed fascination at the clouds as anybody, but you do not dally on Stock Island, you move on. Behind you is the big billboard that says PARADISE WELCOMES THE U.S. ARMED FORCES. You hang on to the wheel as pickups with huge tires and bumper stickers—I LOVE MY COCKATOO, RECYCLE OR DIE, BUY A GUN PISS OFF A LIBERAL—and small fierce Hondas—I'D RATHER BE DRINKING, NOT A WELL WOMAN—rush past you. You plunge over the Cow Key Channel at MM #4, where a tumultuous division greets you.

To the left is South Roosevelt Boulevard, or A1A, the road that goes past little "Houseboat Row" (soon to be disbanded), the airport, the beaches, and the condominiums. The condos are all familiarly banal, one at 1800 Atlantic being particularly contemptuous of the passerby by taking a fascist command of the view.

To the right, and what most naturally sucks you down along it, is North Roosevelt Boulevard, the continuation of Route 1, and of course your heart will sink when you see the sprawl of Searstown, until 1964 a perfectly nice salt marsh. Seagulls soar, still puzzled, overhead. (Up until 1952 there was no commercial activity on Roosevelt Boulevard at all.) This is the strip of discount liquors, discount cars, discount pizzas, and Terminix Pest Control; this is the bawl of consumerism and doubtful services.

Another large shopping mall, Key Plaza, as well as the *really* enormous pink Marketplace, lie ahead. The longer you stay in Key West, the stranger these big malls appear, for they look exactly like the rest of Florida. Kennedy Drive intersects the island shortly. On your left is the ball field, with lighting worthy of the pros. Key West loves baseball, and the number and fervor of Conch fans are large and loud. National TV sometimes comes to town to film this phenomenon. One TV host said he was disappointed with Key West—"I had visions of coming to this lush tropical paradise, but when I got here I saw a lot of asphalt, concrete, and bars. It wasn't what I expected"—but then he met the coach and players and decided there was something special about them, and thus the place must be OK too. So there you are.

Beyond the city pier and the charter boats of Garrison Bight, merge into the left lane if you wish to drop straight down Truman and into the downtown. To the right, Palm Avenue moves around the Bight (*bight* means a bend, after all), skirting the Navy yards off Trumbo Point and the pastel congestion of Peary Court to eventually turn into Eaton. This is, perhaps, the quickest route to the Pier House and Mallory Square if you don't want to cruise Duval, but of course you must introduce yourself to Key West by cruising Duval. This is a big problem for the city's new parking garage, Key West Park 'n' Ride, which is down Eaton and then a right on Grinnel Street, because no one

The southernmost house, at the foot of Duval Street

can find it, much less wants to use it. (Dear, I'm sure we'll find someplace to park downtown, the parking god will provide.) It remains virtually empty, so pristine that there have even been a couple of weddings at the top of it. If you *do* take Truman (not becoming muddled by the overnamed intersection where a medley of political figures are all given their due: Roosevelt Boulevard turns into Truman Avenue as it crosses Eisenhower Drive, which becomes Jose Marti Drive) past Bayview Park and the tennis courts; past the old Truman School, restored now for county offices, with its two gigantic kapok trees, the whole thing lit up at night like Dante's Tomb (in fact all of Roosevelt is overpoweringly lit at night with a row of what surely must have been two for the price of one streetlamps, making the street look like an extremely boring pinball game); past the Chevron station where wonderful Wes, who's repaired half the cars in town, reigns; past the parked car with the three-foot-high fried egg on the roof advertising BREAKFAST ANYTIME; past the Margaret Truman Launderette and the estate that is St. Mary's Star of the Sea Church; past the old and inexpensive motels, the El Rancho, Key Lime Village, and the Red Rooster to the big white sign that says DUVAL.

Yet if you were to pass this temptation nonetheless, in the interest of getting to the rock-bottom end of Florida, and continue one block more to Whitehead, two alternative conclusions to your journey would still remain. A few blocks to the right is the

Monroe County Courthouse with a big kapok tree of its own and a sign, END OF THE RAINBOW END OF THE ROUTE, a sign that could be perceived as being somewhat ominous. Yet you would not think you were at the end of anything here, even Route 1, for Whitehead continues down to the Civil War Monument (a memorial to Union soldiers) and Mallory Square (named for a native son who became the Confederate Secretary of the Navy) and stops, ambivalently, there.

However, were you to travel to the other end of Whitehead, you would be at the real foot of the street, the **Southernmost Point**, which is marked by a large, odd buoy planted firmly in cement. With the water beyond, you will now certainly feel yourself to be at the end of something, even though a painted curb says AMERICA BEGINS HERE.

I know things change now and I do not care. It's all been changed for me. Let it all change. We'll be gone before it's changed too much. I found that if you took a drink it got very much the same as it was always.

—Ernest Hemingway

KEY WEST

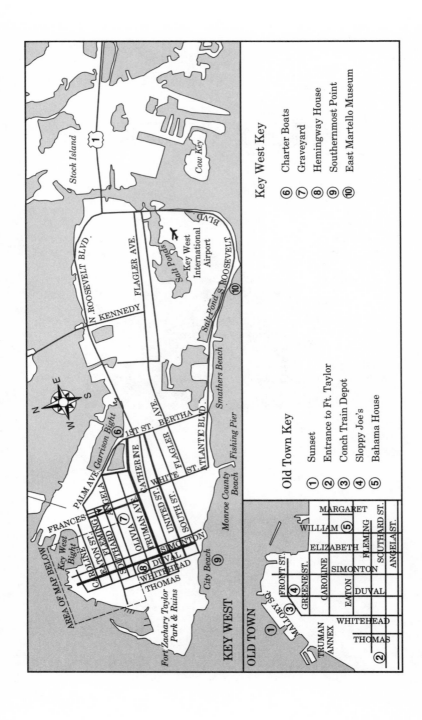

KEY WEST

OLD TOWN

Old Town Key

① Sunset
② Entrance to Ft. Taylor
③ Conch Train Depot
④ Sloppy Joe's
⑤ Bahama House

Key West Key

⑥ Charter Boats
⑦ Graveyard
⑧ Hemingway House
⑨ Southernmost Point
⑩ East Martello Museum

WALLACE STEVENS wrote "her mind had bound me round," and he was speaking of Key West. This peculiar and unlikely town does have a mind quite of her own, with attitudes and habits that can either charm or exasperate, seduce or dismay the new acquaintance. The traveler seldom wants to see what he sees; he wants to see something else. And in many respects Key West, which is so singular in its architecture and attitude, its posturing and fancifulness, its zany eclecticism, its seedy tropicality, is a town come upon unseen, unexpected, the something else almost felt. It is an urbane, isolated, freewheeling, lighthearted, gossipy, and eccentric town. There is a sense of adventure here, of excess and individuality. It's odd. Actually odd. It is a rather dirty town and has very little dignity, but it has style. Its architecture is a charming, intriguing mélange of fine houses and shacks, painted primly white or weathered right down to the silvery bone, a mix of gingerbread grandeur and mañana collapse with an abundance of verandas and porticoes, columns and pilasters and balconies.

Comparison and exception are everywhere. The town can look somewhat like old New England, but with a decidedly unpuritanical cast. Jonathan Edwards would never have slept here. The Navy is a presence, certainly, owning a good quarter of the town as well as two thirds of the waterfront (though the waterfront holdings are increasingly being excessed and sold off) and all of Boca Chica, but it is not a highly visible one from land. From the air and water the extent of its holdings is clearly seen—the piers and berths, the housing, the ammunition dumps, the runways, the radar towers. In the early 1980s, when the military began pulling out of Key West, the former mayor water-skied to Cuba in an attempt to get the Navy to stay in full force by demonstrating how close that island was to our shores. It took him six hours and ten minutes. Key West, being Key West, didn't even think it a particularly strange thing to do.

Homosexuals, who probably command another quarter of the town in terms of real estate and influence, are more visible, providing a sleek and somewhat mordant glaze to the town. Tennessee Williams came to Key West in the 1940s, attracted by the sailors, who all seemed "to be walking to the tune of Managua, Nicaragua," and was influential in introducing the town to artistic gays. Many of the shops, guest houses, and dance halls are owned by gays, and much of the town's restoration is attributable to them. They continue to provide much of the gloss, sophistication, and outrageousness of Key West.

Key West is tropical. Island. Cuban. Black. In the morning one hears roosters crowing, although the sense is not particularly bucolic. The birds pecking in dusty runs beneath towering breadfruit trees are descendants of fighting cocks bred for the gambling pit. A good example of the decadence and innocence that is Key West.

One knows where the city lies in a geographic sense. Forty-five miles north of the Tropic of Cancer. Closer to Cuba at 90 miles than it is to Miami at almost 150. Due south of Cleveland, Ohio. (Cleveland, Ohio!) A glittering, balmy, perhaps not terribly legitimate rock beneath vast sea skies. Key West's economy over the years has been based on a curious and volatile array of occupations: wrecking, shrimping, fishing, and smuggling. In the 1970s certainly most of the money that came into Key West was drug money, but things have quieted down considerably in that regard. Now the money comes from real estate. And things are changing fast.

Key West is a tourist town—one and a half million people visit each year—but also a town of contrast and contradiction, threat and carelessness and charm. The bars should be sampled, of course, and the reef investigated. The gold and emeralds should be seen, and the forts and the galleries. One should dance or stand on one of the balconies that line Duval and watch the prowl of the street. The beaches should be duly attended and a tan obtained. The yellowtail stuffed with crabmeat should be eaten, and conch fritters and Key lime pie and, if you're lucky, guava duff. *Café con leche* or the intense little energizing espresso called *bucce* must be bought from the window of a Cuban grocery. The flowers and trees should be puzzled over and appreciated and their lovely names said aloud. Jacaranda. Bougainvillea. Poinciana. Frangipani. One should catch a fish. One should be in the water and travel over and on the water as much as possible. And, when one is on land, one must assuredly walk. Stroll, linger, wander. For Key West is a walking town, and a bicycling one too. Architectural surprises are around every corner, and other interesting sights less classifiable.

THE STREETS

In Key West, "downtown" isn't in the middle of town at all but up on the northwest corner of the island, on the harbor. All the Keys veer west as they run south, and the streets of Key West, although straight, are laid out on an angle—just about on a diagonal to main compass points; the corners of intersections becoming, in fact, compass points.

Whitehead and White are the parallel boundaries of Old Town. Whitehead is where Hemingway's hoary ghost hovers, in the house where he often experienced "the black lonelies." Then there is Duval, followed by Simonton, a big street which once could have been counted on to hold the post office but no more; the new post office, landmark and comfort to the postcard laden, is on Whitehead. The next streets—Elizabeth, William, Margaret, Grinnel, Francis, and White—can be easily recalled if you put them in the order of three friends—nice old souls who rock and converse with each other across the porches of their white Conch houses: Elizabeth William, Margaret Grinnel, and Francis White. Actually, Francis has a middle name, Ashe, and a lovely street it is to have as a middle name. The island's original coastline marked the intersection of William and Caroline streets until 1874.

Basically, now, you have memorized the streets paralleling Duval. Walking the other way, up Duval from the Pier House to the Atlantic, remembering the streets will be a bit more vexing. You begin at Front, nicely enough. Then there is Greene, a street named after Pardon Greene, an early settler who left his wife and children back in Connecticut rather than subject them to the rigors of the tropics, but this will probably be of little help

to you in remembering that Greene is between Front and
Caroline. Caroline used to be marked on the corner by the Caroline Lowe house, which unfortunately is no longer there. There
are still old Conchs in town who remember the sound of it burning. The house had been built by shipwrights, with heavy timbers that extended from the foundation to the roof. Ablaze, the
timbers "were screaming." Two sequential letters of the alpha-
bet follow next, *E* and *F*. Eaton and Fleming. Eaton has the
Episcopal Church right on the corner, and Fleming has Fast
Buck Freddie's on the corner. Up Fleming a bit and on the left is
Fausto's Famous Food Palace, the town's premier grocery store.
Fleming is easy; the only thing you have to remember about it
is that it's one-way. Southard, marked by the large clock, is the
next street, and that is one-way in the other direction, termi-
nating at the entrance to Truman Annex. Past the white gatehouse there, and about a winding mile farther along is the
entrance to Fort Taylor and the beach. Following Southard is
Angela, then Petronia and Olivia (William Wall, Key West's
original cartographer, named these streets for his daughters in
1832) and Truman. Think SAPOT. It might be best to pause
here, for there is a confusing bevy of young ladies' names ahead:
Julia, Virginia, Amelia, Catherine, and Louisa. In the mind of
the newcomer, they seem simply United. Which is the next
street, just before the last long one, South, which runs down,
appropriately enough, to the Southernmost Point. (Numbers
run upward from the harbor to the Atlantic and from the Navy
base and Fort Taylor northeastward across town.)

CHANGES AND CONFUSIONS

The land of Key West behaves most peculiarly. It cannot quite
be counted upon to be terra firma, for its firma keeps getting
changed, rearranged, created, confiscated. What used to be on
the water doesn't even have a view of it anymore. What used to
be water is now land or concrete. What used to be separated by
water is now joined firmly to land, like Fort Taylor, which had,
in fact, almost disappeared *beneath* the land. Pine trees had
grown on top of it, and the martial mausoleum had to be
excavated, appearing bit by bit.

Weather moved things around a lot. After the hurricane of 1846, the graveyard was moved inland. So was the lighthouse, now one of the most landlocked in America. The military moved things around a great deal, reshaping, building, and abandoning, playing a big role in changing the shape, direction, and accessibility of Key West. On the eve of the Civil War, the Army cut a road through the wild part of the island so that troops could be marched directly from the barracks on one end to the fort on the other; this road was first called Rocky Road, then Division, and most recently Truman.

During World War II the Navy created additional land and islands for munition dumps and housing, including Sigsbee Park, Fleming Key, and Tank and Christmas islands. For years, the reason one couldn't get to Fort Taylor, a state park and a National Historic Landmark since 1973, was because of Naval security for the Caribbean Command enveloping the land around it.

One half of the land area of Key West didn't exist 150 years ago when William Whitehead, brother of one of the four original owners of the island, first surveyed the town. He laid out lots in tiny 46-by-90-foot pieces, and the houses, built mostly by ships' carpenters, were constructed without any particular regard for their relationship to one another, and alleys and paths angled off the main streets and entered the lots at irregular intervals. Whitehead platted everything, including the bottom of a two-acre pond which existed in what was then the middle of the city. The pond was nameless, though described as a "miserable, stagnant lagoon," and was filled in by the rearranging hurricane of 1846. Land in Key West has blown in, blown away, and simply, or not so simply, been made.

Henry Flagler created 134 acres of land on what is called Trumbo Point, Trumbo being the name of the Oversea Railroad project's head engineer. After the bridges of Long, the Seven-Mile, and Bahia Honda, the construction of the railroad approached Key West with no available dry land for the depot. When Flagler was informed of this oversight, he said, "Then make some."

All this is partly why Key West, a busy speck in an abyss of sky and distances, seems so confusing.

But the town is small. If you're invited for dinner and you become hopelessly lost, you'll still arrive only 15 minutes late.

That is unless your hosts have moved their house. For that is
another problem. Key West moves things. The Bahama houses
were moved, plank by plank, all the way from Green Turtle Cay
in the Bahamas. The enterprising David Wolkowsky lifted the
nineteenth-century Porter steamship office off its foundations
on the old Key West–to-Havana ferry dock and moved it 300 feet
out into the water, building first a restaurant and then the
entire Pier House complex around it. The gun turret from the
Maine was moved, all the way from Havana Harbor to an ele-
mentary school on Southard, only to be moved once more to
grace the new post office on Whitehead. The Conch home that
now houses the restaurant Bagatelle on Duval was moved from
its site on Fleming when the library expanded—the library, the
first in South Florida, having moved from its birthplace farther
up on Duval where the Red Barn Theatre is today. The Oldest
House was moved. And E. H. Gato was a big mover. He built a
mansion on Truman in an area which is now Bayview Park, then
moved it to Virginia Street on rollers. The trip took two weeks
and employed one mule and a windlass. His son, E. H. Gato, Jr.,
built a rambling Victorian house at the end of Duval, where it
intersects with South Street (see page 240), but found that he
didn't like the way the sun struck one of his favorite porches, so
he turned the enormous structure around on his yard.

   The only place that seems determined to remain exactly on
the spot where it began is St. Paul's Episcopal Church at 401
Duval Street. Built here in 1838, it was blown down in the 1846
hurricane. Promptly rebuilt, it burned in the great fire of 1886,
a fire which destroyed two thirds of the town. Promptly rebuilt
again, it was toppled by the hurricane of 1909. It took the
parishioners a little longer to get organized this time, and they
did not begin rebuilding until 1914. The white, concrete structure you see today has stayed put now for over 65 years. When
you find the right rock, you stay on it.

MYSTERY AND HISTORY

There is a mystery about Key West, and it is not just behind the
name the Spanish gave it in the 1500s—Cayo Hueso—Island of

Bones. It's true the bones are a puzzle. For whose were the bones, and why were they here? No one knows if the island was actually littered with bones. If it was, they probably belonged to the Caloosa Indians, who used the place either as a burial ground or were massacred here by some other tribe, possibly the Seminoles, although how that somewhat placid group were able to extirpate the ferocious Caloosas has never been explained. In the 1700s the English felicitously altered the sound of *Hueso* to the name of *West*. But the murky etymology of the name is not the mystery. The mystery is in Key West's very self. Why does it look the way it does? And why is it still here? In 1934 the state suggested that the city, which was bankrupt, be abandoned, and that the people be relocated to the mainland. It has endured hurricane, fire, and neglect. It is the oldest city in South Florida, an area known to suffer greatly from the heavy, obliterative hand of speculation, development, and redevelopment; and yet the old part of town, the town platted out by William Whitehead in 1829 and built throughout the nineteenth century, remains startlingly, strikingly intact.

In 1822, the year that the island of Key West was sold by a Spaniard, Juan Salas, to a Mobile businessman, John Simonton, for $2,000, the only beings that frequented the place were mosquitoes and pirates—pirates at the time being a bigger problem in the area than malaria, heat, and lack of fresh water. In that same year Lieutenant Matthew Perry sailed down to raise the American flag over the country's new possession and confirm that it had one of the largest, finest deepwater anchorages in the country. The flag was raised in the vicinity of what is now Mallory Square, the event attended by a few sweating sailors and some black and Cuban fishermen. Several months after the raising of the flag, the energetic Naval commodore David Porter arrived with the ships of his West India Squadron to set up headquarters in Key West and suppress the pirates who had been scooting around the Caribbean and the Gulf in their shallow-draft boats for years, murdering, plundering, and engaging in their sleazy piratical rites. Porter's depredations caused the town more grief than those of the pirates, for he considered Key West a military post and appropriated the settlers' livestock, buildings, and supplies. He wanted to lay out the streets in a star pattern radiating from central plazas which could be controlled by artillery in the event of civil unrest. He even tried to change the name of Key West (as had Perry, who wanted to call it Thompson's Island, after the then–Secretary of the Navy), constantly referring to it as Allentown.

After establishing himself here, however, Porter found that his ships, which were mostly deep-draft frigates, could not pursue the pirates over the reefs and into the winding mangrove creeks where they hid, so he acquired several small light-draft schooners and built five flat-bottomed 20-oared barges, which he called the *Mosquito, Gallinipper, Midge, Gnat,* and *Sandfly*. He also acquired a steam ferry boat, the *Seagull,* that had been retired from the New York–Hoboken service. With the ferry towing the agile bug squadron up and down the Keys, Porter was soon successful in the pursuit and extermination of pirates. He had driven them from the Keys by 1830 and continued to pursue them to Cuba and Puerto Rico. Court-martialed by America after Spain protested his intrusion into Spanish territory—Spain being in the habit of protecting pirates as long as Spanish ships were allowed safe passage—Commodore Porter indignantly resigned, joining first the Mexican Navy, then the Turkish one. Porter never cared for Key West and urged the government not to establish a permanent station here. After the pirates were eliminated and he was court-martialed, the West India Anti-Pirate Squadron was transferred to Pensacola.

With the pirates gone, the only fears the captain of a vessel had were hurricanes and running aground on the reefs, a likelihood that Key West profited from, for it made the salvaging of wrecked ships a regulated industry. Between 1832, the year John James Audubon dropped by, and 1855, the population of the island rose from 500 to 2,700, most of them New Englanders or English Bahamians, almost all involved in wrecking. Millions of dollars' worth of salvage cases involving ships wrecked on the reefs were being adjudicated in Key West courts by the city's own Judge William Marvin, who literally wrote the book on salvage laws, *A Treatise Upon the Law of Wreck and Salvage,* the standard authority in the admiralty courts of both England and the United States. (The judge's other work was on the internal evidences of the authenticity of the Four Gospels.) It was an educated and colorful group on this tiny island far from mainland America, this place the poet Richard Eberhart calls "umbilically extravagant." The men wore silk top hats, the ladies served suppers on fine china—on occasion, gold plates. All the wealth was wrecking wealth. Indeed, much of the exotic furnishings that filled the houses, and the formal clothes the people wore, came directly from the foundered ships.

Ava Parks, in her book *The Forgotten Frontier*, wrote about the Key West of the time, "There was nothing else like it; a city crowded on a small island in the middle of nowhere. . . . This was it—civilization began and ended here."

By the end of the 1850s, however, the first of the reef lighthouses (pages 81–83) was being constructed, bringing the beginning of the end to the profitability of wrecking, and in 1859 the look of the town was changed when the first of Key West's two great fires occurred.

There was no fire-fighting equipment in town. There had been a small hand-pump engine, used mostly for parades, which, failing to be effective against a small fire in 1843, was carried to the wharf by irate citizens and thrown into the water. The fire of 1859 began in a warehouse on Front Street and Duval and gutted two square blocks before it was stopped when a man named Henry Mulrennon got a keg of gunpowder from Fort Taylor and blew up his own house on Greene Street. The town was rebuilt quickly, and many people felt that the fire had been a benefit rather than a liability because the new structures were more "elegant." Key West's newspaper of the day, *The Key of the Gulf,* said the new buildings were "not only an ornamental embellishment but gave an air of permanency and durability to the town."

Wealth no longer came from wrecking but from a new discovery: sponging. Cubans were also emigrating in great numbers from their country's ten-year war with Spain, and cigar manufacturers were establishing large factories here and employing thousands of men. The town was a great mélange and somewhat baffling to casual visitors, one of whom wrote in the 1880s:

It is densely settled, and about as un-American as possible, bearing a strong resemblance to a West Indian town. The houses are of wood, plainly built, and, with few exceptions, painted white. The houses are of all sizes, jumbled up in the oddest way. . . . The interior of each block is filled up with one-story shanties.

On April 1, 1886, the second and great fire engulfed Key West. It started in the Cuban patriotic club and school, the San Carlos, on Duval Street. (The building of today is the third San Carlos to be built on that site.) The town's single fire engine was in New York for repairs and the fire quickly spread, burning the same area as before along the waterfront as well as turning inland, destroying Fleming Street from Whitehead to Bahama. Once more an attempt was made to stop the fire by blowing up houses with kegs of gunpowder from the fort, but this time the blaze raged on and the three sailors who lit the fuse were "blown to atoms." The fire burned for 12 hours, consuming 50 acres of the town. Again, Key West was rebuilt quickly, carpenters working day and night, building homes on the outskirts but bringing them into the burned-out areas once they were cleared. The peculiar thing, of course, is that after both fires, the town was rebuilt in wood, with the wealthier citizens building even grander homes than they had occupied before. There were some commercial, military, or public buildings made of stone and well-laid brick and a few homes made of cast or "rusticated" stone, a concrete block formed in a mold—a fad of the mainland which came quickly in and out of fashion. (Several of these houses, large and side by side, can be found on South Street, near the Southernmost Point.) But Key West was a wooden town, and when it abruptly stopped growing early in the twentieth century, wooden it remained. Silence entered the picture—a deep and sleepy silence. Nothing happened. The Florida land boom boomed but was unheard in Key West. The railroad came and the railroad went and Key West slumbered behind its vines and flowers. The trees grew and blew in the heat-thickened wind, and termites sculpted their own interior columns and castles out of porches undisturbed.

COLLAPSE AND RESURRECTION, COLLAPSE AND RESTORATION

From being the richest city per capita in America in the 1880s, Key West by the 1930s had become the poorest. The sponge industry had declined; the cigar makers had moved to Tampa; the railroad and shipping trade with Havana had diminished; and the Navy and the Coast Guard had pulled out. Henry Flagler's train chugged across the waters "carrying nothing, nowhere, for nobody." Things were so bad that the city's Economic League recommended that only bread baked in Key West be allowed to be sold here and only local orchestras be allowed to play.

On July 5, 1934, with no economic base other than fish, $5 million in debt, and with 80 percent of its 12,000 citizens on welfare, Key West relinquished all its powers of government to the state. The governor, David Sholtz, was aghast. He immediately turned the problem over to the New Deal's Federal Relief Administrator in Florida, Julius Stone. Stone arrived in Key West and saw the abandoned cigar factories and Navy barracks, the collapsed piers and dilapidated houses. He saw the privies, the cisterns, and the trash, and learned that most of the people were living on fish and coconuts. He also learned that Key West was the only city in America never to have frost. He decided that the only way to save her was to turn her into a resort town, a "Bermuda" as it were. Key West's salvation was to be The Tourist.

Stone was a debonair fellow and a flashy administrator, using FERA funds to subsidize air service and to underwrite the rehabilitation of houses and the reopening of hotels. He organized the Volunteer Work Force to spruce up the town, and in six months 4,000 people had donated a million and a half hours, planting trees, building a thousand park benches, painting murals, and shoring up houses. The beaches were cleaned of seaweed and a "smart cabana colony made available." A Maids' Training School was established, with the few remaining grande dames of Key West tutoring young girls in the cleaning and serving arts. There was also a school for fishing guides.

Out-of-work musicians were recruited into the Hospitality
Band, which met every arriving ship and train. The submarine
base, abandoned by the Navy, was turned into a private yacht
basin. (A nice and nasty description of the yachty set is in Hemingway's novel *To Have and Have Not.*)

Key West needed a lot of cleaning up. There was trash everywhere, tons of trash. There is always someone who likes to fig-
ure out the quantity of one thing in terms of the quantity of
another, and trash is no exception. A writer of the time drew
this picture:

> Or, if someone had constructed small bungalows, say, 42 feet ×
> 20 with a 9-foot ceiling, the garbage and trash would have filled
> 176 such bungalows. Figuring eight lots to each side of a city
> block, such procedure would have necessitated five solid city
> blocks of bungalows!

There was a lot of trash and it was hauled off and put somewhere, if not in five blocks of newly built bungalows.

Classes in handicrafts were organized, and people set to work
making hats, pocketbooks, and belts out of coconut fronds and
ashtrays and buttons out of shells. A guidebook was published
touting the attractions, which included the Southernmost
House, the Martello Towers, and the Turtle Kraals as well as
"Raul Vasquez's tame fish." The fish were in a pond at the rear
of his nightclub on Roosevelt, and one could stroke them as one
"would a cat." Also mentioned was the home of a retired school-
teacher, Miss Dunn:

> The house, with Miss Dunn still residing within, stands as a
> monument to the appreciation of her students.

(Actually, Miss Dunn's house, at 420 Simonton Street, may be
the oldest house in Key West. If it was built around 1823, as is
suspected, it would be older than the "Oldest House" on Duval.)

Fifty-three attractions were mentioned; many of them,
including various tropical parks and the magnificent Convent
of Mary Immaculate, are now gone. There were also listings of
fishing guides, churches, and mixed drinks.

Julius Stone even specified how long a visitor should be prepared to stay:

To appreciate Key West with its indigenous architecture, its lanes and byways, its friendly people and general picturesqueness, the visitor must spend at least a few days in the city; a cursory tour of an hour or two serves no good purpose. Unless a visitor is prepared to spend at least three full days here, the Key West Administration would rather he did not come.

Stone's experiment in massive volunteerism, which turned a bankrupt and shabby city into a vacation mecca, was wildly successful. Tourists poured in and the demand for accommodations was so great that residents moved out of their houses and lived elsewhere in order that winter visitors might have the more desirable locations, a practice, certainly, that exists today. But only six months after the best tourist season Key West had ever had, the Labor Day hurricane of 1935 hit the Middle Keys and blew the railroad away. And tourism was forgotten for many years.

Julius Stone, the man who introduced Bermuda shorts to the Keys (Conchs maintained it was his underwear), returned in 1940 to live in the city he had saved, involving himself in investment, banking, and law. In the next 20 years, as leading citizen, he managed to represent and bilk just about everyone in town. In 1960 the master of the shady deal fled, practically as a fugitive, settling first in Cuba, later in Jamaica, and dying in 1967 in Australia.

It took World War II to bring people and prosperity back. In those randy war years Key West became known as the "Singapore of the West." The Navy swept up the town in a dizzying, flustering embrace, but after the war abandoned her once again, and Key West looked more dilapidated than ever. It had entered its own time zone once again—the old houses in Old Town jostling together in eccentric neglect, the roots of banyans erupting through sidewalks, the docks rotting, the streets deserted and silent.

In the late 1950s, things began to change. Action arrived in the guise of destruction. Demolition began to follow dereliction. Fine old buildings were razed and an unseemly demand for vacant lots for parking arose. The handsome Jefferson Hotel on Duval Street, with its cupolas and wide verandas, built in 1886, burned and was demolished in 1958 to create the drive-up window facilities for the Southeast Bank.

In 1958 the Geiger House on the corner of Greene and Whitehead was slated to be demolished so a gas station could be put there. It was this possibility of loss, more than any other, that finally roused Key West. Jessie Porter Newton, a fifth-generation Conch, invited some wealthy and influential people into her garden, and the Old Island Restoration Foundation was formed. With the help of Micky Wolfson, whose astonishing museum—the Collection of Decorative and Propaganda Arts— is located in Miami Beach, the Geiger House was purchased, restored, and transformed into the Audubon House. Miss Jessie was instrumental in saving and moving dozens of houses, but even her energy and the increasing effectiveness of the OIRF as a lobbying and preservationist group could not prevent fire and bulldozers from leveling some of Key West's most beautiful structures.

The huge Curry and Sons Ship's Chandlery, a twin-towered landmark for more than 75 years, taking up an entire block on Simonton and Front Streets, burned in 1963, and the beautiful Convent of Mary Immaculate on Truman Avenue was destroyed despite wails of protest in 1966. The convent is probably the most-mourned lost building in Key West, and Conchs, many of whom were educated here, still speak of its demolition with bitterness. It was made of coral rock and took years to build, first completed in 1886, then enlarged to twice its size in 1906. It was a rounded, graceful, airy structure surrounded by rose gardens and palms. The wounded from the battleship *Maine* were brought here, and it served as a Navy hospital throughout the Spanish-American War before being turned back into a school. There was a large museum inside the convent, filled with relics of the *Maine* and a number of oddities, including a little wooden chest covered with seashells that Dr. Samuel Mudd had made when he was imprisoned in Fort Jefferson on the Dry Tortugas. It seemed that no one wanted the convent torn down except the Catholic Bishop of Miami, who was determined to put up more modern concrete-block classrooms. Many fragments of the convent—fanlights, gingerbread trim, shutters—can be found in various homes in Key West today, and over the convent grounds, beside St. Mary Star of the Sea Church, the afterimage of the lovely structure seems to hover in the empty air.

Each year during February and March the OIRF sponsors house and garden tours as part of Old Island Days celebrations. The houses are shown in groups of five or six and there are three separate tour dates. There have been four categories of houses established: Old Historic, Uniquely Located, Famous Occupants, and Island Living. This covers a lot of territory, so don't expect to see merely "classic" homes: the selections have a fine Key West eccentricity. The OIRF-sponsored **Hospitality House** (294-9501) in Mallory Square can give you current brochures and information on the house and garden tours and other seasonal events. The Hospitality House is the former ticket office for the Mallory Steamship Company, which used to ferry passengers to Cuba.

TOURIST TOWN

Mallory Square is difficult, perhaps impossible, to experience with style. People sort of mill around, waiting to be trundled off by the Conch Train or debating whether they should go into the new corny Shipwreck Historeum, where actors cavort in historical dress and screech, "Wreck ashore!" The area is certainly no place to pretend you're not a tourist. Hundreds of gallons of ice cream and piña coladas are consumed here daily, and the streets are jammed with curio shops and bad restaurants, save for the pleasant, shambly **Rooftop Cafe**, a dinnertime favorite for some of the town's older sophisticates. Ever since Claire's, wonderful Claire's, on upper Duval closed, there's been no place for the old guard to go. At the newly *re*-refurbished Mallory Square Dock, enormous white cruise ships take turns in waiting out the day. Almost 300 of them visit Key West each year. They loom above the town, making everything appear Lilliputian, including the already toylike Conch Train.

Cruise ships only began coming to Key West in 1992, and they get bigger and bigger. The large ones—900 feet, 2,000 passengers—cannot dock at Mallory Square and will be going to the former Navy pier, the mole, near Fort Taylor. The city, deliriously happy to collect more than $1.5 million in docking fees, has as yet not addressed the damage the big girls do to nearshore waters, but residents of posh Truman Annex are finding that their white walls and white furniture and white tiles seem harder to keep, well, white.

The square is named for Stephen Mallory, a prominent Key West citizen who in 1861 was appointed Confederate Secretary of the Navy; a job, it is true, grander in illusion than in fact. The little Civil War monument is dedicated in turn to the Union. In Key West the soldiers who died during the war died from yellow fever.

There are some dignified old buildings here which seem to stand back a bit, bemused at all the bustle. The large brick Romanesque Revival **Customs House** was built in 1891 and served as the federal courthouse during the Keys' wrecking years. On the National Register of Historic Places, it is slowly, slowly being restored. The preservationists' zeal was somewhat dampened when the **Hilton** muscled in beside and virtually around it, diminishing the old building's waterfront presence considerably. Interesting terra-cotta trim decorates the exterior, with five faces being found amid the ornamentation: a lion, a fox, a ram, a human, and a demon. Few people linger to regard these refinements, however. They wander seaward to the broad brick sward of the Hilton and its mall of pricey specialty shops (Panama hats, Key lime fudge, etc.). It all looks rather like Marina del Rey back here. It's the Harborwalk concept. You have the feeling you're not in Key West at all, actually, but somewhere else. They even have a parking garage which looks uncannily like parking garages everywhere. It's the giant, concealing palm trees that make it appear paradisical.

The buff-plastered brick building beside the old Custom House was built in 1856, and was originally used to store coal. It is the sole surviving building from the earliest Naval base in Key West. It is referred to as **Coast Guard Headquarters** for its last tenants, but the building also served as headquarters for the Lighthouse District when that now defunct organization administered the reef system of man-tended lights. The niche above the arch on the buttressed pier façade is filled with the bas-relief decoration of a lighthouse.

Asa Tift (see page 200) built his warehouse here to store

wreckers' loot prior to auction in 1850. The **Waterfront Play-house** now uses the building for its winter theater endeavors. In front of the Playhouse is the town's newest zany production, **The Key West Historic Memorial Sculpture Garden**, which will be full of bronze busts of important Key West people. Initially there will be only thirty-six busts, but there's room for thirty-six more, to be chosen by the inevitable future generations. There are so many vivid, larger-than-life figures who have been part of the city's past, it's apparently hard for the selection committee to choose among them, but for sure one will be a man named Joe Pearlman, who was the owner of a construction company and a developer in the 1950s. He also owned a store on Duval Street. Also in for certain is Sister Louis Gabriel, who served at St. Mary's from 1897 to 1948 and who, when the grotto to Our Lady of Lourdes was dedicated behind St. Mary's in 1922, prayed that the island would be spared from hurricanes as long as the grotto remained standing. (It's too bad she didn't include the convent itself, which might have given the Bishop of Miami pause.)

If you don't want to be subject to committee selection (and maybe get your feelings hurt), you can be part of the Walkway of History by buying a brick. This is more vox populi, as there will be thousands of bricks. They cost $50 each and you can have them inscribed. The possibilities here are thrilling, as you get to put up to 60 letters (including spaces) on each brick. It might possibly be more fun to stroll through the garden of busts than to wander through the Key West Cemetery, but only pos-

---

SPONGES

A sponge is a living marine animal of uniform structure though varying greatly in appearance that grows in a plant-like fashion and is remarkable for its power of absorbing water. Cole Porter remarks upon the sponge's love life in "Let's Fall in Love." Keys spongers would go out in skiffs, spot the creatures in the shallows through a glass-bottom bucket, pull them up with a long-handled three-pronged hook, then beat the bejesus out of them with a paddle. A phosphorous-smelling liquid called *gurry* would ooze out of them until it didn't, then the sponges (now the skeletons of the animal) were rinsed and trimmed.

A lady named Violet Turner recalled her daddy, sponging:

> To identify these horrible-looking black creatures isn't that simple. They are sleeping in the beds at the bottom of the sea. An amateur would assume they were merely seaweed. It is so fascinating to see how the spongers would lower their long poles with a hook on the end to the bottom of the bed and extract the creature with many eyes. After the dinghy is filled, the men head back to the mama boat to kill their catch. They are alive and must die to become useful and beautiful.

Sponging and cigar-making were Key West's primary industries in the last half of the nineteenth century. The city provided 90 percent of all the sponges sold in the United States. There was a great demand for sponges. Everyone used them. There were hundreds of boats employing thousands of men harvesting millions of sponges for a great deal of money. When Greek divers came down from Tarpon Springs to work deeper waters in their suits and helmets in the early 1900s, walking over sponge beds in their heavy boots, the locals blamed them for the fact that there were fewer and fewer sponges to be had. There were battles between the two groups—boat-burning and hose-slashing and the like. In 1953 a movie was made, *Beneath the 12-Mile Reef*. Robert Wagner and Gilbert Roland played two Greeks. Terry Moore and Richard Boone played two Conchs. Robert Wagner and of course Terry Moore fell in love, an event which did not increase the number of little sponges one whit.

The Greeks eventually returned to Tarpon Springs, but the sponge supply remained depleted, and in the 1930s a blight (some said caused by the dredging involved in the construction of Flagler's railroad) and the introduction of artificial sponges virtually wiped out sponging as an industry.

Some of the last to buy them in any quantity were the Japanese. A sponger said in 1935 that he suspected there was going to be a war soon because of all the activity on the Elizabeth Street dock.

> The price sponges bring in Key West right now is fantastic. . . .
> They surely must be planning a war before too long. That's
> always when we get our best prices, when a war is being
> planned. Especially sheepswool and glove sponge. They use a
> lot of those in hospitals. In a hospital they are used only for
> cleaning wounds, no lint to shed! They are much more sani-
> tary and more absorbent than any other material. On the bat-
> tlefield they are used for sponging and cleaning weapons.
> Nothing can stand that rough treatment as well as sponges.
> There are so many foreigners in Key West buying sponges . . .
> gotta be a war coming.
>
> Today, an occasional tourist buys an occasional sponge,
> probably one of three species: the *sheepswool* for bathing, the
> *yellow* for washing up the car, the *grass* for decoration. A
> sheepswool sponge about the size of a grapefruit costs $13.

sibly. Still, one advantage to the bricks is that you don't have to
be dead to get one.

Bricks without messages make up the former **First
National Bank Building**. Built by Cuban cigar manufacturers, the decorative yellow design on red and the ornate balcony
are in the style of Havana architecture. It's now been taken
over by the copycat theme restaurant **Planet Hollywood**.
Opposite the bank is the site of the old Havana-Madrid Club, a
striptease joint and gambling den in the 1930s. Its number
wheel is on display at the **East Martello Museum**. Shops and
another parking garage fail to distinguish the site presently.

Besides the increasing number of franchises, trinket traps fill
the Mallory Market area, and there are also a number of dum-
mies standing about; not dolts, but rather statues of old sea
captains and bearded fishermen holding aloft sponges or shells.
Sponges abound—big drab heaps of sponges. The oversized
ones are splendid to plant ferns in.

Shopping, Warships, Time, the Conch Republic, and the Conch Train

Key West has become the T-shirt capital of the world; it is
believed to have some 45 T-shirt shops, some of them, like

Beach Break at 501 Duval, being highly creative in their pricing. Many European tourists or young female Spring Breakers discover that their credit card has been charged $270 for five T-shirts (it's the monogramming). The "cute" fast-talking boys that work in these shops must get a kick out of this, but if you feel you've been robbed, go to the police station, conveniently located just off Duval on Angela, or call Code Enforcement at 292-8191.

There are some pretty obscene and tasteless T-shirts in the windows of Duval, and a visitor can while away many a moment by being repulsed by them. For the more discriminating browser, there are still a few stores that offer classy merchandise or unique gifts.

The grande dame of the great stores is homegrown **Fast Buck Freddie's** at 500 Duval, with its flashy, ever-changing window displays helping you remember what month it is. Down Fleming at 416 is **Noah's Ark**, a charming plush animal store with hundreds of huggables to choose from. Crossing Duval, at 527 Fleming is **Island Needlework** with beautiful original designs and a friendly, helpful staff. The first place a needlepoint cultist heads for when they're in town. Even beginners can get hooked on the possibility of making their very own CAST NOT THY PEARLS BEFORE SWINE pillow. **Swept Away** has three chic clothing stores at 505, 605, and 1022 Duval, while elegant men's apparel can be had at **Assortment** at 514 Fleming. **Cuba! Cuba!** at 814 Duval purports to sell things Cuban, although they certainly aren't imported from that island. You can get a painting of a rooster (a Cuban rooster) for $800. Best deal is the wonderful book of photographs of vintage Cuban cars with the preface by novelist Christina Garcia. **The Walking Shoe Store** at 335 Duval will help you get around in sleek sandaled comfort while **Machoti** at 721 Duval has fashionable women's clothing. **Kokopelli Southwest Gallery** at 824 brings you New Mexico, while a charming new store, **Curtis & Sons**, beside the **Wicker Guest House** at 913 Duval, sells uniquely designed teak furniture and classy home accessories. **Kudu** at 1208 sells flamboyant African jewelry and lovely kilims from Turkey. **Nannie MixSells** at 1102 is tiny but has a great selection of tasteful clothes and pretty, feminine gifts.

On Whitehead Street, down by the Mel Fisher Museum, is

From the Ruins at 219, with its dramatically singular clothing for women. Maybe you'll find a totally new personality there. Men seem hypnotized by this place. **Native Material** at 605 Whitehead, by the Green Parrot, carries folk art, hammocks, and weavings from Guatemala. Next door is **Kalypso**, a tiny, brightly colored house selling quilts, jewelry, and art created by the owners, a mother and daughter. The gateway, with its hinged picture-book blocks, is a visual treat.

Several worlds apart, for freaky, risky bondage buffs, there's **Leathermaster** (*not* the helpful wilderness tool) on Appelrouth Lane, around the corner from the elegant restaurant **Trattoria** on Duval.

In the Mallory Square–Front Street area, take a listen to the simple and melodious brass wind chimes at the **Shell Warehouse**, a rugged building of coral rock, part of what was once Tift's Ice House, the oldest commercial building in Key West. **Shades** at 306 Front is definitely the place for sunglasses, with a hundred different styles and colors available, whereas **Sweet Mischief** (335 Duval) is where to go for the niftiest bikini. **The Cigar Factory** in Pirate's Alley is a microscopic touristic representation of a Key West industry that in 1890 employed more than 6,000 workers and produced 100 million hand-rolled cigars yearly. Two men now roll Honduran tobacco in the dim light. A box of "El Presidente" will set you back $50, but you can have "El Hemingway" for less. **Key West Hand Prints** at 201 Simonton is a silk-screening institution. The colors are mixed up in old Navy soup kettles.

If you enjoy watching paint dry, you'll like seeing the printers working behind glass at 60-yard-long tables. There are a few chairs around in which exhausted men sit while their wives and granddaughters browse through the delicately colored skirts and sundresses. Lots of tea towel specials here. (A place for bolder hand-painted fabrics is the **Sign of Sandford** at 328 Simonton Street. Sandford designs fabrics for the decorating trade, but everything in the window is for sale, including the bright and witty hand-painted canvas beach chairs.) The **Saltwater Angler** at 219 Simonton is a sophisticated fly-fishing store with the best selection of reels and custom rods in town. The owner, Jeffrey Cardenas, a former flats guide, is an expert on the fishing art and the waters. As well as gear, there are clothes and books and even accommodations in this old, very well located building (294-3248).

Key West Aloe at 524 Front is a Key West institution, even though the aloe, that soothing succulent, is imported from Haiti. The sights and smells in here are a bit overwhelming—so many perfumes vying for dominance, so much White Ginger, Black Coral, Frangipani, and Sexy Afternoon—so many immaculately complexioned girls with long bright nails sweeping about in white lab coats. When one regains the street once more, the homely smells of seaweed, engine oil, and frying fish seem refreshing.

There's a tiny public beach and boat ramp squeezed between the **Pier House** holdings and the high-Bermuda design of the new **Hyatt** at the end of Simonton. **The Galleon** now takes up a lot of space, its dockage fees perhaps the highest in all Florida. There used to be nothing down here but gasoline storage tanks and the decidedly midscale **A&B Lobster House** on the water at the end of Front Street. Opened in the 1940s, it was a favorite for many years, one of the few restaurants in town. Its modernity consisted of an elevator that went up one entire level. No one was known to have patronized the A&B for the last decade or two, but it persisted, and now finds itself perfectly situated for the regenerated Bight. The new manager also runs the **Half-Shell Raw Bar**. Entrees are rather pricey, but a tourist could do far worse. Very well-prepared conch steak here.

Another old-time restaurant on the opposite side of the island, nailing down the other end of Simonton where no one was known to have gone for years, is Logun's, now the **Edge**. Still no one goes here. There's patio dining on the water, but you can't shake the feeling that you're opposite the Reach's trash bins, which you are. There's a little dance floor, a big parking lot, and even a few rooms for rent above the bar.

In the 1950s, the car-ferry *City of Key West* took passengers from Havana Docks (where the Pier House is now) to Cardenas, Cuba. She was later replaced by the *City of Havana,* which left from Stock Island. Many are looking forward to the resumption of ferry service to Cuba, although if Cuba does open up to

American tourists, Key West may become a backwater once again, a transportation turnstile. Why come to car-clogged Key West and buy a dirty T-shirt when you can go to exotic, mysterious, unmodernized Cuba? Others make the bet that after Castro, Key West will be to Cuba what Italy is to Albania, where hordes of refugees create a chaotic interface between capitalism and communist peasantry.

Things come and they go; needs arise, then they wane. In the '80s people lounging around the Pier House could see Navy hydrofoils churning past. Stationed at Trumbo Point, they prowled back and forth, to and from maneuvers in the Gulf, where they made their acrobatic turns and reversals and barreled about at classified speeds. Hydrofoils are agile and fast war vessels, each equipped with eight computerized surface-to-surface missiles and an assortment of rapid-fire machine guns. Because, thankfully, they had nothing to shoot these weapons at, they cruised the waters off Key West and intercepted drug boats, making the town no longer the primo port of call for drug smugglers that it once was. As a psychological weapon against a coke-laden cigarette boat, the hydrofoil was without peer. When the foils of these flying ships are deployed, they generate lift that raises the craft a few feet above the surface of the water, allowing it to move unhampered by the waves. A Navy commander said, "The Navy built this ship and now they're trying to find jobs it can do." They either never found out exactly what those jobs were or the hydrofoils were so expensive to operate that they became high-tech dinosaurs. In any case, all six of them were decommissioned in 1993 and you will no longer see them passing by in their sinister fashion. They certainly were arresting-looking, but you're just going to have to enjoy your shockingly red strawberry daiquiri mid-morning waterside—without them.

At 512 Greene Street, a little behind Sloppy Joe's on Duval, is the handsomely restored **Old City Hall**. Built just at the turn of the century, it replaced a wooden City Hall that had burned in the fire of 1886. Only ten years before, that structure had been dedicated at the centennial Fourth of July celebration for which W. C. Maloney, a prominent citizen of the town, had prepared a speech. The speech, entitled "A Sketch of the History of

A Navy hydrofoil

Key West," which he later published, would have been three
hours long. Midway in his presentation, however, a bar caught
fire from one of the celebratory rockets that were being shot off,
and Maloney's audience ran off to see the blaze, never to return.

Something called the Key West Torture Museum once had a
stint here on the ground floor, and we all wish we had been
around for that.

The Old City Hall has four large clock faces in its tower. Few
people glance at them, though, thoughts of time being eschewed
here. Too, the clocks seldom reflect the correct time. Their old
Seth Thomas façades conceal newfangled electric innards
which do not coordinate well with Key West's frequent power
outages.

The Conch Republic

The Conch Republic was born in April 1982, in reaction to road-
blocks set up by the border patrol near Florida City. The federal
government maintained they were screening for drugs and illegal aliens, and everyone leaving the Keys was stopped and
questioned. After insult came annoyance at the long delays,
then protests in the form of lawsuits and letters to the governor. Then came inspiration, the idea of secession, followed
immediately by plans for a party. On April 23, at high noon in

Mallory Square, there were secession ceremonies. A Key West flag was invented and raised; the establishment of a new republic was marked with speeches; a loaf of stale Cuban bread was tossed in the air as a token shot declaring war against the United States; and then the Conch Republic quickly surrendered in order to be eligible for foreign aid from the state of Florida. There were T-shirts, of course, and flags and border passes and passports. And there was a party which lasted a week. "Conch Republic Days" have now become an annual event each April, with parades, dances, powerboat races, and a very peculiar *bed* race in which teams of five people decorate beds which must consist of four wheels, a mattress, and themselves; they race down Duval Street with four team members pushing the bed and one riding on it. Prizes, of course, are awarded to the winner as well as for the most creative bed.

Fifteen years after its founding, the Conch Republic turned from quippy Dada to boorish complaint. It declared war on the Nature Conservancy, war on the National Park Service, war on the Florida Keys National Marine Sanctuary. The Conch Republic, or at least the individual who considered himself to be the Secretary General of the Conch Republic, declared war on the federal government and its "unholy alliance" with "so-called" environmentalists. War, war, war. He wanted to bomb Fort Jefferson with biodegradable toilet paper, whatever that is. He flew to the state capitol with an anti–Marine Sanctuary activist who wore a frock coat and carried a loaf of Cuban bread as a sword. The City Commission of Key West actually had a meeting where they voted to secede from the Conch Republic, even though, of course, the Conch Republic is . . . imaginary. One commissioner even bared his chest to disclose his Conch Republic flag tattoo and said he was embarrassed by the antics in the Republic's name. The Conch Republic seems to have become entangled with the "Conch Coalition," a clone of the Wise Use Movement. But the devil's in the details. Another commissioner voting for independence from the Conch Republic pointed out that the sword taken to Tallahassee was not a loaf of Cuban bread at all, but a baguette. He said, "If the man doesn't know the difference between French bread and Cuban bread, I don't want him representing me."

The Conch Train

The Conch Train is a pretty curious number. Imagine a little amusement park train with open cars and a fringed top, pulled by a Jeep camouflaged to look like a locomotive, rattling through the streets of a living town (not a theme park, not a wildlife safari, but a *real* town), the driver babbling about trees, houses, gingerbread, cisterns, hydrofoils, presidents, and emeralds. The Train goes past bars, and little old men rocking on porches, and ladies watering palms in the graveyard, and mustached cruisers wearing shorts and thigh-high black lace-up boots, the driver babbling all the while. You don't have to imagine this, of course, because the improbable thing exists and has since 1958 been faithfully serving tourists from 9 A.M. to 4 P.M. daily.

The Train was Bill and Olive Kroll's idea. They were running the Aquarium, the first tourist "attraction" in town and just about the only one in the 1940s. Built in the '30s with Federal Emergency Relief Funds, it was abandoned during World War II and the Navy used it as a pistol range. The Krolls took pictures of the way it had been and put it back together again, stocking it with the funny-looking fish that the local fishermen would bring them. People would pay a quarter, stare at the fish, and ask the Krolls what else they could do to while away the afternoon. Where do we eat? What else is there to look at around here? They had a lot of questions. What is that weird tree with those *things* dangling from it? Where does Harry Tru-

The Conch Train

man get those shirts? What's that big pile of bricks out by the beach? Why isn't the lighthouse on the water? Such a tiny town and so many questions! Bill Kroll realized that there was a thirst for information, *accurate* information if possible, that the town's cabdrivers were often loath to provide. (For a taxi today, info still not 100 percent guaranteed, call 296-6666 or 294-2222.) He decided to get into the sight-seeing business, patterning his vehicle on something he had seen once in, of all places, Helena, Montana. The Conch Train, hauled by its little propane-powered Jeeps, proved to be far more profitable than Henry Flagler's venture.

The Krolls long ago sold the Train to a local businessman with the somewhat Dickensian name of Ed Swift. Swift now owns a great deal of Key West, including many of the attractions like the Aquarium and the Historeum in the Mallory Square area. He also owns the Trolley. The Trolley is warmer in cold weather and drier in wet and is somewhat more nimble than the Train, but the itinerary and route are similar. Compared with the Train, the Trolley is mundane, but the business has spread rapidly elsewhere, including to the avenues of our nation's capital. If you go to D.C. after a visit to Key West, it's almost alarming to see trolleys, identical trolleys, motoring slowly past the monuments, their drivers talking, talking, talking. Swift has an exclusive sight-seeing franchise with the city and has thus far managed to repel all like-minded entrepreneurs, most recently the DUCKS. The DUCKS were gen-u-ine converted World War II amphibious vehicles which would lumber around town, then splash down at the Bight and churn around the water for a while. The drivers had their own spiel about Key West's peculiar history, but the odd, kind of darling, DUCKS were driven off and out of business. The Conch Train rules here, and is everywhere.

You needn't feel embarrassed riding the Conch Train. A strange cloak of invisibility is dropped over your self as you board. Once in a while a tourist will take a picture of you, a tourist on the Conch Train, but mostly no one pays the slightest attention to this contraption whirring down the streets, the driver repeating outlandish jokes without the slightest trace of shame. "On your right is the only free hotel in Key West, the county jail . . . and on your left is a famous old bar which used to be the city morgue. You'll still find old stiffs hanging out there."

On one modest little street the driver talks about crotons. Unfortunately, there is a clump of crotons growing on this street. Now, crotons grow all over Key West, indeed all over Florida, but this is the street where all the Conch Train drivers, a dozen times daily, mention the croton and its medicinal properties. Its purgative qualities actually. Its use in a tiny chocolate bar called Ex-Lax. "Don't laugh, folks, you didn't laugh when you needed it."

Sixty subjects are covered in the course of the tour, including a listing of all the ways in which the word *Conch* is used: the high school athletic teams are called Conchs, the drill team Conchettes, a Conch Cruiser is a dilapidated Key West car bought for less than $500, and so on. Pirates are mentioned, and sponges and cigars and Ponce de León. The passengers listen, earnestly invisible. "See," the driver states, "Ernest Hemingway's home and feel the personality of the man radiate around you." It's hard to know how much radiating gets through. What you see as a passenger on the train are people milling in the Hemingway gardens, taking pictures, milling. After passing the airport and the houseboats nosed up to the sidewalk on South Roosevelt Boulevard, the Train takes a boring jog down Flagler through the development of new homes there. There is not much to talk about here. The driver is reduced to talking about fill. He talks quite a bit about fill and how much of the island is built upon fill, and what fill is. The driver never stops talking, actually. You will deboard almost refreshed, invisibility being quite relaxing. **Conch Tour Trains** once left from only two locations, Mallory Square and Roosevelt Avenue. New depots are now appearing all over, and the trip includes trinket stops at the Bight and on Petronia Street. One and a half hours. Frequent departures daily. Adults $14.

Sunset

In the Keys the best place to ponder the descending globe of gas, our sun, is just about any place other than Mallory Square, where actually only a small wedge of horizon is visible. Audubon beheld a few sunsets in the Keys and couldn't get over them. "A blaze of refulgent glory streams through the portals of the west," he wrote, "and the masses of vapor assume the semblance of mountains of molten gold." The sun, as we know, appears to grow larger as it sinks in the west. This is one of the many illusions which nature presents, perhaps, as a children's astronomy book suggests, "to sharpen our wits in deciding between sights that are real and those that only seem to be."

At Mallory Square the Sunset definitely plays second fiddle to the unreal people and events that accompany it. In order to get your attention a young man will lie on a bed of nails, place a concrete block over his groin, and have someone shatter the block with a sledgehammer. You can buy a freshly woven palm hat and see some white cockatoos. You can't pet an iguana anymore because the Iguana Man died and the iguanas don't come down to see Sunset by themselves. You can buy a chocolate chip cookie. You can watch rather saucer-eyed cats jump through a flaming hoop. You can watch fire-eaters and jugglers, some of them quite talentless. Everything is giddy and determinedly carefree. And everyone is there: break-dancers and frightful bikers, little kids and deeply tanned weirdos, old ladies in their Lily dresses and guests from the Casa in their tennis whites, college students with their beer buzz.

The hippies began this Sunset viewing in the 1960s when they congregated here to pound drums and smoke dope. Now the camera is king. If you don't have a camera you will probably be elbowed away from various sights by those who do. The pier itself has been refitted for part of the new cruise port facility. The mayor had to promise Sunset devotees that whatever gargantuan ship will be docked there will have left each day before the sun goes down. The crowds mob this congested spot. Street entertainers quarrel with merchants, who quarrel with street vendors. (Over at the Bight, similar "schooner skirmishes" are increasing in season between spit-and-polish grand mogul vessels and the hippier ships. "Maybe pigtails down to your ass and girls with their tits hanging out are all well and good, but not everybody likes that and you won't see it on my vessel," *America*'s owner snarled, possibly to *Appledore*'s owner.) Performers muscle into other performers' territory, and some are not as charming as others in the way they solicit donations. Grease is spilled, curses are flung. There are, regrettably, often

bad vibes. The City Commission, wanting Sunset to be maintained, had to set up a committee to explore the possibility of an
alternative site for all the activities. Sunset had become something of a problem.

Now performers are chosen and positioned by a complex lot-
tery system, a $2.5 million face-lift (more bricks, more lights)
has been accomplished, and some of the bigger acts (those flying cats, that living statue) have been lured over to the Hilton,
where they actually get salaries. For the moment, at least, Sunset has been stabilized.

Key West Aquarium

YOUR FAVORITE SEAFOODS ALIVE! The oldest attraction in Key
West, it was once open to the sky, with individual coral tanks
for the fishes. An admission ticket is good for several days, so
you can wander in more than once if you're at terribly loose
ends. Kids come back often. It's one of the few things available
for them in Key West—the town is not exactly Toys "R" Us.
There are some very wiggy fishes in here. The big-eyed, flaccid
porcupine fish, for example, which has no fish enemy. If anything tries to swallow it, it just puffs up and the predator gags
to death. The Atlantic guitar fish, the sawfish, the peculiar reef
squid, all representing life as we certainly do not know it. The
butterfly fish, with splotches of color near the tail resembling
eyes, draws would-be attackers to the wrong end of itself. The
coral-crunching colorful parrotfish, with its big bright lips,
wedges itself between rocks and secretes a gelatinous cocoon of
mucus around its body when it goes to sleep at night. Fish, if
not exactly leading rich emotional lives, have developed some
very peculiar characteristics.

The old shallow coral pools are still used, along with glass-
wall tanks and a deep outside pen for turtles and tarpon. The
tarpon have been here for years but are small, not growing
because there's no room for them to grow. At one point there
was a good-sized permit, which some selfless angler had
donated, in the enclosure. Outside there's the usual array of
cats and pelicans.

There are half-hour tours four times a day, much of the talk

eliciting enthusiastic "yarggghs" and "yuks" from the kids.
There's a touch tank, and the feeding of lemon, blacktip, and
bonnethead sharks. You can pet a barracuda, and pick up a sea
cucumber and watch it squirt—the Conchs don't call them "sea
pissers" for nothing. You might be able to identify some of the
fish you've seen on the reef in here, but the multitude of wild
waterlife in the Keys is vast and enigmatic, and the number of
species in here represents only a small percentage of the variety out there. People often come in and try to explain what it
was they saw, not realizing how strange it actually was, or how
difficult to describe. Open 10 A.M. to 7 P.M. Adults $7. Kids
$3.50.

Truman Annex

Just off Mallory Square, behind the iron gates on Greene
Street, is **Truman Annex**. The Navy annexed the land piece by
piece for over a century and it was off-limits to the town for
almost 50 years; then it was deemed surplus property and 43
acres of it came up for sale.

The oldest building in the annex is the **U.S. Marine Hospital**, built in 1844. It was designed by Robert Mills, who was the
architect for the Washington Monument. The high, steep steps
which distinguish it seem ill-suited for a hospital entry, but the
building originally stood directly on the water and patients
were brought by boat to the rear.

In September 1986 the Navy conducted an auction of the land
and all its buildings. Many came ready to bid, including a group
of Eskimos, but it was purchased by a 36-year-old rich Sikh
from Maine named Pritam Singh for $17.25 million. Singh
seemed a democratic sort, although he frequently, unnervingly,
referred to his "covenant" with the people of Key West. He wore
a turban and had a sparse beard even though he hadn't shaved
it since he was 17. He razed a number of buildings that had
been running down for years with Key West panache but rehabilitated the ones most important from a military or historical
perspective. His plan was a mix of condos and residences, all
mixed in with amazing trees (two of the most fabulous banyans
in Key West live in the Annex), white-picket fences, walkways,

THE LITTLE WHITE HOUSE

Built in 1890 as the Naval Commandant's Quarters, this comfy structure is recognizable by its symmetrical double façade and its encircling porches enclosed by wooden louvers. President Harry Truman first came here in 1946 and returned ten times for vacations during his administration, arriving at the Boca Chica air station on the presidential plane *Sacred Cow*. Truman enjoyed walking around town, buying coffee with autographed dollar bills, eating coconut cake which was made especially for him by a Miss Etta Patterson, and playing a great deal of poker. His habits also included swimming (no one in the Little White House was allowed to flush during these ablutions) and coming downstairs to the kitchen every morning at 7 for a shot of bourbon followed by a glass of orange juice, a practice which, it was said, "always astonished" the Filipino housekeepers.

The tour, including a video, is half an hour and costs $5. The guide is earnest. Truman the Human played Chopin, he'll say. Truman the Human wrote Bess every day, every day without fail when he was away from her. He and Bess were poor, humble, simple folk, he'll say. Bess wasn't poor, a woman from Independence says. Yes she was, the guide says. No she wasn't, she was certainly not poor, she was very well off, the woman says. Oh well, the guide says. Another tourist, a boy in a JUST DO ME T-shirt, doesn't know whom to believe. He studies the poker table, a magnificent poker table. An alarm is supposed to go off if you sit in any of the chairs but it usually doesn't.

President Dwight Eisenhower came to Key West in 1955, three and a half years after Harry's last visit, but he wouldn't stay at the Little White House because he didn't want to sleep in Truman's bed. He felt very strongly about this. He slept in the surgeon's house in Quarter L instead.

Another structure that more peculiarly carries the old haberdasher's name is the **Harry S. Truman Import Center** on Fleming Key, off the Trumbo Point Annex of the Naval Air Station. This considerably creepy-looking structure is a quarantine center for animals imported into Florida. Its uneasy guests have included llamas, hogs, birds, and water buffalo.

and parks, everything architecturally correct and lavishly landscaped. He promised not a chicken in every pot but a hibiscus
bush in every yard.

Other plans included an 80-slip marina (flanked on one side
by the town's cruise-ship dock and on the other by the Navy's
port, recently expanded and deepened to accommodate war-
ships—pleasure and war having apparently been judged
compatible); the transformation of the Romanesque Revival
Customs House, the most imposing structure on Mallory
Square, into a yacht club; and the development of Tank Island,
the 27-acre spoil island created by the Navy to hold its fuel
tanks. Singh's plans were for a hotel to pop up here—a Ritz-
Carlton hotel, no less—all turreted white clapboardy gingerbread Victorian. Mullions and millions. His plans were for
aviaries and croquet courts and instant jungles too. He worried
that the "sleaze factor in Key West" would keep all this from
happening, but the sleaze factor just wasn't enough to leash the
dogs of progress.

Singh sold Tank as well as the land next to the Customs
House (which was just getting its new screaming watermelon-
pink roof) to Ocean Properties, which owns the Hilton chain.
Tank is 500 yards offshore and nine feet above sea level and
will have 110 houses on it, with the usual amenities: French
doors, French doors, French doors, volume ceilings, dormer sky-
lights, and spa tubs. Prices start at $700,000 and go up to $1.5
million. The owners of these houses will shuttle back and forth
to the mainland—Key West—via a 30-foot mahogany 1936
reproduction Chris-Craft yacht called the *Mae West*. "People
want the sense of getting away from the crowds," the developer
says. Only golf carts and bicycles will be allowed on Tank,
renamed Sunset Island, except for service vehicles like garbage
trucks which will arrive by scow from the Bight. Owners' cars
will be sheltered at the Hilton.

Meanwhile Singh, whom some Conchs referred to unkindly
as "Diaper Head," followed his heart and sought other properties to develop in Key West, most immediately the Key West
Golf Club on Stock Island, where "Conch vernacular" houses
are being thrown up rapidly. Singh no longer wears a turban,
and now has donned a mustache. He explains that he is striv-
ing, with his nineteenth-century folk village look, to "touch the

village image and village mythology within us." He says, modestly, "I try to be very enthusiastic with the seeds I choose to grow." He has theories on how the tallest tree in the forest gets to be the tallest tree in the forest. There are two ways apparently. Sometimes he gets mixed up and talks with a Grateful Dead sort of sentimentality, but he has settled into the fin de siècle nicely. He now likens his developments to Wal-Mart, extremely large scale operations who compete with smaller sellers by means of lower prices.

The Annex has now been built out. There are no open spaces.

The Treasure Salvors

The large raised stone building near the Greene Street gate to the Annex is an old Naval storage building, home of **Mel Fisher's Treasure Exhibit**. Fisher, once an Indiana chicken farmer, became a successful computer-age salvor whose most spectacular discoveries were the gold-and-silver laden Spanish galleons the *Nuestra Señora de Atocha* and the *Santa Margarita,* which sank in a hurricane in 1622.

The Spanish referred to all the Florida Keys as Matecumbe, and for some time Fisher and his Treasure Salvors searched the waters off Matecumbe for the *Atocha.* Wrecks which had previously been discovered were in an area between Key Largo and Long Key, and most had been salvaged by the Spanish themselves, who had mapped their locations. The correct sites of the *Atocha* and *Margarita* wrecks, 100 miles south of the area in which they had been searching, were discovered by a historian going through seventeenth-century Spanish documents in archives in Seville. The manifests of the ships indicated that they had been loaded with over 47 tons of gold and silver from the mines of Potosí, Lima, Mexico City, and Bogotá. The galleons had gone down within miles of each other, the *Atocha* on a shallow reef in 55 feet of water, the *Margarita* on a wide shoal, an area referred to as the Quicksands. Fisher discovered some of the wealth of the *Atocha* as early as the 1970s—gold and silver bars, gold chains up to eight and a half feet long, coins, crucifixes, and navigational devices, the most important being the ship's astrolabe, a precursor to the sextant.

As of early 1985, however, only a small portion of the *Atocha*'s treasure had been found. The wreck had scattered, most of its cargo lying beneath 20 feet of sand and shell. Most of what had been retrieved was contraband gold, smuggled on board and not listed on the manifest at all. Still to be found too was a suspected but unlisted 70 pounds of raw emeralds. Almost daily the Treasure Salvors were out searching for the "Big Pile" with their divers, ships, and planes, plotting and mapping, scanning inch by inch the ocean bottom with magnetometers, subbottom profilers, and side-scan sonar, and moving sand with their "mailboxes," a device of Fisher's which forces the wash from a boat's propeller down through an elbow-shaped tube aimed directly into the sand. These things could blow out craters in the ocean bed down to 20 feet.

On Memorial Day 1985, 13 gold bars, 16 emeralds mounted in gold, and piles of pieces of eight were discovered, but it was not until July 20, when divers found a telltale wall of ballast stones about five feet high and began bringing up hundreds of silver bars, that it was known that the "Big Pile," the mother lode, the largest shipwreck treasure in the world, had at last been found.

The yield—large, loaf-shaped silver bars (47 tons of silver alone have been recovered), gold bars, and chests of coins—is all being cleaned by an electrolytic reduction process and cataloged on the upper floors of the Treasure Exhibit with typical Key West insouciance by a large staff. More exciting even than the gold was the recent emerald bonanza; thousands have now been found. The divers put their first discoveries in a Mr. Peanut quart jar. As for the site itself, 40 miles southwest of Key West, it is protected from possible piracy by a great deal of potential

Pieces of eight (Spanish silver)

muscle. Mel Fisher says, "We have instant direct scrambled communications and on a moment's notice can have Navy dive-bombers and radar blimps, Coast Guard helicopters, marine patrol boats, and lots of other security on the spot."

All this is heady, even giddy, stuff, but the typical visitor to the Treasure Exhibit does not, in fact, see a great deal of the *Atocha* discovery. It is a huge building, and one might think one would be wandering around for hours viewing tons of artifacts, but the exhibit is small, all taking place in a single, curving, dark room. There is some gold and silver prettily displayed on sand and velvet, and some impressive globs of silver coins fused in the shape of the mahogany boxes they had been carried in. Each chest contained 2,500 coins. There is also a gleaming exhibit of silver bars. The most interesting items are a gold bar which one can heft by worming one's hand through a small hole, a solid gold "antiassassin" cup with handles in the shape of dolphins and space in the pedestal to hold a bezoar stone, which was meant to absorb and be an antidote to arsenic, and an eight-and-a-half-foot gold chain brought up by diver-photographer Don Kincaid. Kincaid was new on the job as Treasure Salvor when he discovered the heavy chain bright as the day it was in 1622 when the *Atocha* went down. He thought that the other divers had planted it there to tease him. Gold remains impervious to time and seawater, but silver will corrode—thin silver coins becoming big as biscuits from calciferous buildup. As part of the exhibit there is also a long-winded National Geographic film concerning the Treasure Salvors which plays all day with a wheezing soundtrack, and a gift shop where you can buy shipwreck coins and T-shirts with Mel Fisher's trademark cry TODAY'S THE DAY imprinted on them. Most of the treasure remains at the bottom of the ocean still, to protect the value of what has been brought up.

The "mailboxes" proved to cost Fisher and his company, Salvors Inc., dearly when they were used to efficiently blow away an acre of protected sea grasses in 1992. Five years later the Treasure Salvors were fined $600,000. They also had to turn over the silver forks and plates, and the cannonballs and anchors they found beneath the sea-grass bed.

Mel Fisher's Treasure Exhibit, 200 Greene Street. 10–6. Admission: $5. Children under seven, $1. Telephone: 294-2633.

The Audubon House

Across the street at 205 Whitehead is the **Audubon House**. Audubon was ubiquitous, seemingly sleeping in as many places as George Washington. But the fact is, Audubon did not sleep here, in the Geiger Home on Whitehead Street, nor did he even step inside the door. According to a sketch made by William Adee Whitehead in 1838, no two-story house existed on the site. Audubon spent only a brief time here in 1832 and probably spent most of his time on the vessel *Marion.* There were but 500 people living in Key West then, and only 81 buildings of any note. Captain John Geiger is not so much as mentioned by Audubon in his journals, even though he had been a pilot for Commodore Porter and was supposed to be such a wit that his sayings were referred to as "Geigerisms."

The Audubon House *was,* however, built by Captain John Geiger sometime in the 1830s and possibly moved to this site. Geiger was a wrecker who furnished his home with treasures salvaged from foundered ships. He introduced the Geiger tree (*Cordia sebestena*) to Key West from the West Indies. He must have been interested in this tree, since it possessed the same name as he did (no one knows who the *real* Geiger was). He planted it in his front yard, where the much-pruned specimen with its pretty orange blossoms is extravagantly noted today. The captain had many children, and his descendants lived in the house until 1956, the last one being a drunken hermit named Willy Smith.

Audubon's host and helpmate in Key West was one Benjamin Strobel, a doctor, newspaper editor, and amateur ornithologist. It was Strobel who procured the Geiger twig that Audubon used in his painting of the white-crowned pigeon. In his newspaper, Strobel enthusiastically wrote of Audubon:

> It is impossible to associate with him without catching some portion of his spirit; he is surrounded with an atmosphere which infects all who come within it, with a mania for bird killing and bird stuffing.

Audubon indeed had a mania. Though his name has become synonymous with wildlife preservation, he was in no way at

any time concerned with conservation. He killed tirelessly for
sport and amusement as well as for his art, and he considered it
to be a very poor day's hunting in Florida if he shot less than a
hundred birds. From St. Augustine he wrote:

> We have drawn seventeen different species since our arrival in
> Florida, but the species are now exhausted and therefore I will
> push off. . . .

Audubon shot thousands of birds and never in his mind made
the connection between the wholesale slaughter he so earnestly
engaged in and their decreasing number, although in his forties
he did begin complaining about the scarcity of mammals and
birds for his studies. "Where can I go now," he grumbled, "and
visit nature undisturbed?"

It is ironic that the Audubon House, which is worthy because
it began the preservation and restoration movement in Key
West, was a home Audubon never visited, and that the
Audubon Society has taken as their standard the name of a
man who had no interest in the survival of the birds he so
painstakingly drew. Certainly one of the archangels of the organization is a young warden, Guy Bradley. In 1901 the fledgling
Audubon Society pressured the Florida legislature into prohibiting the taking of plume birds. Killing the birds was an
extremely profitable undertaking because fashionable ladies
liked to affect whole birds on their bonnets. They'd pay anything for those pretty feathers, but Bradley was hired and dep-
utized to enforce the seemingly unenforceable law. In the
summer of 1905 he was killed near Flamingo in Florida Bay by
a plume hunter named Walter Smith, but a Key West grand
jury failed to indict Smith for the murder, rookery protection
laws not being greeted warmly by people in the Keys at that
time. The deputy's death, however, essentially brought about
the demise of the plume business. His tombstone is displayed at
the Everglades National Park station at Flamingo.

The two birds which are connected to Key West in *Birds of
America* are both pigeons, although the Key West pigeon, which
he named for the town, was actually a dove. The detailed background painting of Key West that is behind the great white
heron, Audubon's prize find on his trip to the Keys, was done

separately by George Lehman, a Swiss landscape painter who
accompanied Audubon on his southern trip aboard the *Marion.*
Three of the birds done on the trip were sketched in the Dry
Tortugas—the noddy tern, the sooty tern, and the brown booby.

In all, 1,065 birds appeared on 435 plates in Audubon's mas-
terwork, the Double-Elephant Folio (so called because of the
size of the paper, 40 inches by 30 inches, double the size of an
ordinary folio sheet) of *Birds of America.* The engraving, print-
ing, and coloring of the plates took 11 years and was done in
England by Robert Havell and his son. Around 175 complete
sets were published, and the Audubon House had one on display for a while but someone stole it. It was later recovered but
is now being exhibited at an ostensibly more secure location in
Miami.

What you do see in the Audubon House are delicate ceramic
pieces of warblers, flycatchers, and wrens by the English artist
Dorothy Dowdy, who was commissioned by Royal Wooster in
London after World War II to produce collection sets to be sold
to help relieve England's war debts; a dozen framed bird prints;
and antiques "typical of the period." You're given a cassette
player and headphones and can listen to a taped tour. Local
actors had a lot of fun pretending they were the Geiger family.
It really is a somewhat bizarre recording. The sonorous voice
that introduces them all is that of John Malcolm Brinnin. A
film describing the Double-Elephant Folio is shown on a small
screen in one room. A small, very pale, and very dusty stuffed
roseate spoonbill perches disconsolately on a desk just inside
the door of another room. Its presence here is carefully
explained. It was not tracked down and shot by a bird fancier
but "found in Key Largo, tangled in wires and choked to death."
There is also a photograph of Audubon's shovel-jawed wife
Lucy, who once wrote, "I have a rival in every bird." Audubon
House and Gardens, corner Whitehead and Greene. Daily
9:30–5. Adults $7.50. The gardens are lovely.

Caroline Street

Caroline begins in official pomp at the wrought-iron presidential
gates on Whitehead Street, moves regally past shaded, stately

homes for several blocks, turns abruptly into homely marine practicality, and dead-ends at the City Electric stacks. Its variability is pure Key West, for here is a history of mansions and rough bars, turtle slaughterhouses and pretty little lanes.

Just opposite the gates is the old Airways Building, the former home of Aero-Marine Airways, which flew passengers and mail to Cuba in the early 1920s. Each flight would carry a passenger pigeon, to be released in case of trouble over the open water. As part of the operation, the trained birds were kept in cotes in the Pigeon House. Aero-Marine went out of business in 1924, to be replaced by Pan Am, the first international airline recognized by the Post Office. It made its first flight from Key West in 1928.

The restaurant in this great old building is called **Kelly's**. It's pleasant to sit outside here on the spacious patio, though the food can be as memorable as an airline meal. Next door is the rickey-green **Heritage House Museum**. Robert Frost apparently visited at the cottage more than a dozen times. You shouldn't say, "Who cares?" It is said that he enjoyed it here (though not at first) but didn't talk about it much. The stately house was built by a British barroom owner in the 1850s. He boasted that his ancestors could write evenly on paper without lines, but only when drunk. The house as a museum is interesting because it is Conch shambly with lots of odd collectibles, "treasures," and antiques from seven generations of a Key West family. In one of the tiny rooms, displayed on the bed as though he were going to totter into it at any moment, is the tiny suit of lights worn by the "Brooklyn Bullfighter," Sydney Franklin. It was a gift to Jessie Porter, the house's late gregarious owner, from Pauline Hemingway. How Mrs. Hemingway acquired the whole suit rather than the more traditional hat, or ear, is a mystery. Look at it and ponder the fleetingness of glory. The house and engagingly overgrown garden is open from 10 to 5, and you can tour it for $5.

The second block of Caroline is perhaps the prettiest in town, with eight splendid wooden houses and one, at 529, made of brick, complete with tin roof and turret, built by a Turkish sponger in 1906. The **Milton Curry Mansion** at 511 is a miniaturized version of a Newport cottage, with all the expected excessive embellishments. Milton built this home in

The Patterson House

1905 as a wedding present to himself and his new bride. He was
the son of William Curry, who had come to Key West from the
Bahamas as a child in 1837. It is said that the elder Curry's
"capacity for making safe and lucrative investments amounted
to genius." He became owner of the largest ship's chandlery in
town, and when he died in 1896 he was considered the wealthi-
est man in Florida. More than 70 carriages accompanied his
body to the graveyard, although the solid gold dinner service he
had purchased from Tiffany and Company in New York over
the years stayed at home. The mansion is now open to the public from 9 to 5. Adults $5. Behind it is a recently built, wickered-
up inn (see page 236).

At 522 is the most graceful example of Queen Anne architecture in Key West, the **George Patterson House**. It was built
immediately after the annihilating fire of 1886, as were many
of the grandest homes in town, including the **Richard Kemp
House** at 601. This beautiful home has an elegant simplicity of
style and proportion and represents the "Conch" style at its
very best, employing shipbuilding techniques as well as Classic
Revival and island architectural design. The house was built by
John Sawyer (who also built the twin-towered Armory on White
Street) for the Kemp family, who had become wealthy in the

sponging business after William Kemp introduced Key West sponges to the New York market. Great care and detail was given by the builder to the outside appearance of the house. Inside, old odd lumber was frequently used, for wood was dear in Key West and little of it was wasted. Many of the beams had been salvaged from other structures and show old square holes, caused by a previous use of pegs rather than nails. Today the Kemp House, which is built of pine, is called the **Cypress House** and is a guest house (see page 240).

The following block of Caroline offers a lovely array of Classic Revival homes before the street opens up into the more utilitar-

---

TURTLES

The life of the green turtle in the vast oceans is mysterious, but not mysterious enough to insure its survival. Its behavior on land is better known and has steadily doomed it. The turtle's fate is to come ashore to lay her eggs—a hundred of them at a time, several times a year—in a deep sand nest which she covers up with her flippers before returning to the sea. She always nests on the same beach, and her female hatchlings, those that survive, will come back to the beach where they were born when it is their time to lay eggs. Male turtles never return to land.

Nests are dug up by raccoons, dogs, and men. But if they are not discovered by the second day, the eggs are usually safe for the following 60 days; then the nests erupt and little turtles emerge en masse and make their rush to the sea, a dash which is often cut short by hordes of feeding birds. Hatchlings instinctively head for the brightest spot they see, and for millions of years this was the reflection of moon and stars on the water. Now, however, street and house lights often attract them to death on highways and lawns. If the water is reached, the first wave releases in the baby turtle its sea knowledge—it is the water that teaches the turtle how to swim—and it is then only a matter of luck how many survive the onslaught of predatory fish.

The green turtle is considered to be the world's most valuable reptile, and it is a form of life that has almost been extinguished. The United States banned the import of all sea turtle products—meat and shell and calipee—in 1979. The calipee is the gelatinous cartilage cut from the bones of the bottom shell and is used to flavor soup. Huge nesting turtles are often killed on the coasts of the Caymans, the Caribbean Islands, and Costa Rica for the sake of a few ounces of calipee alone—the rest of the turtle left for buzzards.

Protection of the hunted and harassed and exploited sea turtles has probably come too late. In remote areas they are still killed regularly and all the eggs in a nest taken. In built-up areas tenderhearted condo dwellers guard the nests of turtles who stubbornly return to beaches now bright with the lights of development. They protect the eggs, even taking them back to their balconies where they try to hatch them in cardboard boxes. If the turtles hatch, they feed them raw hamburger for a while before releasing them into the sea. It isn't known whether this sort of assistance raises or lowers the incredible odds against their survival. The fact is no one knows where young turtles go. They are seen only after some years have passed and they are old enough to mate, the female then making her perilous journey ashore.

A Key West newspaper of the 1890s, *The Daily Equator Democrat,* wrote:

> Thousands of these monster turtles weighing from 100 to 1200 pounds are taken in these waters. They are shipped to the larger cities in the U.S. and command a high price. The turtle business is growing rapidly on the coast and seems to be, like the fish business, inexhaustible.

ian, humble, and often raucous structures that, past and present, have served the fishing and shrimping docks. Look into the marine hardware store at 818—a great supply store with everything for the boater. Across the street is **Land's End Village**, all part of the Bight. The *Yankee Freedom* (see page 265) departs from here for a full-day trip to Fort Jefferson. **Seasports Dive Center** goes out to the reef twice a day. Here too is the popular **Half-Shell Raw Bar** and the old **Turtle Kraals**, a former butcher shop and cannery, now a restaurant of scant excellence where you can "drink your way around the world" with a staggering selection of imported beers. The Kraals once maintained a clouded pen where a few green turtles, those fabulous travelers, drifted aimlessly, but it no longer has the permits to keep this species. Down a short pier is the old slaughterhouse, now a "museum" devoted to the artifacts of what is often referred to as the "colorful" industry of turtling, although the only color which comes to mind is red. Here are axes, grinders, photographs, and a painting of an old turtle schooner, the *A. Maitland Adams.*

Green turtles, a species virtually extinct, were hauled back to Key West from the coast of Nicaragua until the late 1960s, when tourists would still gather eagerly at the docks with their cameras to see them being butchered. The butcher would sometimes have a bit of fun with his "neat trick" of slitting the turtle's throat so that the blood would spring 20 feet toward the insatiable observers' eyes.

The **Key West Bight** was home to the shrimp fleet in the 1970s. There were hundreds of boats, so many that you could

A shrimp boat

SHRIMPING

Nocturnal shrimp were discovered off Key West in the 1970s, and for a while it looked as if the good times would never end. More than 400 boats worked the waters from November through July, dragging 65-foot-long cone-shaped nets behind them. It was a boom, it was wild. Pink gold. Now shrimping is, as they say, in decline, the catch down 60 percent in the last decade. The Bight harbors no working boats; the much-diminished fleet is on Stock Island. The business has become very competitive, and the not-so-plentiful shrimp now costs $10 a pound.

In 1980, during the Mariel boat lift, initially called the Freedom Flotilla, then Operation Alien Assist, ultimately A Disaster, shrimpers abandoned their nets and went to Cuba to bring back refugees, sometimes at $2,000 a head. "Hauling Cubans paid a lot better than shrimping," one captain said. Boats left Garrison Bight by the hundreds and returned with thousands of people, depositing them on the pier at Truman Annex from which they were sent by bus to an old railroad shed converted into a hangar on Trumbo Point, from which they were airlifted to Homestead and Miami. President Jimmy Carter, after first declaring "an open arms, open heart policy," changed his mind when it appeared that a considerable number of emigrés were deranged, or were thieves and murderers, the latter being marked by tattoos on the inside of their lips. When he declared a halt to the flotilla, Key West fishermen ignored him, preferring to continue their lucrative missions of mercy. Forced by the Cuban authorities at Mariel Harbor to take on increasingly unsavory individuals, the shrimpers returned home and had their boats seized by the U.S. government. Boats rather than people started piling up at Truman Annex. At one point 80 percent of the commercial fishing boats of Key West were red-tagged and impounded on the docks. The seizure was later declared unconstitutional, 100,000 Cubans were absorbed into the city of Miami, and Key West's shrimp boats returned to their former occupation. There hasn't been one of those sentimental Blessing of the Fleet ceremonies in town for a long long while. At the last one only several local boats showed up. The rest were out shrimping.

walk the Bight's length—all the way from Elizabeth to Grinnel—across their decks. A statue of Henry "Shrimp King" Singleton, who invented the flash-freezing of shrimp, thereby
bringing it to the menus of thousands of mediocre Midwest
restaurants, has been erected here, though Singleton never
lived in Key West. Singleton's estate sold the Bight to the city
in 1992 after a public referendum was passed for its "preservation," even though the public is seeing it being paved over and
knickknacked up like everyplace else. Singleton's wife, who
never lived in Key West either, said, "Who would have dreamt
that a smelly shrimp-boat docking area called the Bight would
exemplify Key West and all its splendid charm?" The old Singleton ice plant down here may have a new life as a conch farm.

A WALK UP DUVAL STREET

One mile long and certainly no *zona rosa*, Duval stretches from
the glass-bottom boat *Fireball* docked on the Gulf to a little
beach beside the Southernmost House on the Atlantic. Perhaps
the most interesting strip in Florida, Duval has it all—emeralds and chicken wings, dance clubs and missing elks, fake
butterflies and party baskets, lewd underwear, failed foun-
tains, and uninspired psychics. It's got chic shops and forbid-
ding hotels, twinkling galleries, bars, and scrub clubs. In
dawn's sweet light, it's lined with beer trucks making fresh
deliveries. It hums at night and in the sun. In the rain it
appears less than electrifying. Old-timers feel they've lost the
real Duval, which was darker, danker, noisier, had even more
bars and certainly fewer postcards. The Duval Crawl is a must.
It's done in a car at any time, slowly, very slowly. Be cool now.

The street was named before Florida even became a state, for
William Pope duVal, the first governor of the territory. It was a
dirt road until the 1920s when it was paved with brick. People
bought milk from vendors who milked their cows and goats at
the door. Much of Duval burned down, was rebuilt, and burned
down again. In the 1950s it was wild, in the 1960s dirty, in the
centennial year of 1976, after rejecting a plan which would turn
it into a canal with Venetian gondolas poling people around to

the shops, it was not exactly rehabilitated—and certainly not restored—but made more reputable. False fronts appeared. Brick planters. Balloons and cookie and croissant shops were invited in—particularly in the 600 and 700 blocks. Beyond this, well into the '80s, was terra incognita to the tourist. It was a mixture of cans, cats, old convertibles, a few Cuban groceries, and many empty lots, as derelict buildings burned down with regularity. Other than La-Te-Da and the marvelous old-time Valladares newsstand, which carries more magazines than could possibly be published each year, it seemed the Big Empty.

But now retail has moved in and there are malls and squares and shops, shops, shops. Cigar makers' cottages now sell lingerie, soft pretzels, and kayak trips, and the dour Holmes Auto Body building is an art gallery. Upper Duval is gaining the distinction of being the "upscale" part of town. Usually, those disembarking from the cruise ships don't stray this far, content with a burger at the ubiquitous **Hard Rock Cafe** on lower Duval. (Oh look, there's a Hard Rock Cafe. Thank goodness. . . .) (See also Where to Eat, pages 241–52, Art and Antiques, pages 189–91, and Bars, pages 252–56.)

The 200 block is the bar block. Always carnival time here: **Durty Harry's**, **Rick's Cafe**, **Bull and Whistle**—they all rock and roll. The Whistle and Rick's have skinny upstairs porches and do well for hollering and howling. **Sloppy Joe's** hammers down the corner at Greene. "I'm going over to Sloppy's" you hear from the most elderly and exhausted tourist as well as the most energetic short-shorted youth. Everyone makes the pilgrimage to Sloppy's, "Hemingway's favorite bar." Parachutes billow from the ceiling. Pictures of the writer beam or brood from every cranny. The waitresses clang a cowbell every time the Conch Train goes by (as does the funkier **Green Parrot**). **Rumrunners** has innumerable bars squirreled away in a shambly building. There's a psychic next door for those who are aware they're lost.

On the corner of Caroline, opposite the Bull and Whistle, is the **Fogarty House**, built by yet another son of William Curry, Key West's first millionaire. The walrus-mustached President William Taft was once entertained here, as was Henry Flagler during the festivities accompanying the arrival of the first train into town. The Fogarty House has been reclining in its decline for years, ever since a group of French sailors on shore leave used the fountain as a pissoir. The restaurant here need not be investigated.

In the 300 block the **Joseph Porter House** on the corner of Caroline reflects the best of Conch formidable design—taking the architectural flavor of the Bahamas as well as New England and New Orleans. It is now apartments, and houses two small specialty shops which are worthy of approach if only for the opportunity of being able to linger for a moment on the wide cool veranda. Up and across the street and down a little alley is the **Red Barn Theatre**. Tiny (85 seats) and terrific, with skilled professional performances. Energetic cast, great sets, delightful variety. Call 296-9911 for information on their seasonal offerings. Tickets are around $15. The melancholy **Southern Cross Hotel** is at 326 Duval. Built in the 1920s, it has been held together for years by its intense mustiness. Some adventurers enter the lobby to buy a cigar. More adventurers than you might think, actually. The new owner plans renovations. A funeral home operator from Wisconsin, he said of his new acquisition, "That lobby turns a pretty coin." Next to the Southern Cross is the Oldest House.

The Oldest House

As mentioned, this may not be the oldest house, but it is the one researched, restored, and made accessible, and it is old enough, certainly, having been built only a few short years after John Simonton bought Key West in 1822 and found "no living person" about. The house was built by Richard Cussons, a grocer, and probably moved here from Whitehead Street. It sits on unusually tall, three-foot piers to protect it from the storm tides which used to flow unimpeded up Duval, and it has low ceilings and shuttered windows. The early scuttles on the roof were later replaced by dormers, and these are the house's most peculiar characteristic, for they are wildly dissimilar in size, the sort of dormers fairy-tale bears might fancy.

The house is pleasantly askew and homely. Another house was added to the original structure early on, probably around the time Francis Watlington bought it in the 1840s. Watlington was a wrecker who raised seven daughters here. During the Civil War, when he was in his sixties, he went off to fight for the Confederacy, but he returned to Key West and is one of the few early settlers buried in the graveyard.

The house is now a museum and is open every day from 10 to 4. The "Rules of Wrecking" are on display, and upstairs there is a dollhouse furnished as eclectically as the house itself. On the grounds there is a cookhouse, the only outside kitchen remaining in Key West, and a surprisingly large yard.

Anchoring the corner of the 400 block is **St. Paul's Church**, with its towers from which hurricane-cracked bells peal daily. There are ten bells at St. Paul's, the largest weighing 1,800 pounds, and chime recitals are played for 15 minutes at both noon and 5 P.M. Each Christmas a wonderful choral program is presented where everyone from the Fabulous Spectrelles in their beehives to gospel choirs perform in one of Key West's marvelously nontraditional traditions. The **La Concha** (see page 235) has held down the other side of the street since 1924. Redone as a Holiday Inn, it's now well run and quite elegant, pretty and tropical de rigueur pink. At the top there is **The Top**, with its three-sided view of the town. (From here a local lawyer, Counselor B., known posthumously thereafter as No Bungee B., jumped, having waited until the place was totally renovated. In 1995 someone else jumped, after ordering a glass of white wine. "He seemed normal when he ordered the wine," the bartender said.) A new restaurant on the street called **Celebrities** is very black-and-white-and-mirrored handsome. Salads, sandwiches, pizza, and a fresh raw bar in smooth surroundings. The food makes robust literary references, though the Short Story has been reduced to a couple of scoops of ice cream.

Here, Fleming is the cross street of the 500 block, up which is renowned **Fausto's Food Palace** and the nice pink library. Commanding the corner is sleek, slick **Fast Buck Freddie's**, where in the shimmering, heady recesses people are heard to cry out, "I have to buy something from here!" Fast Buck's has great clothes, toys, jewelry, kitchen equipment, and flashy souvenirs. Nobody misses Fast Buck's. See if they still have the battery-run, super-realistic writhing rat in a trap that was the

Fausto's Food Palace

sensation of a Christmas past. "People *love* them," a salesman said. "Those things just *fly* out of here."

The San Carlos (516 Duval)

The original San Carlos was built in 1884 and named for Carlos Manuel de Cespedes, the father of Cuban independence, a plantation owner who in 1868 cried *Cuba libre!* from the balcony of his estate. He wasn't talking rum and Coke; the cry sparked the Ten Years' War against Spanish rule, a war which the patriots ultimately lost. (Cespedes's son, Carlos, became the mayor of Key West in 1876.) Cubans who fled to Key West founded this political and social club, financing it with the abundant profits of cigar-making.

The fire of 1886, which destroyed most of the town, originated in the San Carlos, which was then located on Fleming Street. It was rebuilt three years later on Duval and became as well a political club (José Martí, the architect of Cuban independence, often spoke here), a school, a cultural center, and an opera house. Anna Pavlova and the Russian Ballet danced here in 1915. In 1919 it was virtually destroyed by a hurricane, and in 1924 it was rebuilt with money donated by the president of Cuba.

Designed in the Cuban-baroque vernacular of that time—
spacious rooms, high ceilings, graceful arches, marble stairways, handcrafted mosaics, and floors of checkered Cuban
tile—it was considered the "jewel" of Key West. But Cuba
ceased funding the San Carlos after diplomatic relations with
the United States were severed in 1961. The school closed in
1973, and by the '80s the building had been invaded by
vagrants and was at the point of collapse. A portion of the
façade fell off at one point, braining a German tourist. Shortly
afterward, $10,000 was spent on restoring the façade, most of
the money being used for an injection process which literally
glued the building back together.

There was much dispute at the time whether the San Carlos
was owned by the Republic of Cuba or belonged to a Miami-
based board of directors. In 1994 a Miami man, Armando Ale-
jendre, clearly in favor of the board of directors idea, drove
down and began smashing the institute's big glass doors. Sixteen months later he was one of four men killed by Cuban MiGs
when an organization called Brothers to the Rescue flew into
Cuban airspace to pamphleteer. The incident resulted in this
country's controversial Helms-Burton Act, a restrictive
embargo that threatens to punish other countries for trading
with Cuba. Today the restored San Carlos is proudly open, providing today's *veladas*. It has suffered no recent vagrant or militant attacks.

Stop by and see the historical displays, the wonderful prints
of Cuban birds, the theater with its intriguing backdrop painting of the tree on the farm of de Cespedes. Concerts, recitals,
and other events are presented at the San Carlos frequently.
They are always preceded by a scratchy tape recording of the
American national anthem followed by the Cuban national
anthem. This provides the listener with a global moment. The
San Carlos is open every day but Monday.

The Strand (527 Duval)

A movie house built in the 1930s, its "boomtown" front is elaborately decorated with lions, Roman legionnaires, and bowls of
fruit. After a fire destroyed the roof, the building was used for a
while as a boxing ring beneath the stars. The sherbet-colored

circusy façade was painstakingly restored recently, and inside, for a time, the interior became a state-of-the-art video, dance, and music complex with ever-changing shows—rock, reggae, blues, mud wrestling, male strippers for the ladies, etc. Food was also served here—most particularly sandwiches named for local politicians. For example, there was the "Bum Farto," in honor of a former Key West fire chief. All this was just too good to last, of course. The money ran out, and the Strand shut down. It has now come back as a **Ripley's Believe It or Not Odditorium**. It's too politically correct in all regards to be truly odd or thrillingly creepy, and somebody keeps stealing the shrunken heads, but going there does seem like a madcap thing to do after dinner or on a rainy day. Pricey at $9.95 for adults, $6.95 for children. Open daily 10 A.M. to 11 P.M. (293-9686).

The 600 block is the area snatched from the skids in 1976. Merchants and politicians had the year 1910 in mind here, but they wanted the block to appear as it "should" have appeared, not the way it actually did appear. The result was this street of appearances, sticky with fudge and ice-cream nooks, only a pawnshop clinging to the brassy taste of yesterday. A co-op art gallery is here, near to where the old Picture Show *used* to be. The theater sold beer right along with the popcorn and showed a variety of old, flaky, and message flicks as well as the very funny homage to Key West, *The Key West Picture Show*. You can catch it now only on video.

The Copa (Epoch)

In July of 1995 the Copa, along with the chic restaurant Antonia's, burned to the ground in the traditional suspicious, middle-of-the-night fire. Built in 1917 as a movie theater, it had been wearily showing *Deep Throat* for a decade before it was transformed in the '80s into a glossy gay cruise bar. There were flickering lights and heavy-duty dancing, with bars below and male erotic videos above. There were Wet Jockey Short nights and Doris Day nights. The Copa was crazy and wild and kept up nicely with the times before it was torched, introducing such European notions as descending bubbles of slippery foam that enveloped the dancers after midnight in an unspeakable mélange.

The fire was so hot it blistered the paint on the fire trucks, and the *Miami Herald* utterly lost its composure with the headline: TEN YEARS OF DEBAUCHERY GOES UP IN FLAMES. The Copa has now risen again as **Epoch**, and the wet jockey shorts contests are back, along with Take Off Tuesday (take off your shirt and drink half-price all night) and Drag Night (everyone in drag drinks free, but it has to be *full* drag). Epoch has a fabulous road-warrior decor complete with guttering candles in studly chandeliers. (Surely, with what happened to the Copa, they can't be *real* guttering candles.) The controversy about Epoch is its clientele. Has it become too straight? This is a sticky problem. Straights have apparently discovered the best dance club around. The management plans a phase-two environment—a garden area in back of the building set aside for intimate conversation, *gay* intimate conversation. Cutely cruel bartenders here. Great lighting and sound. 623 Duval. 296-8521.

The 700 block once had the distinction of having the dustiest and most forlorn collection of seashells in town at the Key West Conch Shell, but someone discovered Windex, then found they didn't want to sell seashells at all. There's something for everyone on this street, even a car at **Pandemonium**, tiled like a Cuban patio, that enjoys being photographed and hasn't, at least of yet, asked for donations. The shops and restaurants of upper Duval have all been wrested from what was once a Cuban enclave, but the gentrifiers met resistance in **Bahama Village**, the area that Hemingway, in his way with words, called "Jungle Town." Change is now imminent, however, particularly with the excessing (and soon-to-be availability) of Navy property adjacent to Fort Taylor known as the Seminole Battery.

Back on Duval, just up from Truman, you will find yourself at the newly concocted **Duval Square**, with its fashionable gym, its fashionable hair salon, and its fashionable restaurant, **Square One**. Beyond is the irresponsibly delicious ice cream at **Flamingo Crossing** (do the fresh coconut) and the kayak outfitters of **Mosquito Coast**. They have two dockages, one on Geiger Key and one farther up on Sugarloaf. You're taken there by van and have about four hours of water time among the mangroves. Cost is $45. Call 294-7178.

BAHAMA VILLAGE

Bahama Village is in the southwest corner of the island, bordered by Angela, Duval, and Louisa streets. On most tourist maps Bahama Village does not exist, the town seemingly ending at Whitehead, but it is very much a distinct, special part of Key West, with simple houses and broom-swept dirt yards, crowing roosters, tiny groceries, and many churches. People dress up and go to church in this neighborhood. There're also some less than innovative public housing, an industry that involves kids (the "chicken boys") catching roosters with nets to sell for $20 to high rollers from Miami who in turn sell them to cockfighting rings for $200, and a New Year's Eve tradition of firing off guns.

In the 1980s a colorful wrought-iron archway was erected at the intersection of Duval and Petronia and adorned with a flamingo, a marlin, a demi-sun, and conch shells. FORWARD, the swirling iron spelled out—FORWARD TOGETHER UPWARD ONWARD. But through the splendid passageway moved— nothing. In fact, the adornments were periodically found missing from the gateway, and now the arch itself has vanished.

When it was suggested in the '90s that Petronia Street be renamed Martin Luther King Street, some black Bahama Village nascent developers protested, saying that the new businesses here would suffer. Apparently many travel agents tell their customers, particularly European ones, to avoid areas with streets named King.

Blue Heaven, a restaurant and seeming time and space warp at the corner of Thomas and Petronia, introduced many people to the specialness of Bahama Village, and although not patronized by exactly the real neighborhood, it has thrived here. Chickens, dogs, a friendly, easygoing air, and wonderful food have made it very popular, particularly on Sunday. For some reason *The Tempest* was once performed here. The entire play! Sensational. Aristophanes' ancient Greek comedy *The Frogs* is going to be next. Across the street is cool blue **Johnson's Grocery**. Coldest beer and freshest snack cakes in town. The Johnsons have recently opened a café that serves breakfast and lunch out of a tiny window. Homemade soups and hearty down-home lunch specials. Friday and Saturday there's conch, brilliantly prepared conch. **Johnson's Cafe** is all closed up on Sundays, as is the tiny **Conch Shop** next door, which has been operating in the neighborhood for 40 years. Fabulous fritters. They're open nights Thursday through Saturday, but call to be certain: 294-4140. **Island Breeze Cafe** down at 1003 Emma is casual island yard, with vocals coming from the radio. Very Bahamian, actually.

More and more people are sallying forth on their bicycles through these streets, and you can almost hear them saying, Why, this is delightful, it's so ungentrified, so real. Look at those gentlemen playing cards, and look at those baby chicks—why, she's got 12 of them. . . . Look at that shoe repair shop . . .

On the weekends many of the churches sell fantastically tasty barbecue. With the flocks of wild parrots flying overhead, the obscure weed-covered Cold War battlements behind the Navy's fence, the metallic twinkling of the church's spires, you feel you've discovered something. Something that blissfully for now, but probably not forever, the Conch Train has not.

The **Community Swimming Pool** at the intersection of Catherine and Thomas is a terrific place for doing Olympic-length laps. The pool is clean and alfresco and has a great view of the ocean.

Kayak trips are fun but can sometimes make even the inner child within you feel a little childish. Long longueurs followed by frantic paddling. Intense examination of worms, slugs, and odd life forms with hundreds of tiny tube feet. For lunch there's water and a dense nut bar from The Nut House on Big Coppit. Then the van ride back to Key West where the adult within you can have a glass of wine at **The Grand Vin**, a tony little wine bar/shop that shares the building with Mosquito Coast. Marvelous wines, and a genial manager. Test a "flight," which is a sampling of three different wines grouped roughly by their type (296-1020).

More peculiar land tours are springing up in Key West's rocky soil. "Catch Donald," someone will say. "He's very sweet, knows a lot, and probably will split when his probation is up."

You don't really need all that much help here with guides—Key West is not, after all, Morocco—but it's interesting to be instructed by someone other than the Conch Train. Lloyd, for example, hosts a bike tour. He takes you through the quieter parts of town. He chats with Conchs on their porches and invites you to eat peculiar flora as though you were lost in the desert. Sometimes you can meet a fellow whose skill is pulling his bottom lip over his nose. It's 90 minutes of relaxing fun, but Lloyd (294-1882) might not be offering this service forever.

The automobile graveyard that used to nestle against La-Te-Da is gone, as are the beyond-seedy Casa Blanca Apartments (now the William House, a guest house that warrants no interest, one of those places that believe some muslin hanging around a bed and a Jacuzzi raised on a bald wooden deck connote romance). New visions are the Miami-style furniture at **Fletcher** (lots of fossil accessories).

Duval is a street one should see through from start to finish. At night it's a carnival, but a street that runs straight to the sea is a fine street, and **South Beach**, the little beach that fits so easily on a postcard, is the seaweedy termination to Duval. The pink-and-green Queen Anne mansion beside it at 1400 is the J. Viking Harris House, built before the turn of the century by a

Key West transportation

judge. For a time it was a nightclub, Casa Cayo Hueso, then was a private home. The plan now is to turn it into a bed-and-breakfast with a small private club within. "Our goal for the club would not be street traffic," the owner, Charlie Ramos, says. "It would be a very private place." This is the **Southernmost House**.

The Southernmost Point

This is not at the end of Duval at all but over on Whitehead, at its intersection with South Street. You would logically think the low pink house, lushly compounded and sticking out into the Atlantic beside it, would be the Southernmost House, instead of the turreted, tottering creation on Duval. And it is! But it's not really because it's not the *original* Southernmost House. The same kind of spirited controversy that swirls around the problem of the great white and the great blue heron (Is the white just a color phase of the blue? Or is the white a distinct species? If the white *is* just a color phase of the blue, why do they hate one another so much, unlike other herons which get along quite amicably?) muddies the waters around the *real* Southernmost House.

However, we do have, without question, the Southernmost Point in the continental United States, which allows us to exclude Hawaii. This point is marked with a black, red, and yel-

The southernmost point in the continental United States

low object of many tons constructed to resemble a nun buoy.
The Director of Monuments in Key West, Billy Pinder, designed
it. People kept stealing the sign that said SOUTHERNMOST POINT
IN THE USA, so the town decided to install something that sou-
venir-mad tourists couldn't carry off. It is painted in ribbons of
bright colors so that it will show up well in photographs. Billy
Pinder invited President Reagan to the dedication ceremonies
for the buoy in 1983, suggesting that if the president came, the
town would rename South Street President Ronald Reagan
Street. The president did not grace the proceedings, however,
and South Street remains South Street. The lady who lives in
the house diagonally across from this peculiar and very permanent object that marks the Southernmost Point was so upset by
its shape, color, and enormity that she hung her American flag
upside down during the ceremony.

Tables are set up here each morning laden with shells. There
are, too, lamps made of shells—complete with plastic flamingo
and palm tree, ready to brighten your life with a tiny red
Christmas tree light—and an assortment of dried and pickled
things from the deep. "Honey! Look at this little shark or something in the formaldehyde!" Sponges and shell necklaces hang
from the chain-link fence separating the street from Navy property. (Many people bike or Rollerblade back here as it is now
open to the civilian populace via the gates on United. Nice '50s
feel here.) The conch shells are very rosy, very pretty, but it's
supposed to be bad luck to put them in your home, or so the
Conchs say. It would be the only revenge the conch could have,
in any case. On stormy days, waves crash against the seawall
and surge into the street, soaking the Conch Trains as they
make their turns past. Harley guys love to take their hogs and
their chicks down here and have their pictures taken. Sometimes the rumble of their machines is so loud that it sets off all
the car alarms in the neighborhood.

BEACHES AND SALT PONDS

Key West's beaches are not her crowning glory. They are mostly
man-made, marly, bumpy, and covered with seaweed, and the

waters offshore are shallow. The longest, skinniest beach on the island is **Smathers**, which begins just west of the airport on A1A (South Roosevelt Boulevard). Fresh sand is constantly trucked onto it from elsewhere. It's lined with cars, taco trucks, and raft and Windsurfer rentals, and parasailors (no age limit, no dress code, and no skill required!) take off from a float on the southern end. All this considerable activity is bleakly gazed down upon by the nervous inhabitants of condominiums.

On the other side of the beach and the highway are the remnants of salt ponds which were once scattered over 340 acres. Evaporation of seawater to make salt, an important preservative before the advent of ice, was an intermittent business here until 1868. Airport construction and condo development have reduced the ponds and the flow of water, but there are still a number of feeding birds to be found back here, particularly early in the morning. The ponds themselves contain extensive grass beds and are filled with blue crabs, shrimp, minnows, and killifish, all being lunched upon by herons, egrets, and migratory ducks. A portion of the land is the **Riggs Wildlife Refuge**, and behind a green gate is a small observation deck.

The salt ponds link up with **Little Hamaca Park**, accessible off Flagler. This is a very weird area peopled by an assortment of unsavory individuals—druggies and gay cruisers for the most part. People get a kick out of dumping stuff here, too— sofas, sinks, batteries, broken toys. (There was the box for a Barbie's Housekeeping set out there once, although the set itself wasn't. Some lucky little girl had it elsewhere probably.) The airport is breaking up some of the dirt roadways that isolate the ponds to enhance tidal flow, but it's going to be some time before this becomes a beauty spot.

Just beyond Smathers on Atlantic Boulevard is an area now rudely jammed with condos but once known as Rest or Picnic Trees Beach. Despite its placid names, it has long been a troubled and disturbed area. Early on it was a dump, then the butchering pens for cattle were located here (livestock was also kept in the abandoned West Martello Tower). The pens were torn down in the cleanup of the 1930s and for years it was a spot not for sunbathing but for digging. People would hunt for old bottles here, the aficionados of that art wielding shovels and picks. Intersecting with Atlantic is White Street, which terminates in the **White Street Pier**, now renovated, to the thrill of Key West citizens. For years people would drive to the end of it, try to catch something with a chicken gizzard on the end of a line, take a few gulps of the salubrious sea air, and then drive away again. Because it was constructed as a road, however, with no place for the water to go but around it, the air became less salubrious with the passing of time. It's been redesigned and is now closed to cars. The second largest beach in town is **Higgs Memorial** right alongside. There are picnic tables, showers, and a pavilion, and the public buildings sport freshly painted murals of fish on the walls. Families with children like the little playground across the street. In the winter some peculiar but generally benign characters stake out the covered picnic tables on the beach. There's also a beachside restaurant here, somewhat reminiscent of a beachy restaurant in Mexico (see page 242). Large flocks of skimmers and seagulls gather at one part of the beach near the West Martello Tower during windy winter months, while the rebuilt and oft-described "well-extended" Reynolds Street pier nearby ("Dick Dock") sports a less gay clientele these days.

There are also two tiny patches of landfill where the undaunted seeker of waterfront can go. Then there's the famous Dog Beach at the end of Vernon, just beside **Louie's Back Yard**, where the dogs come to play. It's *the* place to see the rakish canines of Key West. Cool people come here too. As one human habitué said, "Anybody who comes to a beach that's peed on all day has to be OK." At the end of the sternly unimaginative **Casa Marina** complex on Seminole Street, there's a slice of concrete and a slice of sand. Snorkeling around the remnants of an old pier is fun here, and a little farther out, just to the east and west of markers that mark a channel through some scattered coral heads, are some nice patch reefs.

The best beach in town and really the best place to see the sunset is at **Fort Taylor** (pages 206–9).

Two surrealistic sights are offered for your delectation here. One is the departure of the mammoth cruise ships, suddenly materializing at the jetty. Surely this is an absurd vision. The other, at the opposite end of the beach, is the sight of Navy commandos practicing their amphibious landings in full battle gear. The Navy's beach is separated from the park beach by a stop sign. European visitors seem to get a particular kick out of this. The entrance to the Fort is through the Southard Street entrance to Truman Annex. (Presently it's quite a long and circuitous walk from the Annex gatehouse to the Park's gates and then to the beach itself.) The beach is open from 8 A.M. to sunset and has picnic tables and grills. The fee is $1.50 per person, or $4 a car and 50¢ a person. Bring sneakers or amphibious sandals because the beach is rough coral. It's difficult getting into the water gracefully at Fort Taylor. People teeter, hobble, crawl. Once in, the tendency is to stay in for a considerable time, putting off the teetering, hobbling, and crawling out as long as possible.

Jeanna's Courthouse Deli on Whitehead delivers tasty sandwiches and sodas out here. Call them at 294-2929.

ART AND ANTIQUES

Lucky Street (1120 White Street) was forced out of its gallery on Duval by rising rents only the T-shirt shops could afford and is now in the hinterlands near the Cuban bakery La Dichosa and the wash and wax lot Quality Auto Care, which used to be called the far more interesting Y. B. Dirty. Pottery, jewelry, paintings, constructions, great receptions. Local sculptor John Martini, whose studio is an old movie theater in Bahama Village, shows his witty giant metal sculptures here. Slender, near mythic, neurotic creatures all. **The Harrison Gallery** (825 White on the other side of Truman) has lovely wooden sculptures for sale. In winter, numerous low-key friendly openings showcase a remarkable range of local talent. **Gingerbread Square Gallery** (1207 Duval) is the longest-running gallery in Key West. It frequently shows the soft, otherworldly acrylics of the artist John Kiraly, whose work has been described as "idealized realism" and even "attainable fantasy." **Island Arts** (1128 Duval) is an artists' co-op, more varied and exuberant than the original artists' co-op, Guild Hall. **Bordello Gallery** (Thomas Street at Blue Heaven) and **Village Art** (around the corner at 309 Petronia) are both very much worth investigating. Fresh and fun. The latter has some wonderful wooden fish and raised sculpted paintings in the manner of Mario Sanchez.

The Haitian Art Company (corner of Francis and Southard). Several rooms jammed with Haitian primitives. Voodoo bottles, spirit flags, gloriously painted boxes. Very reasonable. Open 10 A.M.–6 P.M.

Perkins and Son is a salty store at 901 Fleming. Great shorts and shirts as well as brasswork, ships' clocks, models, charts, and a nice selection of books about the sea.

The Sea Store (614 Greene). A nice little store, but be sure to call first as they're erratically open (294-3438). Bottles and old coins. A variety of Keys hardwoods which could possibly become something handsomely custom-made for you. The owners, Bill and Fran Ford, are gregarious and knowledgeable about poking around the Keys. They are great birders. If Fran can't get you excited about the Birdathon, the Keys' bird-count day that happens each May 1—"We start in the Dry Tortugas at dawn, spend an hour there, then fly back to Key West for breakfast in the Indigenous Park, and then work our way up the Keys, and by nightfall when we hear the screech owl in Key Largo, we could have one hundred thirty species!"—then nothing ever will.

Whitehead Street Pottery, at 1011 Whitehead, has an elegant offering of original works in stoneware and porcelain, while around the corner on Catherine Street is an entirely different experience in the modest home of Makiki, with its little hand-lettered sign, ART FOR SALE. Makiki (a childhood nickname that means fighting rooster) has turned the front room into a shrine to his mother, who died 19 years ago. Glittering with thousands of pieces of glass, candles, and Christmas tree lights, it shines quietly each evening. The rest of the house holds work that he is willing to sell, all framed in wedges of colored glass. The subjects include churches, fish, roses, Everglades deer, and guardian angels. There is also a very robust Adam being expelled from the Garden of Eden.

There are several antique shops between Fleming and Simonton. **Sam's Treasure Chest** has tidied itself up considerably and you no longer have the feeling that you're going to rescue something that has languished there for years. Still, many is the old foot from a claw-footed bathtub that has found its way here. **Joseph's Antiques** is down at 616 Greene with a great many nautical items and other things the eclectic-eyed owners have collected.

NEWSPAPERS

The *Key West Citizen* is Monroe County's only daily newspaper, although it does not appear on Saturday. It is a thin paper, sometimes astonishingly thin, and poker-faced in its accountings. It is known as the mullet-wrapper, and the staff depicted it thusly in papier-mâché during one Fantasy Fest parade. A now-departed editor investigated, with two reporters, rumors of occult disturbances at the Little White House. They spent the night in the house where Harry once slept, equipped with high-speed film, a tape recorder, a German shepherd, and notepads. The trio experienced two ghosts. One was a lady named Rose. The other was a slight man with blue eyes named Tom. Tom wore a brimmed felt hat, a cardigan sweater, had thin bony fingers, an eye for the ladies, and owned a green parrot. It is not known what the German shepherd thought, but the reporters' observances were duly reported in the *Citizen*.

The pictures of babies, newlyweds, and high school sports are nice, and, of course, the drug trials of prominent local citizens, including police officers and real estate ladies, are followed with great interest, but the most fascinating section of the *Citizen* is by far the police blotter on Page Two. It is here where Key West sings her strange song. It is here where much is exposed but little explained—the complaints to the police of break-ins where pots of black beans vanish and wet clothes are rearranged. The thefts of car bras and meatball subs. The reports of voodoo roosters and murdered palm trees, the arrests of individuals opening coconuts in a dangerous fashion. The headline of choice on Page Two is THIEVES, WACKOS KEEP POLICE BUSY. Or, MINOR BURGLARIES GALORE.

Solares Hill began in the 1970s as a monthly free paper. It was named in those heady days for the "highest" point on the island, a bit of land 16 feet above sea level at the intersection of Elizabeth Street and Windsor Lane. (The lowest point in Key West, at least for the undercarriages of cars, is at South and Simonton.) *Solares Hill* is a paper with style and conviction, a community paper of the very best sort, with articles on local concerns, politics, and personalities. In 1995, when the mayor and a commissioner were indicted—the mayor for accepting payments from a jet-ski operator, the commissioner for soliciting money from someone who wanted to start a pink Cadillac tour business—*Solares Hill* ran the federal indictments verbatim in a "special souvenir issue." As well as such souvenir issues, there are helpful supplements for the visitor, such as a walking and biking guide to Old Town. The paper is now published weekly and can be picked up at almost any store or guest house, although some establishments banned it after it printed a picture of fun-loving Spring Breakers on the cover, one of whom, under closer perusal, was starkers.

People get the *Citizen* for Page Two, but they have to pay 50¢ for it, and lately Page Two is not the place you want to begin your day. Muggings and beatings, people screaming obscenities or making "illegal deposits"—it's beginning to lack . . . charm. The polite Citizen of the Day column beside it has as yet not elicited one interesting quote. Livelier is *Solares Hill*'s Our Weekly Reader box, where the chosen say things like "Nothing confirms life's worst expectations better than *Solares Hill.*" Another good free paper is *Key West: The Newspaper.* Pick it up for reviews, disclosures, the style of the rock, and in-depth eristic attitude.

WRITERS

It is known that writers hang out in Key West, and after the brisk, rather flamboyant tour of the Hemingway House, one might be curious to catch a glimpse of the other homes where novelists, playwrights, and poets ply their grisly, solitary trade. The Hemingway House is, of course, big business. The other houses can only be reflected upon from outside. Why people are fascinated with the shells these souls inhabit is curious. Per-

haps they're actually not that fascinated but have been encouraged to believe they are.

Key West writers have done well. Many of them have won the
Pulitzer Prize, including Ernest Hemingway, Philip Caputo,
Elizabeth Bishop, John Hersey, Wallace Stevens, Joseph Lash,
James Merrill, Richard Wilbur, Tennessee Williams, Allison
Lurie, and Annie Dillard. (Robert Frost won several Pulitzers
as well but came here for the climate rather than the cama-
raderie, and Key West is rather hesitant to claim responsibility
for him.) It almost seems as though with the Pulitzer comes an
irresistible urge to move here. Writers like Key West—there
may now be more writers in town than bars—but many of them
are faithless creatures and they come and they go. One of them,
Hart Crane, often mentioned as a Key West writer, was in fact
never here at all. The nearest he came was the Isle of Pines in
Cuba, although a grouping of his poems was entitled *Key West
Sheaf.* Tom McGuane, Jim Harrison, Thomas Sanchez—all are
associated with this strange rock, Mile Zero. Through the
decades they pass. Macho, gay, hip, the intellectual elite—their
reigns overlap. Their houses of Pepto-Bismol pink and lime
green and proper white could be duly noted and located, but
this guide, believing that all living writers have enough problems, most of which are still with them, prefers to address only
those who have passed on in a permanent sense. More specifically, the former homes of two of Key West's fixed and illustri-
ous dead, Elizabeth Bishop and Tennessee Williams.

Elizabeth Bishop and Tennessee Williams

The **Bishop House** is at 624 White Street, not far from the
pale yellow, twin-towered National Guard Armory, now a
Senior Citizens' Center, at 600 White. It is a fine, simple,
weathered structure, almost hidden behind palms and plantings but sporting a new bronze tablet on the gate that quotes a
line from one of her poems: "Should we have stayed at home,
wherever that might be?" Bishop lived here between 1938 and
1942, and many of the poems in her first collection, *North and
South,* winner of the Pulitzer in 1956, were written here and
are about Florida, the state which she considered to have "the

prettiest name," a "careless, corrupt state, the poorest postcard of itself." She would be less than inspired, no doubt, by the view across the street, at the wasteland the Navy has made of Peary Court, but she would probably not have been surprised. In 1942 she wrote to a friend,

> It's impossible to live here any longer. The Navy takes over and tears down and eats up one or two blocks of beautiful little houses for dinner every day. One poor old man committed suicide two days ago because he heard they were going to take his house. And the point is that it is unnecessary—you have all these vast tracts of land in other parts of the island. . . . When the war is finally over, Key West will be more ruined than ever— nothing but a naval base and a bunch of bars and cheap apartments.

Actually, Bishop was frequently glum about Key West. She wrote to Robert Lowell,

> When somebody says "beautiful" about Key West you should really take it with a grain of salt, until you've seen it for yourself. In general, it is really *awful* and the "beauty" is just the light, or

Bahama anole lizard under a periwinkle

something equally perverse. . . . The harbor is always a mess, junky little boats all piled up, some hung with sponges and always a few half-sunk or splintered up from the most recent hurricane. It reminds me a little of my desk.

Elizabeth Bishop was a poet of stunning gifts. Read her poem "Seascape," about a Keys lighthouse's knowledge of Heaven and Hell. Key West and New England were the early compass points of her work, although after leaving here she lived for 18 years in Brazil. Two of her wonderful prose pieces concern Key West: *Mercedes Hospital* and *Gregorio Valdes*.

Gregorio Valdes was a Cuban sign-painter whom she met after purchasing one of his paintings out of a barber shop on Duval. The painting was of a neat row of royal palm trees and was in the window of the shop, covered with dust and termite wings.

Bishop wanted him to paint a picture of her green-and-white White Street house, but she wanted him to add more flowers and a parrot. She also wanted him to include a monkey that lived next door, and a traveler's-tree. She liked the appearance of the traveler's-tree, which she described as looking like the "fan-filamented antennae of a certain gigantic moth." There being only one such palmlike tree in town at the time, Valdes

---

TRUMAN CAPOTE IN KEY WEST

Truman Capote was in a bar in Key West with Tennessee Williams when a woman came over to the table where they were sitting and asked Capote to autograph her navel with an eyebrow pencil. She handed him the pencil and pulled up her T-shirt. "Just write it like you would the numerals around a clock," she said. So Capote wrote his name around her navel. T-R-U-M-A-N-C-A-P-O-T-E. She returned to her table, but her husband got up, seemingly quite enraged. He came over to Capote, eyebrow pencil in hand and, as Capote relates, hauled out his "equipment" and howled, "Since you're autographing everything, how'd you like to autograph *this*?" Truman paused and said, "Well, I don't know if I can autograph it, but perhaps I could initial it."

sketched it separately, then worked from an enlarged photograph of the house Bishop gave him. She was delighted with the final result. "He put in flowers in profusion and the parrot on a perch on the verandah and painted the monkey, larger than life-size, climbing the trunk of the palm tree." But Gregorio Valdes was apologetic because the living tree he had copied had seven branches on one side and six on the other, but in the painting he gave both sides seven to make it more symmetrical.

The **Tennessee Williams House** at 1431 Duncan Street on the corner of Leon is noted for the large, highly *a*symmetrical traveler's-tree in the front yard. A writer of genius in his early years and considered by many to be the greatest living playwright since O'Neill, Williams continued to write prolifically even though his later plays were poorly received, one critic referring to them as "mere mystic mazes of lyrical mumbo-jumbo concerning human despair." Bought in 1950, this little house with its tomato-colored shutters is almost a miniature house, reminiscent perhaps of one of the small torrid symbols of *The Glass Menagerie*. On the lot he added a white gazebo, in honor, he said, of his friend Jane Bowles; a pool; and a studio where he produced some of his best-known work, including *The Night of the Iguana* and *The Rose Tattoo*. The movie version of *The Rose Tattoo,* with Burt Lancaster and Anna Magnani, was filmed in Key West, at this house and on the Casa Marina grounds, in 1955. Williams loved his studio, pointing out its "complete bath-shower and female sockets for electric grills."

Tennessee Williams was born in Mississippi in 1911 and christened Thomas Lanier. His father more than once called him "Miss Nancy." His older sister, Rose, was a little odd and was in and out of sanatoriums until she was given a lobotomy at the age of 28. The procedure was safe and sure, the physicians assured the Williamses, and they offered to do it for free because Rose would be one of the first persons to undergo it. The operation could not be considered a complete success. Tennessee was devoted to mad Rose throughout his life, and she visited him in Key West often, along with their grandfather, the Rev. Walter Edwin Dakin. The Reverend, elderly and almost blind, was extremely sanguine about his grandson's lifestyle, considering homosexual bonding an elite and rather stylish manner of living. Rose occupied her time by watering the trees in the garden with glassfuls of water from the kitchen sink. Tennessee, the master of duality, took up painting here, as did Elizabeth Bishop. He was tutored by the flaming eccentric Henry Faulkner, who lived on Peacon Lane with his goats, with whom he loved to take showers. Williams said that painting was relaxing and didn't wear him out like writing did.

In 1969 Tennessee's younger brother Dakin visited him in Key West and could not help but notice that Tennessee was heavily beholden to drink and drugs. He fell down a lot and could barely complete a coherent sentence. Dakin's solution was to have him convert to Catholicism, which he did, at St. Mary's church on Truman Avenue. He was even baptized there, which shocked the faithful. Tennessee later said, "I loved the beauty of the ritual but the tenets of the Church are ridiculous." Later that year Dakin returned to Key West again, this time to take Tennessee back to St. Louis, where he committed him to a psychiatric hospital. Going through total withdrawal of all drugs (he was particularly fond of Doriden), he suffered three grand mal seizures and two heart attacks. (The family seemed to have difficulty with the treatment of doctors.) He was cured, more or less, however, and returned to Key West later that year, where he had only one drink a day and "limited" pills, at least for a while.

One of Williams's more interesting infatuations was with Fidel Castro. He had in fact a fantasy of being kidnapped by Castro and Che Guevara. He visited Havana several times from Key West and chatted with Castro, whom he found very gentlemanly and charming. Castro referred to Tennessee as "that cat," and was knowledgeable, at the very least, of the titles of the playwright's classics.

Tennessee wrote that ordinarily his life was "50 percent work and worry about it; 35 percent a struggle against madness, and 15 percent devoted to friends and lovers." Williams was happy in Key West. Early on he felt that it was the most fantastic place he had ever seen in America, more colorful than New Orleans, San Francisco, or Santa Fe. In the pictures taken of him here he is always smiling, happy with his pet bulldogs, his houseguests (who included Carson McCullers and Gore Vidal), his writing (in which the town never figures), and his friends.

By the '70s, however, Key West's huge parties and catty social intrigues were wearing Tennessee out. Donald Spoto in his book *The Kindness of Strangers* notes that "Key West, once a quiet retreat where he could work well and live a reasonably ordered life, was now really no longer suitable for him. The crowd around him gave him nothing but a phony admiration and took whatever they could get."

There was an incident in the late '70s where Williams and a friend, Dotson Rader, were roughed up late one night as they walked drunk and singing up Duval Street. They were singing the old gospel hymn "In the Garden":

> *Ohhhh He walks with me*
> *And He talks with me*
> *And He tells me I am his own*
> *And the joy we share as we tarry there*
> *No other has ever known*

The lyrics achieved certain implications never dreamed of by their creator. Some young toughs pushed the men down and kicked them, and although the incident was highly publicized and caused considerable concern among Key West gays, Tennessee dismissed the misadventure. "Well, I suffered no injury," he said. "Fortunately, an ice-cream shop was being shut right behind us and a man picked up the phone, called the police, and said, 'Some men are attacking Mr. Williams on the street.' " Williams later mused that his attackers might not have been punks at all, but New York theater critics.

Three weeks prior to the incident, the caretaker of his house on Duncan Street had been shot and killed. While going through his effects, the police found that he had pilfered many of the original copies of Williams's manuscripts. "Well," Tennessee said dryly, "I guess he thought he was going to die after I did."

Tennessee Williams's talent died 20 years before he did and he knew it. His travels became constant and neurotic and Key West just another place where he failed to find inspiration or peace. Near the end of his life he was living on wine, Seconal, and coffee, writing every day, all of the work hopeless and virtually unperformable. He died alone in New York City at the

Hotel Elysee at the age of 72. His wish to be "buried at sea between Key West and Cuba, dropped overboard in a clean white sack" was not granted. His brother arranged that his body be buried in the city he loathed, St. Louis.

Not long ago in New Orleans, someone moved into the tiny apartment in the French Quarter where Williams wrote *A Streetcar Named Desire* in 1946. The new tenant set off six roach bombs in the eight by ten kitchen and the place blew up. This should have happened in Key West, of course.

The **Key West Literary Seminar** takes place each January with panels, readings, and, of course, parties. This has become quite a sophisticated event, with well-known and articulate participants and interesting themes. Past topics have included Literature and Film, Travel Writing, and Biography. Call 293-9291 for information. By calling the same number you can get information on the **Writers' Walk**, a one-mile guided tour of literary sites. Tickets are $11.

The **Hemingway Days Festival** was a rowdier event that took place in the doldrums of July. Begun in 1981 and snow-balling nicely for 16 years, with Papa look-alike contests and arm wrestling contests and short-story contests and costume parties where one had to dress up as a Hemingway character, the winner one year being a fluttering Portuguese man-of-war from *The Old Man and the Sea,* the event was axed in 1997 by its local founder after Hemingway's sons, Hemingway Ltd., threatened to sue unless they got royalties from the event. Hemingway Ltd. already licenses a number of products, including Mont Blanc pens and shotguns. One of the sons, Patrick, even went so far as to say, somewhat accurately, that Key West projects a cheap, derogatory image of Hemingway. Oddly, a new celebration of the writer, endorsed by Hemingway Ltd., will take place annually on the west coast islands of Sanibel and Captiva—very tony places where Hemingway never set foot. Reorganized in Key West under the auspices of the Hemingway Home and Museum, the festival hopes to continue. There will be look-alike contests and arm wrestling contests and short-story contests. There will also be the "running of the bulls" around Sloppy Joe's, where festivalgoers can be chased around the block by fake bulls and bullfighters.

Foremost of the bookstores in town is **Key West Island Books** at 513 Fleming, just off Duval. On the walls is a rogues' gallery of local authors' photographs, and on the shelves there is an excellent selection of their work and books of local interest. There's also a rare-book room and carefully chosen used books. Throughout the winter there are readings and signing parties here. **Blue Heron Books** at 1014 Truman (296-3508) is a well laid out, personable store that has a good selection of recently published books. Fans like it because the enthusiastic owners will actively pursue special orders. Independent bookstores are treasures.

In a class by itself is **Bargain Books**, nearby at 1028 Truman (294-7446). Open late, perhaps to tempt the patrons of Teaser's Lounge across the street who might want to pick up a "preread" copy of *Under the Volcano*. A great jumble of a used-book store. There aren't enough rainy days in town to explore this place. Newspapers and magazines too.

The pink **Monroe County Library** was built in 1959 and has been recently spruced up. In 1994 a benefactor gave several hundred thousand dollars, not for books but specifically for a palm garden to the side. Overnight, and to considerable amazement, an oasis appeared. Ask the librarians about it and they'll say, "Oh, *that* . . ." A visitor's library card costs $15 and is good for a year. On the first Saturday of each month there's a book sale behind the library. During the winter there are weekly coffees and talks, some of them *most* intriguing. How could one resist, for example, early on a Monday morning, the desire to hear one Poochie Myers discuss "The Serpent-Handling Religions of West Virginia."

Hemingway and His House

In 1851 Asa Tift, a "brainy, cultured, suave gentleman" from Groton, Connecticut, a merchant and builder of Confederate ships, built a limestone mansion from native coral rock at 907 Whitehead. With its mansard roof and iron-flanged pillars, of vaguely Second Empire or Spanish Colonial design, the **Hemingway House** is unlike any other house in town.

Ernest Hemingway and his wife Pauline bought the house in 1931 for $8,000, a monetary gift from Pauline's wealthy Uncle Gus. The house was in a gross state of ill repair, with a grassless yard dotted with a few scraggly trees. It was a "miserable wreck," according to Pauline, who also referred to it as a "damned haunted house" after a piece of plaster fell from the ceiling and lodged in her eye. Nonetheless, just before Christmas the Hemingways, with their two small sons, nurses, and cooks, moved into rooms still jammed with carpenters, plumbers, plasterers, and crates of furniture shipped from France. Hemingway worked here winters in a small room over what had once been a carriage house until his divorce from Pauline in 1940. At that time he crated all his belongings— papers, books, guns, and hunting trophies—and stored them in a back room at Sloppy Joe's. (When Mary Hemingway, his last wife, went into the room in 1962 and opened the boxes untouched for decades, she found original manuscripts blackened with mildew and eaten by rats, uncashed royalty checks, and rotted animal skins.) He then went off to Cuba for a new, if brief, marriage with Martha Gellhorn, and a new house, the Finca Vigía or "Lookout Farm," nine miles outside of Havana. It was at the Finca where the ghastly collection of inbred cats roamed and not in Key West, where the pet population, which numbered several peacocks, included only two cats, one of which the children once dyed a dark green, producing unknown consequences. Hemingway, however, did have over 50 cats in Cuba and once boasted of shooting a peasant's dog who had molested one of them. He had intentionally gut-shot the animal so that it would take three days to die.

Ernest Hemingway, as every schoolchild knows, fished, drank, and wrote in Key West. He wrote *Death in the Afternoon, The Green Hills of Africa,* and *To Have and Have Not,* as well as a play, *The Fifth Column,* and a considerable number of short stories, including "The Short Happy Life of Francis Macomber" and "The Snows of Kilimanjaro."

A Farewell to Arms was completed in 1929 in a house he and Pauline had rented at 1100 South Street, the same house where his mother had sent a chocolate cake and the Smith & Wesson revolver his father had used to commit suicide.

"Christ, this is a fine country!" Hemingway wrote a friend,

enthusiastic about Key West. Between trips to Arkansas, to shoot grouse, pheasant, ducks, and geese; Wyoming, to shoot bear, elk, mountain rams, and eagles; and Africa, to shoot elephant, lion, rhino, buffalo, and kudu, Hemingway fished the Gulf Stream. As the biographer Carlos Baker remarks, in somewhat of an understatement, he "enjoyed life immensely without being sensitive to it." Once, when the poet Archibald MacLeish visited him and they went kingfishing, they found the fish weren't running so Hemingway "took to shooting terns, taking one with one barrel and the grieving mate with the other." Besides shotguns, he also carried on board a harpoon and a machine gun for sharks and the stray pod of whales.

Hemingway liked marlin fishing best, for marlin were "fast as light, strong as bucks, with mouths like iron." Tuna, perhaps, were not so exciting, even though they could take just as long to catch. It took him seven hours to land one 11.5-foot, 540-pound tuna, and after getting drunk he strung it up and used it as a punching bag. Hemingway also once used the poet Wallace Stevens as a punching bag in Key West. He blackened his eyes and fractured his jaw after the older man had apparently remarked that Hemingway's writing was not his "cup of tea." One mystified biographer wrote, "For reasons that remain obscure, the poet seems to have baited the novelist into some

The oldest house in Key West, on Duval Street

THE TOUR

You will enter the grounds. The plantings are nice. It is lush.
Figs, elephant ears, a magnificent date palm. Then you will
see the excessive inauthentic collection of cats, clumping
around on their malformed toes—cats eating, cats brawling,
cats having more cats in little cages. You will take the tour. It
will cost you $6 (children $1.50) and it will take 30 minutes.
Four people give tours ten times a day. The most eccentric
tour is given by a tiny man with a tiny belly in tiny, tight,
shiny black pants. You will be in a mob and he will call you
"beanies," he will call you "little sparklers," he will tell you to
keep it "flowing and glowing" as you follow him tripping
through the rooms. He is a movie buff and you will hear
about Loretta Young and Rock Hudson and Lauren Bacall.
There's a chair in the bedroom which he will point out
because Franchot Tone sat in it in the production of *The Fifth
Column.* Franchot Tone was married to Joan Crawford at the
time. The bedroom abounds in strange little chairs, uncom-
fortable chairs, keyhole chairs, even a midwife's chair. Later,
of course, you are shown *the* chair, the cigar-maker's chair
Hemingway wrote in. The books of the house are all enclosed
behind wire mesh, although there is a good selection of his
works in paper for sale in the drawing room. "I had no idea
he wrote so much," you'll hear. Glance inside the pages.
Other than this, his life's work, Hemingway is dead as a
doornail in this place.

kind of fight." Stevens was 20 years older than Hemingway, a
portly insurance executive, and certainly no boxer. When he
threw a punch at Hemingway's jaw, he broke his hand in two
places.

During his first years in Key West, Hemingway chartered the
boats of Bra Saunders, Charles Thompson, and Sloppy Joe Russell. In 1934, at the height of the Depression and in the same
year that the town had declared bankruptcy, Hemingway
bought his own boat—a 42-foot black cruiser with mahogany
trim built to his specifications in a New York shipyard. "A
really sturdy boat," he described her, "sweet in any kind of sea,
and she has a very low-cut stern with a large wooden roller to

bring big fish over." He called her the *Pilar,* one of his early names for Pauline, as well as the name of a Catholic bullfight shrine in Zaragoza, Spain. He docked her at the Navy station, in the submarine pen where he and his friends, the "Mob," liked to swim. She rode out the 1935 hurricane there.

Hemingway did a lot of fishing on the *Pilar.* In 1942 he employed her in a daffy manner as a submarine hunter in the Caribbean, having convinced the Navy to equip her as a Q-boat with a supply of bazookas, grenades, and short-fuse bombs. The *Pilar* was seized by the Castro government in 1960, a year before Hemingway's death, and is now rotting on the lawn in front of the Finca in Cuba.

Hemingway thought his house on Whitehead Street resembled "Joan Miro's 'The Farm' as it might have been painted by Utrillo." If that does not exactly crystallize the vision for you, imagine it being, in the 1930s, the finest house in town, a mansion with tall French windows, staffed with servants on an acre of land and possessing the only basement, bathroom, and swimming pool on the island. The pool is 60 feet long and was dug by pick and shovel for $20,000, an amount which, the guides like to point out, would be equivalent to spending over $225,000 today. Hemingway lived very well here. In 1936 he was putting the finishing touches on his Key West book, *To Have and Have Not,* a novel that showed the poverty-stricken plight of islanders during the Depression as well as Hemingway's considerable disdain for fellow writers, literary hangers-on, Gulf Stream yachtsmen, and tourists. *To Have and Have Not* is actually an unsuccessful attempt to fashion a novel by taking three previously published stories about a fisherman and smuggler named Henry Morgan (based on Sloppy Joe Russell) and attaching them to subplots of love triangles and capitalistic boorishness. But it's Hemingway's Key West book, and it captures the jarring rhythms of a town on the skids.

Hemingway became Key West's most famous citizen and immediately fell prey to his fans. "Have been driven nuts by visitors this last ten days," he wrote to the editor Maxwell Perkins. "Everything from movie stars up and down and they have cost me a week's work except for one good day. The people all come at once and always in the cool season when I have to get my work done." In 1937 Toby Bruce, a driver, friend, and general handyman for the Hemingways, built a privacy wall around the property from bricks salvaged from Duval Street, dug up when the town laid down its first sewer system. By 1940 Hemingway was gone. "Those who live by the sword, die by the sword," he said rather uninspiredly, explaining Pauline's replacement by Martha. After all, Pauline had replaced Hadley. And Mary was to supplant Martha. Pauline, who had provided him with the wealth he so enjoyed and despised, died suddenly in Los Angeles in 1951. When asked by Tennessee Williams, who had met her in Key West, how she had died, Hemingway replied, "She died like everybody else and after that she was dead."

FORTS, TOWERS, AND MUSEUMS

The Lighthouse Military Museum

Close across from the Hemingway House, this museum is housed in the lighthouse keeper's cottage. It used to be more interesting, but unfortunately in 1988 a great deal of well-intentioned housekeeping took place and the rooms lost their messy, intriguingly atticy quality. The grounds were once cluttered with various torpedoes, depth charges, and gun mounts, even a Blue Angel stunt jet, all innocently moldering. All of this has been carted off now, even the oddest object of all, a miniature Japanese submarine from World War II. This captured sub (small windows cut in the hull and two mannequins in Japanese uniforms placed inside) toured the country during those war years collecting money to raise the ships sunk at Pearl Harbor. It will be returned there to be part of the *Arizona* memorial. The museum still includes many artifacts from the *Maine,* including life preservers and a capstan to which the nuns of the Convent of Mary Immaculate added a spire. The new emphasis is on lighthouse history and memorabilia. The impressive original Fresnel lens from the Sombrero Key light is on display, and more interpretative exhibits are planned.

You can climb 88 steps to the top of the lighthouse and get a good gull's-eye view of Key West. When it was built in 1847 it was 58 feet tall, but it had to be raised over the years so that the

light could be seen over growing trees and the new buildings of
an expanding town. The tower stopped growing at 78 feet, and
the light was extinguished in 1969. Open 9:30–5. Admission is
$5. Children, $1. Telephone: 294-0012.

Fort Taylor

The Fort is scarcely visible from the exterior, either from the
land or from water. It is not imposing until one is inside.

Begun in 1845 as part of an ambitious coastal fortifications
system and named five years later for President Zachary Taylor,
it was originally built 1,200 feet from shore (sand and fill eventually connected it to Key West) and had two tiers plus a top
platform for cannon just behind the parapet. The Fort is built in
the shape of a trapezoid and rests on a foundation of Keys limestone and New England granite. Millions of bricks, shipped
down from Pensacola, were used in the 21-year project, set by
slaves and German and Irish masons. (Ironically, the slave pop-

The lighthouse at Key West

ulation of Key West increased fivefold when Union authorities imported them to work on military fortifications during the Civil War.) Construction was plagued by strikes, shortages of material, the antipathy of European craftsmen toward Negro laborers, and hurricanes. Most important, there were the vicious periodic attacks of yellow fever, blamed on "miasma" in the air. Indeed, the only time the Fort's cannon were fired was in an attempt to dispel this "miasma." A swamp close to the workmen's quarters and teeming with mosquitoes was not suspected.

On the night that Florida seceded from the Union, January 13, 1861, a small group of Union soldiers marched to the Fort and, with the assistance of a Lieutenant Edward Hunt, in charge of the Fort's construction, secured it for the Union, delivering an immediate blow to the Confederacy. Less than 50 Union men held a crucial fortification in what was the largest town in Florida. Sentiment in town was mostly Southern, but there was no attempt to take the Fort by rebel sympathizers, although many of the young men of Key West sailed away immediately to join the Confederate army. Several months later, with the arrival of additional troops, the Union blockade of the Confederacy began, and captured blockade runners with their ships and cargoes were brought into the harbor and anchored beneath the massive guns of Fort Taylor, guns which now numbered almost 200. An average of 32 ships were stationed here during the war years, and at one time there were 300 vessels of various description held captive.

Key West was the only city south of the Mason-Dixon line to remain in the hands of the Union during the Civil War, but Washington officials did not consider it that important militarily. Frantic requests for supplies and reinforcements were largely ignored. Many Union commanders considered it a fetid place of disease and desired neither their ships nor their men to come near Key West. In 1862, of the 448 men garrisoned at Fort Taylor, 331 contracted yellow fever and 71 died.

The Fort was still in the process of being constructed in 1866 when it was declared obsolete. The innovation of rifled cannon, which projected a spinning cannonball that dug into masonry rather than bounced off it, made huge brick fortresses useless. Only a few soldiers remained stationed here, and it became a favorite spot for the townspeople to picnic. A local druggist,

J. Otto, made a written request to the authorities for picnicking privileges using his letterhead:

Apothecaries' Hall
Pharmaceutists and Embalmers
Bodies Disinterred
Hermetically Sealed
and Forwarded to Friends.

In 1867 the president of the defeated Confederacy, Jefferson Davis, visited Key West for a day on his way to Cuba, where he hoped to regain his health. He did not picnic at the Fort, but while here he was given a sapodilla to sample. He broke it neatly in half, took a small bite, and put the halves back together again. When asked if he liked the fruit, he said politely, "I cannot say that I care for it particularly, but I fancy some people are very fond of it."

In 1898, for the Spanish-American War, the Fort was reactivated. It was also modernized by cutting it back a level and equipping it with newer weapons. This new emplacement of guns was called Osceola Battery. The refuse from the demolition was packed into the casemates with all the obsolete Columbiad and Rodman cannon, cannonballs, and gun carriages, and the whole thing was covered with cement and sand. Over the years, through World Wars I and II and the Cuban Crisis, other weapons, radar, missiles, and antiaircraft guns were mounted and removed, but the treasury of Civil War artifacts, including the Parrott rifle, the type of cannon that had reduced Savannah's Fort Pulaski to rubble, remained untouched. (The Parrott can be identified by the wrought-iron jacket shrunk around the breech and the grooves inside the muzzle.)

By the mid-1960s Fort Taylor was abandoned, forgotten and buried beneath dredge material and weeds. Then in 1968 the Navy (the Army had turned the Fort over to the Navy in 1947) directed their base architect and historian, Howard England, to investigate the site, although they did not want to spend any money for excavation. It is to Howard England that the "discovery" of Fort Taylor should be attributed. With borrowed equipment and volunteer help from townspeople and Navy personnel, including, perhaps most enthusiastically, men from the brig, Fort Taylor emerged. After months and years of hand shoveling, the beautiful vaulted brickwork of the gun rooms was exposed and cannon unearthed. Also discovered was America's first water desalinization plant—Dr. Normandy's Patent Marine Aerated Fresh Water Apparatus—which had once produced 7,000 gallons of fresh water daily from the sea. The military artifacts you will see have been recovered from only two of the fort's 24 casemates and represent only a fraction of the buried arsenal, which is the largest collection of Civil War cannon in the United States.

The Fort and 50 acres of surrounding land are now under the management of the Florida Park Service. The Fort is interesting, with great views, and the volunteers throw themselves into their reenactment roles, appearing only mildly perturbed that you are seemingly inhabiting a time 130 years after their affected one. The picnic grounds are shaded by hundreds of casuarinas (which you're not supposed to like but can't help liking here), and the swimming is splendid, though conditions are infrequently calm. Don't miss Fort Taylor. Truman Annex at Southard Street. Telephone: 292-6713.

East Martello Museum and Art Gallery

A charming museum and a great place to acquaint yourself with Key West history.

The Martello Tower was an ancient Corsican means of defense, a cylindrical structure often described as an "upside down flowerpot." Key West's two nontraditional towers were constructed during the Civil War to assist Fort Taylor in repelling a coastal landing force. Begun in 1862, work on them ceased two years later. The towers, like the rest of the Keys' huge brick fortifications, were never completed. Cannon were never installed here. Before the Art and Historical Society took over the East Tower in 1950, there was not even a roof.

The museum has exhibits depicting sponging, turtling, pirating, and whatnot. There's a tiny portion of an Indian midden, discovered when the golf course was being made on Stock Island. It sports a small trowel so you can paw around in it.

PEARY COURT

Key West is an emotional, obstreperous town, its citizens continually in a lather about something. Everything becomes an issue—sidewalks, the Bubba system, Houseboat Row, the San Carlos, the airport—but nothing has divided the city more than Peary Court, Key West's last green space, 30 acres of sloppy but cherished parkland on the edge of Old Town near Garrison Bight. It had been an Army parade ground, cavalry barracks, and military cemetery for 106 years when the Navy took it over after World War II and used it pretty much as a dump site, then built cement bungalows which they later razed before "giving" it to the city in 1974 for $1 a year. The city cleaned it up, made a couple of softball fields, mowed the grass, and let the trees grow, some sapodilla, fig, and frangipani reaching considerable size.

By 1988, when the Navy decided they wanted to build 160 units of military housing there, citing a desperate housing shortage, the town had pretty much forgotten that the park wasn't really theirs. ("This is what happens when you give something to the people. They don't want to give it back," a counsel for the Navy said.) Since the military had been downsizing in Key West for the last decade, the "desperate need" rhetoric seemed a little inflated, but the town, which has long loved the Navy here, supported them—though possibly they could build someplace else? On one of their many unused or underutilized sites? In a less socially and ecologically sensitive location? KEEP PEARY COURT GREEN signs appeared all over town, ratified not only by environmentalists but by a lot of carpenters who liked to play softball. Military cutbacks continued. But it seemed the more the Navy families left Key West, the more determined Naval base commander Michael Currie became.

Peary Court was going to be built out, and since it was a federal project, exempt from municipal control, building codes, taxes, and all but the most perfunctory environmental survey, it was going to be built out to the max. Fences went up and most of the trees came down. Bases all across the country continued to close, and in Key West the hydrofoil fleet left, as did two fighter wings from Boca Chica.

In 1992 the General Accounting Office concluded that

Peary Court was unnecessary. It was still somewhat green, though inaccessible, and could in theory be excessed to the city for a dollar, but slabs were poured, the first frames of the eventual 160 houses appeared, and the remaining trees didn't look so good. Captain Currie, in his role as juggernaut (and a successful role it was), maintained that there was a housing shortage until his retirement in 1993, a few months after which an internal Navy report was released saying that the military had a huge surplus of rental units in Key West but planned to demolish or excess them and continue to construct Peary Court. They wanted higher-quality housing for their personnel. Building began in earnest, the locals marveling at the use of something called oriented strand board instead of plywood in the construction. It looks somewhat like head cheese and was banned in Dade County after Hurricane Andrew because it absorbs moisture and disintegrates when wet.

This was all too much for Harry Powell, a City Commissioner from 1987 to 1991 and leader of the dogged but dispirited Keep Peary Court Green crowd. At eight in the morning on January 14, 1994, he walked into an empty construction trailer just opposite the old armory on White Street with a stick of dynamite and a gallon of gasoline, threatening to blow it and himself up unless he was promised a federal investigation into Peary Court—another GAO audit. The standoff, immediately dubbed Key Waco, ended ten hours later when Powell surrendered. He was jailed for ten months. Further debate and inquiries into the necessity of the housing is now moot, since all the houses have been built. Only a few Naval families live there, since the Naval presence in Key West was considerably scaled back in 1996.

There's Robert the handmade doll, who belonged to a local boy in 1904. Robert seems strangely, expectantly alert even now, though a psychic who visited the museum recently made the judgment that his spirit was dying. There are the little woven palm frond hats that the iguanas wore when the Iguana Man took them down to Sunset. Here, too, is a Cuban life raft, found floating empty ten miles south of Key West in 1969, made of bamboo, wire, and tractor inner tubes and bearing a feed-sack sail. In the great exodus of 1994, more rafts appeared in the Straits of Florida, some consisting of little more than a wedge of Styrofoam powered by a grass-trimmer engine. U.S. immigration policy changed toward Cuba that August, when automatic asylum was no longer granted and thousands of rafters were returned to Guantánamo Bay by the Coast Guard.

The gallery has rotating shows of contemporary and local art as well as an interesting permanent collection where "the welded found materials" of Stanley Papio of Key Largo and the wood carvings of Old Key West by Mario Sanchez can be found.

Papio was a junk dealer and welder, despised for years by his neighbors in his little concrete house near MM #100. After he was arrested six times for violating local ordinances concerning orderliness and neatness, a friend suggested he claim the junk-yard as an art museum and charge 25¢ to see the peculiar and parodic conjunctions made between bedsprings, toilet fixtures, and Buick chrome. "Dishpan Annie" is a charmer made out of a kitchen sink body, hubcap hat, and gas-stove-burner breasts. "The Bowlegged Bride" has chrome bumper slippers, a wire net veil, and chain earrings. Papio is the Keys' John Chamberlain, and his works are witty, crude, and very charming. Papio said about his work, "I can't explain it. I have no idea what I'm doing. I see something lying in a pile and I want to make something out of it." When he died suddenly in 1982, Key Largo, home of the movie lie and Port Bougainvillea, still had no interest in the collection, and Martello was eventually able to purchase the pieces.

The Cuban primitive Mario Sanchez was born in Key West in 1908 in what was known as Gato's Village, an area bounded by Truman Avenue and Whitehead, South, and Simonton streets. This is where the flourishing cigar industry was located—one of the larger rebuilt factories still exists today as the abandoned Navy Commissary—and the heart of the Cuban community. It is this lively and departed village that Sanchez re-creates in his meticulous, colorful carvings. What is nice about his work is that he, like a kind angel, restores lost things. The Convent of Mary Immaculate was demolished, but Sanchez re-creates it, complete with its stupendous plantings. To the sightseer at the corner of Amelia and Duval, the Cuban Club is nothing but a simulation (more shops!)—just a bit of hygienic faux, but

Sanchez paints it as it was when it was the soul of the neighborhood, beside the long-gone El Anón Ice Cream Parlor.

Sanchez first draws his scenes on grocery bags, then transfers them to wood with carbon paper. His tools are chisels, a mallet, a piece of broken glass, and a razor blade. Sometimes he uses coffee grounds, coral rock, or kitty-litter to make streets. He likes horses, parades, funerals, pregnant ladies, chickens, and clouds. In the amazing clouds of Key West he carves things too—doves, blossoms, trumpets, and even the themes of Mr. Hemingway. In one of the explanatory notes to his carvings in this carefully presented exhibit, Sanchez says, "I have featured two of his best-known works in the clouds: *For Whom the Bell Tolls* and *Death in the Afternoon.*" And there they are.

East Martello Tower, its museum, gallery, and garden, is right in front of the airport on South Roosevelt Boulevard. Open daily 9:30 to 5:30. Adults $6.

West Martello Tower

The West Tower, on Higgs Beach, between the picnic grounds and the White Street Fishing Pier, is the home of the Key West Garden Club. It is far more low-slung and battered than the East Tower because bored soldiers stationed at Fort Taylor used it for target practice, and since it was closer to town, people pilfered many of the bricks for their walls and gardens.

Within the garden center at West Martello are plant-identification books, seed-pod exhibits, and a tattered arrangement of stuffed birds. There is also a checklist of plants, 92 of which are marked in the rambling, ruined confines of the tower's grounds. Below the mounded fortification on the beachward side are topless sunbathers, and above you, according to the season, is flowering or fruiting this and that.

The West Tower is free and erratically open. Each year, in March, there is an orchid show, and on the last Sunday of April there is a large, lush, and frantic plant sale. Open Tuesday through Thursday and Saturday and Sunday, 10 A.M.–noon and 2–4 P.M.

OLD TOWN

Conch Houses

Most of the beautiful old homes and intriguing lanes and alleys of the town can be found in the blocks between Caroline and Angela (which borders the graveyard) and Duval and Francis, and many of these buildings are well documented. *The Pelican Path,* a free descriptive folder published by the Old Island Restoration Foundation, is available from the Hospitality House in Mallory Square. The route is marked with directional yellow signs and the buildings sport neatly numbered plaques. (So much of the Keys seems recently numbered. Even the birds of the air are sometimes seen bearing pancake-sized discs on their wings, numbered, by those great numbers, the field researchers, who roam armed with nets and tranquilizing darts.)

Extremely helpful is Sharon Wells's *Walking and Biking Tour to Historic Key West.* This is published by the Island City Heritage Trust and is free and widely available. Key West has three historic districts with many hundreds of historic structures. The guide has good maps and succinct histories. Old buildings in this town have had many, many lives.

"Conch" architecture is the indigenous look of Key West. It is what's here. One of the prettiest houses in town, passionately regarded as "Conch," is the violet-hued **Artist House** (a guest house) at 534 Eaton Street, which can only be described as Key West–West Indian–Colonial-Victorian in design. Conch too is the dignified rawboned **Albury House** at 730 Southard, as is the modest **Eyebrow House** at 1025 Fleming, its attic windows tucked beneath the shelter of the roof; a most efficient breeze-capturing and air-circulating architectural eccentricity and one not found elsewhere in Florida. With this exception, however, the Conch style is not one unique to the country—it is a coalescence of styles, a high density of nineteenth- and turn-of-the-century classically built wooden houses that give the town such an appealing and distinctive appearance.

The practicalities made necessary by a remote, hot, and wet location were combined with mainland fashion and local wealth.

Many of the houses have thermally efficient roofs of galvanized steel, embossed with a pattern, and virtually all have porches. In the case of the larger houses, the porches often curve around three sides of the house with the pattern being repeated on the second story. Top-hung shutters are prevalent as a blind to the sun, and ventilating scuttles (simply a hole on the roof, with a lid) are outlets for hot air. Frequently, houses large and small are built not on foundations but on piers, which may explain why Key Westers so enthusiastically undertake the task of moving them around. Piers are slabs of coral rock which elevate the house, protecting it against rot, flooding, and even hurricane winds.

Paint was not employed until the cleanup of the 1930s. Houses were left to weather and silver in the sun. Plaster was never used. Inside, the wood of preference, pitch-rich pine from Pensacola and Dade County, was used on floors, ceilings, and walls, often hand-planed and fitted without nails. Dade County pine has become extinct, Dade County being Miami now, but the wood lives on in Key West houses, beautiful wood, personalized by each home's resident termite population. Chimneys are rare, except on those Queen Anne mansions whose all-embracing style insisted upon them, but there are a number of cupolas to be seen, resembling the widow's walks of New England coastal towns. Here, however, they should be referred to as wreckers' walks, for they were not employed so much by desperate ladies awaiting the return of their men from the sea, but by anyone with an eye out for ships which would hopefully run aground on the reef, providing the household with a variety of new possessions.

Another vessel eagerly awaited by all in the 1800s was the ice boat, delivering its precious and disappearing cargo all the way from Maine ponds. Ice was also often used as ballast in ships traveling from the North. Good examples of wreckers' walks can be seen on two houses built before the 1886 fire, the Albury house at 730 Southard and the John Lowe house at 620 Southard. The **Lowe House** is built of heart of pine and Honduran mahogany with all mortise-and-tenon joints secured with wooden pegs so that the house would give in strong winds. An early historian noted that Lowe was rich because he never embarked on a "bubble enterprise." He owned a sponging fleet and enlarged his home as he grew more prosperous. Sponges

A GONE GARDEN AND THREE GROWING ONES

People used to love to drop by Peggy Mills Garden, once open to the public at 700 Simonton Street, and confer with the awesome plantings. There were real treasures here—huge earthenware jars called *tinajones* from Cuba, orchids and lilies, rare old palms. The plants grew so vigorously inside Miss Peggy's that it was said if you parked your car outside on the bougainvillea cuttings, you'd get a flat tire. Over the past years the most intensely planted acreage in Key West has had a series of owners, each adding extensive renovations, which were usually of a nonorganic nature. For example, a tennis court. The tennis court has since been felled, and Miss Peggy's place now exists as the very pricey Gardens Hotel (see page 234).

The **Botanical Gardens on Stock Island** was the pride and joy of horticultural ladies of the 1930s. An intriguing spot with a varied number of trees in a natural hammock setting, it was allowed to decline, its rare and indigenous species pushed out by Brazilian pepper and neglect. Difficult to find—it is behind the golf course, sandwiched between the Easter Seal Society, the dog pound, and the jail annex—it has been cleared and replanted, now the pride and joy of the horticultural ladies of the '90s. It boasts three Florida "Champion" trees (which means they're *big*), the Arjan almond, the Cuban lignum vitae, and the Barringtonia; and, once again, the oddities of monkey's dinner bell, egg fruit, horseradish, and soapberry trees grow here.

The **Indigenous Park** at the end of White Street opposite the pier and next to the bocce courts is only a little over three acres but seems much larger as you wander and linger among these palms and trees—the real natives here. Everything is identified but, relaxingly, not explained. There are over 125 different species of trees and shrubs. The place is not very polished—there seems to be no master gardener in residence—but for a Key West park it's nonfestival oriented and thus pleasantly parklike. There's even a little pond—a "water garden"—where you might see a visiting merganser. Behind the park is **Wildlife Rescue of the Florida Keys**, which cares for injured animals (294-1441). Hawks, herons, pelicans, a barred owl, even abandoned exotics like iguanas, hedgehogs, and snakes reside here, all with their dietary needs—mealworms, mice, fish, and salad.

Of great interest is **Nancy Forrester's Secret Garden**, on Free School Lane opposite the Heron House on Simonton Street. There are ferns, orchids, and over 150 species of palms on one acre of lofty and lovingly tended jungle. Ask to see Nancy's collection of exquisite antique botanical and zoological art prints—animals, corals, strange odd things, great fishes. She even has some of the work of Mark Catesby, who came to the Keys before Audubon to document the natural history here. The garden is open 10 A.M.–6 P.M. $6 buys you an enchanting respite from the street.

were responsible for much of the wealth and many of the fine homes of Key West, as were foundered ships, turtles, and cigars.

An ice palace, indeed, having been built in 1885 by George Curry, the president of the ice company, is the large classical home at 620 Eaton Street—a temple of columns, porticoes, and entablatures, all tropically garnished with louvered porches and Canary Island date palms.

Eaton Street presents many beauties, the lovely triplets at 401–405–409, and the equally impressive clutch at 511–517 and 523. The "tropical Greek Revival" **Donkey Milk House** at 613 is open to the public. Built in 1868, it's been meticulously restored and has hand-painted ceilings (the Italian artist gave Key West four seasons), century-old Barcelona tile, and distinctive antiques. Open 10 A.M.–5 P.M. Admission is $5. The octagonal tin-towered **Richard Peacon House** at 712 Eaton is somewhat notorious for the price it once commanded. It was originally built by a banker and grocer in the 1890s. Key West realtors went into deliriums when it was bought in the 1980s by Calvin Klein for close to a million dollars, approximately $700,000 more than everyone admitted the house was worth. Klein said it was "probably crazy" but he "wanted it badly." (Million-plus houses are now routine in Key West, particularly in Truman Annex and the Hilton's new "Sunset Island.") The

NOT ON THE PELICAN PATH

Just past Cafe Sole at 1017 Southard is a dignified, pretti-
fied-to-the-max Conch house. It was not always thus, however. Once it was quite overgrown and run-down. On April
30, 1992, police even found a man who had been dead for two
months lying on the floor there. His roommate, a 78-year-old
gentleman named Thomas Warren, thought he was just
being "stubborn" and ignored him, though occasionaly he
asked him if he wanted something to eat or drink or wanted
to go to the hospital. Annoyingly, the body didn't reply. As his
roomie moldered and melted into the linoleum, Mr. Warren
went about his business, stepping over the body, which lay
facedown between the kitchen and a bathroom. He told
detectives that he thought the fellow, an unlucky man
named Delaney, was alive because he appeared to change
positions and, even, stretch his legs.

handsome house at 724 is of Bahamian style with Victorian
influences, adorned with flourishing columnar trim and cranberry glass.

Two of the most remarked upon homes in Key West were
brought here from somewhere else. The **Bahama Houses**, one
at 730 Eaton, the other directly behind it at 408 William, were
made in the Bahamas, dismantled, brought over by ship, and
reconstructed in 1847, after the hurricane of 1846 had
destroyed much of Key West. Wood was scarce, so two brothers-
in-law, Joseph Bartlum and Richard Roberts, returned to their
home in Green Turtle Cay and sailed these structures, made
simply of random-width, hand-beveled pine boards, back. The
twin-gabled roof, with the valley in between to collect rainwater
for the cistern, and the large shuttered windows are of typical
Bahamian design. The low ceilings inside indicate the age of
the houses, for the cooling benefits of high-ceilinged rooms were
only recognized by later Key West builders. Bartlum was a
shipbuilder who built the only clipper ship ever made in Key
West, the *Stephen Mallory*. The ship was launched in 1856 and
bore a life-sized figurehead of the cherubic Mallory upon her
prow. The Roberts House on William has been very little

altered over the years. Crowded at right angles to the street, its double porches run the length of the house on two sides and are built under the roof. Both houses are rather unassuming, intriguing primarily because of the journey they once took.

Gingerbread, Courtyards, and Shotguns

Key Westers love their gingerbread. The town embraced this fanciful fashion of the mid-1800s, and people today are still gleefully remodeling by slapping up baluster patterns of pineapples, fleurs-de-lis, and urns. Most of the elaborately turned railings of Old Town were not made locally but were brought here as stock items for the building trade, although there were several local craftsmen who did scroll-cut work from flat boards. One of these was John Carroll, who set up his turning lathe near the lighthouse in the 1880s and produced brackets, cornices, and trim according to the customer's whim. Another was Francisco Camellon, a black Cuban whose lathe was turned by a blindfolded horse. His shop was on Simonton Street under a big Spanish lime tree.

There are more than 60 different baluster patterns to be found in Key West, the most popular being Grecian urns, diamonds, hearts, ship wheels, and—after the railroad reached Key West in 1912—viaduct arches. Lovely examples of scroll-

Examples of gingerbread trimming

cut ship wheels can be found at the **Cuban Consul House** on the corner of Eaton and Grinnel. The same gingerbread string-course adorns the house at 615 Fleming.

One of the most intriguing examples of personalized ginger-bread and a design that was used for professional advertising is found on the old Conch house at 1117 Duval. The saloon keeper who once lived here had this pattern of whiskey and wine bottles and the hearts and diamonds of playing cards sent from Cuba and installed as balusters.

Two of the most elaborate gingerbread dwellings in town are the gray Victorian **George Roberts House** at 313 William Street (its beauty assisted in the late spring and summer by the blooming of a towering poinciana tree) and the **Benjamin Baker House** at 615 Elizabeth Street. Baker was the owner of a lumberyard, a contractor, and an undertaker, and he built this house for his daughter in 1885 as a wedding present. His workmen, freed from the rigors of nailing together coffins, spared no flourish here—the trim is all scroll-cut. The house was so well built that when a tornado moved it seven feet off its foundation in 1972, not a single wall or window cracked.

The **William Kerr House** at 410 Simonton Street has gingerbread embellishments of a more Gothic sort. The style of this little house is unclassifiable, put together by a carpenter-architect who designed many of the striking buildings of Key West in the last 20 years of the nineteenth century. Born in Massachusetts, Kerr became one of the town's most versatile and original builders, responsible for the design of the convent as well as the Customs House and the Old Stone Church at 600 Eaton Street. The house is heavily ornamented inside, with hand-painted landscapes over the doors and indented panels in the ceilings.

A building of erratic history, so common in Key West, is the structure at 314 Simonton, the old Trev-Mor apartments. Built with bricks taken from the ruins of Fort Taylor, the first Ford dealership in Key West was located here in 1919. There were apartments upstairs, and it was here where Hemingway and his wife Pauline, fresh from Paris, stayed for several weeks as they awaited the delivery of a new car. It remained a rooming house and hotel until the 1970s when it was completely gutted by fire. The new owners kept the core empty and it is now a one-bedroom private home with a vast inner atrium. The old cistern in the middle of things is used as a swimming pool. A number of water craft continue their lives most peculiarly behind these walls. An Ecuadorian canoe is used as a planter, a glass-topped Haitian dory serves as a coffee table, and a wet bar and dumb-waiter have been created from a lifeboat off the yacht of one no less than Adolf Hitler. It's now called Casa Antigua and you can see the gardens for $2.

The old Mercedes Hospital, or Casa Gato, at 1209 Virginia Street, just around the corner from the Gulfstream Market on White, is out of the way but noteworthy. It too has a courtyard, of an initially more intended sort, and a history even more eccentric and variable.

Eduard Gato was a wealthy Cuban cigar manufacturer who had come to Key West in 1868 at the start of Cuba's Ten Years' War with Spain. The town was jammed with wealthy Cuban cigar manufacturers building factories, banks, and mansions and hiring and housing thousands of their fellow emigrés to work as strippers, trimmers, rollers, pickers, and packers. Gato built his mansion, embellished with balconies and cupolas, and enclosed a patio, in the Spanish style, but it appears a little odd because it was built out of wood, covered with clapboard, and

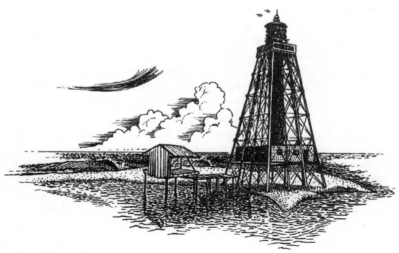

Sand Key light

decorated with a bit of gingerbread. It is a high, square building with long Gothic windows and large, dark, tall-ceilinged rooms (eight to a floor) that look out onto the somewhat stern court-yard. It was said that after Gato got his Spanish courtyard he was puzzled as to what to do with it, so he stabled his horses there for several years.

Gato and his family did not live here long. He returned to Cuba after the Spanish-American War of 1898 (the war in which Teddy Roosevelt disappointed Key Westers by having his Rough Riders sally forth from Tampa) and gave the house to the town to be used as a hospital. The hospital was named for his wife, Mercedes, but it was locally called Casa del Pobre—the house of the poor. It remained a poorhouse until the 1940s. Elizabeth Bishop, once paying a call, described a patient as possessing an "apocryphal appearance," her bright, milky blue eyes seeming "like the flames of a gas burner when they have just been turned off and are about to sink back into the black pipes." The Mercedes Hospital had a reputation of harboring gloomy ghosts, and there are still some old Cubans in town who refuse to walk on the Casa Gato side of the street.

When its days as a poorhouse had passed, it became an arena for cockfights and a storage area for newspapers collected during World War II paper-drives. It was "a monster nobody wanted" until the 1970s when it was restored as apartments.

Many cigar barons like Gato built houses for their workers, creating instant neighborhoods around their factories. (The large concrete edifice on Simonton and Virginia was built in 1916 after a fire destroyed the original wooden factory. Purchased by the Navy in the '40s for a barracks, then a commissary, it's about to begin service as county offices.) Most of the other factories are gone, but many of the little company houses remain. These narrow houses were simplicity itself, consisting of three rooms, one behind the other, the front and rear doors in alignment with the door connecting the rooms, and were called shotgun houses, perhaps because of the narrow and uninter-rupted passage the space allowed. Most were no more than 12 by 30 feet in floor area and had galvanized steel roofs and little porches. Tired of termites, many shotgun owners later replaced the wooden pillars and porches with concrete ones. Tidy, cherished examples of shotguns can be found between 822 and 834

The graveyard

Olivia, where the street parallels the graveyard, and in the 400 block of Truman.

THE GRAVEYARD

"I'd rather eat monkey manure than die in Key West," Ernest Hemingway said. He said this one summer day, sweating in the sulfurous, warm, and brownish waters of his swimming pool, years before he chose to die in Idaho. But people not as fortunate, one would assume, have died in Key West, and it is here where they remain, smack in the middle of things on the lip of Old Town. This is referred to formally as "The Cemetery," but what it is is the graveyard. It was established here in 1847, although some of the graves date before that. The original burying ground was closer to the lighthouse but was moved here when many of the graves were disinterred in a hurricane. There are still funeral marching bands in town that will play the dead home. There are approximately 70,000 inmates in this necropolis, or about three times the number of those who reside in the living city. No new plots can be purchased here.

The graveyard is hot, white, and built up, the graves all in aboveground vaults, because of both the water table and the toughness of coral rock, and it is virtually treeless, although some citizens are hard at work planting frangipani cuttings and mock oranges in available scraps of ground. "Palm Avenue," which intersects the graveyard, is now neatly lined with tiny Christmas palms. Other citizens, however, are just as determinedly cutting down large, bearded, Washingtonian palms, fearing that a high wind will bring them crashing down on what James Merrill described as "whitewashed hope chests." Neither Conchs nor Cubans care for trees as a rule, and in fact the graveyard is a fine, impressive place without them. There are flowering shrubs planted here and there and something is always in bloom. White egrets drift among the markers, giving an Egyptian effect.

This is a wonderful place to see birds, particularly at the end of the day. This is the nighthawk's territory, for instance. The large, mottled bird is known in Key West as the mosquito hawk, although it is not a hawk at all but belongs to the voracious insect eaters known as goatsuckers. A flying mouth, it darts and scoops at twilight here, saying *piskkk*.

A sausage tree, notorious for its preference to be pollinated by bats, stands at one of the entrances on Angela Street opposite the remains of the "bottle wall," a Key West landmark demolished by its creator one dark afternoon, to the horror of its fans. Look upon the tree and be grateful that once again it appears to be fruitless. If R. C. Perky had been successful in raising bats on Sugarloaf, Key West would have been up to its rooftops in sausage trees with their weird seed pods swinging on long stems.

The 15-acre graveyard is crisscrossed with paths that bear concrete road markers. For example, the brick Otto plot which contains the graves of three Yorkshire terriers—Sunny, Little Boy, and Little Derry Otto—as well as the one of a pet deer, Elfina, is located at the intersection of Second and Laurel. (Sunny might have been something of a pest; his inscription reads HIS BEAUTIFUL LITTLE SPIRIT WAS A CHALLENGE TO LOVE.) A varnished marker on the crypt of B. P. Roberts which complains I TOLD YOU I WAS SICK is at the end of Seventh Street just before the fenced Jewish plot. There are angels small and large, including the beautiful Gladys, swans and lambs, open books, and amputated tree trunks. There is a full-sized cement sculpture of a man, done by his friend, utilizing the boots of the deceased. His name is Earle Saunders Johnson and he is smiling. THE BUCK STOPS HERE one gravestone says. HERE LIES OUR HEART says another. A DEVOTED FAN OF SINGER JULIO IGLESIAS says a third. People *think* there's a plaque that says AT LEAST I KNOW WHERE HE'S SLEEPING TONIGHT, but there isn't, though there is the famous "bound woman" near the fence at the intersection of Angela and Grinnel. She's no angel certainly, and her posture seems to suggest something other than grief, but Archibald John Sheldon Yates really really wanted her on his grave, and there she is. Wander and read epitaphs of loss: WE MISS YOU AT HOME; longing and regret: YESTERDAY IS GONE AND TOMORROW SHALL NEVER BE MINE. Even gratitude: GOD WAS GOOD TO ME. There are pictures of some of the dead in small plastic frames. There are benches beside some of the graves and wrought-iron fences around others. There is a pretty plot which contains the graves of the victims of the *Maine* with a handsome statue of a sailor holding an oar. And there is a monument to *Los Martires,* Cubans who died during the Spanish-American War.

An infamous grave that is not marked is the one of Elena Hoyos Mesa, a Cuban girl who died of tuberculosis in the 1930s but who even more unfortunately was the object of affection of an elderly and lunatic X-ray technician named Carl von Cosel.

The dead are always with us, some more than others.

The graveyard's gates are open from sunrise to sunset. Walking tours of one and a half hours are given for $10, and leave from the Margaret Street entrance. There's even a breakfast tour on Memorial Day. Have a pastry and contemplate the ever-approaching nothing. Contact Sharon Wells, a knowledgeable historian and historical preservationist, for reservations and times. She also conducts architectural strolls through town (294-8380).

WHERE TO STAY

There are many quaint, elegant, and/or decadent places to stay in Key West. There are guest houses and motels (chain and

COUNT VON COSEL

The count could merit a tour of his own. He was everywhere—the Marine Hospital at Truman Annex, Rest Beach (now so creatively landscaped), the Lopez Funeral House, Lime Tree Village, and, of course, the graveyard. The count was a proper little man with a goatee and a walking stick who always appeared natty and self-assured. Before he met Elena he was obsessed with airplanes and was building an experimental craft that would land on either water or land. The plane had huge wheels made of wooden slats which were covered with paper.

Elena was a very pretty girl who died in 1930 at the age of 22 at her home on Watson Street after Von Cosel's bizarre, whirring "inductor box" and "shocking coils" had failed to arrest her TB at the Marine Hospital. Von Cosel was mad for Elena. He bought her little treats and trinkets, even the bed she was to die in. He paid for the funeral, the casket, and the tomb, and after her death he was seen visiting her elaborate mausoleum more than frequently. He played records and sometimes ate breakfast there. He described it in his memoirs as being more of a "pleasant summer residence than a burial place." Nonetheless, after two years of this he decided to "re-bed" her, and with the approval of the state of Florida and Elena's family, he disinterred Elena and fixed her up somewhat in the funeral parlor. ("Decay," he wrote, again in his memoirs, "had set in in a most disheartening manner.") He placed her in a nicer casket. He then decided he didn't like her "little house" in the graveyard and moved her, in his wacky airplane which he towed behind a truck down White Street, to Rest Beach, where he refurbished a shack that had once been part of the old cattle-butchering pens.

He lived with, loved, and experimented on Elena there for several happy years, having a particularly nice time at Christmas, decorating the Christmas tree with silver tinsel, cotton snow, and small wax candles instead of electric bulbs. He presented her with little gifts such as picture books, chocolates, and face powder. The count bought throughout the years a great deal of soap and eau de cologne. Even Jimmy Weekly, a city commissioner in the '90s, remembers his mother reflecting on how much soap Count von Cosel bought at their family's grocery store, Fausto's. WPA workers were increasingly on the beach, however, raking up the seaweed and building cabanas, so the count packed Elena in his airplane and towed her off to new accommodations on Flagler.

His days with his bride were numbered, though. Her tomb was vandalized and it was discovered that Elena had not been there for some time. The count admitted, somewhat proudly, that she was safe with him, and Elena was carted off once more, rather unceremoniously this time, in a wicker basket by the morticians and the sheriff's department. Von Cosel was jailed, but no one in Key West seemed to find the story particularly repellent. He had the town's sympathy, in fact, with the ladies in particular finding his obsession sort of romantic.

There was a viewing of Elena at the funeral home seven years after she died. She wore a kimono and a pleasant smile. She sported all her own hair. Held together with wire and waxy compounds, the corpse had glass eyes, fabricated breasts, and, according to a doctor who testified at the count's trial, "a tube in the vaginal area wide enough to permit intercourse." Almost 7,000 people came out to see her, and many felt she should be on permanent display, something to kick off the new tourist industry. Elena, however, was dismantled, placed in a smallish container, and buried again, though not in her tomb. No one knows where she actually is buried.

Von Cosel was generously ruled sane by a court-appointed Key West lunacy board and was never found guilty of anything. He was bailed out of jail by friends and spent some time at the Cactus Terrace Motel, now known as Key Lime Village, before returning to his house on Flagler, where for a few months he entertained visitors who came by to take pictures of him and his airplane and wheedle him out of souvenir nails and screws from his laboratory. He charged 25¢ to talk to them. He tired of tourism eventually and left Key West in the spring of 1940 for Zephyrhills, Florida, towing his airplane behind him. Elena's empty mausoleum blew up several hours after his departure, destroyed by two sticks of dynamite. One can only assume that the creative count was responsible.

The marker from Elena's tomb can be seen at the always fascinating **East Martello Museum**.

unchain) and condominiums, as well as suites in time-share resorts that can be rented by the day or week. The Key West Visitor's Bureau puts out an accommodation directory with rates and a helpful visitor "type" category. You can get one by writing to Box 1147, Key West, FL 33041 or calling 294-2587.

If you're planning a longer stay you may be interested in renting a home by the month or for the season. Most of the real estate agencies have furnished houses for rent. **Key West Realty** (294-3064) specializes in "historic hideaways" in Old Town on the quieter (more or less) streets. Also specializing in vacation rentals is **Property Management of Key West** (296-7744). They have about 40 houses in and out of Old Town that they'll rent daily, weekly, or monthly. They provide maid service, have their own maintenance department, and will try to match your vacation needs, even your desires, with present availability—just like a dating service.

Remember, prices here are probably already history. Undoubtedly they have risen. And will rise. In season, nonrefundable deposits and two- or three-day minimum stays are often required.

Chains

The chains are on North Roosevelt Boulevard as you come into town. The prospect—a jumble of the familiar, plus a highly harrowing four-lane highway teeming with illogical and neurotic traffic—is not pleasing. It's awful. There is the water, but it looks so *sad*. Beware of ads promising Gulf views in this area. It's not that they're lying exactly, it's merely that you might be disappointed. Here are **Holiday Inn**, **Howard Johnson**, **Quality Inn**, **TraveLodge**, and **Days Inn**. Prices are usual for chains in resort areas—$140–$200 a night, $75–$125 off season.

On South Roosevelt Boulevard (A1A) the expected appears much nicer. Set back from the ocean, by the airport, in pleasantly landscaped grounds are the **Best Western** (296-3500), $150–$185 a night, and the **Key Wester** (296-5671). The Key Wester, with its spacious grounds, tennis court, and big pool, is soon to be run as a time-share resort.

South Street–Simonton Street Beach Area

There are a number of reasonable motels here, all within walking distance of town, including the classic, old-timer **Santa Maria** (296-5678), now dwarfed by the pink four-story **Reach**. The Santa Maria has nice rooms overlooking a huge pool with a tiled Santa Maria at the bottom of it. The Queen's Table Restaurant attracts many with its cozy dignity, particularly later in the evening when a jazz quartet sometimes plays. Rates are around $145, out of season $75. There are the swimming-pool-in-the-middle-of-the-parking-lot variety like the **Blue Marlin** (294-2585), and the swimming-pool-on-the-street variety such as **Southernmost** (296-6577) and the **Spanish Gardens** (294-1051). Rooms here run $110–$150 a night for a double in season, slightly more for an efficiency, and drop $20 in price from June until December. **Atlantic Shores** (296-2491) is a big place, no beauty on the street side but with a handsome swimming pool decked out on the ocean and a 150-foot pier. Rooms around $125, $50 in summer. Sunday night there's a rambunctious "tea dance" at their bar, **Club Atlantic**. (A tea dance in Key West is bare-chested bump-and-grind boogie.) The **One Saloon** at 524 Duval gets right down to it and just has Sleazy Sundays, in their desire to make Sunday night the naughtiest night of the week. The more subdued and better-designed **South Beach Motel** (296-5611) is next door, with a huge pool, pier, and balconied rooms. Rates are $160–$197, Christmas through April; in summer, $100–$140. **La Mer** (at the same number) is a turn-of-the-century home renovated as a small hotel with 11 rooms. Once somewhat dreary, it has been recently redone and it sparkles—the only bed-and-breakfast on the ocean. It has a swell little beach, and some of the rooms have efficiencies. It's gotten a reputation as a honeymoon destination, and children under 12 are not permitted. Around $150 in summer; $250 in season. Next door is the **Dewey House**, part of the same complex, with eight rooms. There's a continental breakfast, tea, and the use of the big pool at South Beach. This is a nice area of town—jammed, but somewhat less jammed.

Posher and pricier is the **Coconut Beach Resort**, run as

a time-share at 1500 Alberta Street near the Casa Marina (294-0057). Very pretty, sophisticated rooms on a hidden beach. All in a three-story complex. All are similarly furnished, but the top floor is the best. All the suites have ocean views and complete kitchens. A one-bedroom suite is $310 in season, a two-bedroom $440. Smaller studios are $185–$240. A pretty free-form pool and Louie's are only a few steps away. There are minimum stays during the holidays, and prices go up for Christmas, New Year's, and, as in the case of most hotels and motels on the island, Fantasy Fest.

FANTASY FEST

Takes place the last week of October and has developed a quite indescribable life of its own. Invented 15 years ago to celebrate the end of hot and sulky September, arguably the most tiresome month in the Keys, this festival has many events connected with it, so many in fact that it now takes place over ten days in October, kicked off by the more down-home Bahama Village Goombay Festival. Then there's a Pretenders in Paradise costume party—tons of feathers, foil, and Mylar, much smoke and many mirrors; a Sloppy's Toga Party; a Masquerade March that begins at the Cemetery; and a culminating large parade up Duval Street. This parade doesn't necessarily get better as the years go by. Sometimes it's outrageous, sometimes raunchy, sometimes just corny. Each year there are arguments about how "nice" Fantasy Fest should be. Nobody wants it to be too nice, of course. "But surely," a festival coordinator said, "people can have a great time without dressing up as a sex organ."

  In 1997 some outrageously garbed revelers (they looked suspiciously as if they'd been imported from Miami) were milling around the streets eight months *before* Fantasy Fest. It was in fact Fat Tuesday, the day before Ash Wednesday and the beginning of Lent. Sponsored by (as you might suspect) a number of bars, including the town's little newcomer the Hard Rock Cafe, the barkeeps hope to bring Mardi Gras to Key West and make it large and official.

Deluxe

Henry Flagler planned a chain of luxury resort hotels, which he referred to as "Halls of Joy," along his Florida train route. The **Casa Marina**, with its Spanish Renaissance design, tiled roof, arched windows, colonnades, and loggias, in a beautiful garden setting at the end of the road on the Atlantic, was to be the ultimate. The Casa opened New Year's Eve 1922, eight years after Flagler's death. It was a popular spot for the rich and famous until 1943, when the government leased it for Navy housing during the war. (Thousands of mines were placed by the military in the Florida Straits during the war, 15 miles offshore, to blow up German submarines—*Unterseeboots*. No German subs hit the mines, although three wayward Allied ships and an American destroyer did.) It returned to hotel status in 1945 but was taken over by the Army in 1962 during the Cuban missile crisis. Sentries replaced doormen, missile battalion troops were quartered in the rooms, and the beach was strung with barbed wire. After the Army left, it was declared out of commission as a hotel. Indeed, it was described as a "termite-ridden firetrap." For the next ten years only the dance patio and the Birdcage lounge remained open, and it was messy and popular until 1978, when the Marriott chain took it over, renovating it completely, tearing down the Birdcage and adding a new, ugly four-story wing. The elegance is all beach-side. They don't do pretty for the street. The old building is grand, its walls "battered in" for hurricane proofing, receding in thickness from 22 inches at the foundation to 12 inches at the roof. The black cypress lobby is impressive but lacks grand furnishing. The grounds are immaculate. The Casa has a 1,100-foot beach, tennis courts, and several bars and restaurants, including **Flagler's**. Thirty-dollar lamb chops here in a reserved, even solemn, setting. It seems very far from town. And it is. In fact, going downtown from the Casa feels like a foray into exotic, uncontrolled, and unsecured territory. The Casa is great-looking but can't quite shake—despite her pig roasts and steel-drum music—her reputation as being a bit . . . boring. Locals can buy beach and tennis privileges here for around $70 a month. There are many people here, the smell of tanning oil intense. The fine old lobby is furnished with small pallid wicker chairs and does not project the glamour of yesteryear. Ocean-view rooms range $206–$349, oceanview suites $288–$419; without the glimpse, $170–$309 and $231–$349. Actually, if your time and space requirements are right, you can spend up to $795 a night here. There are also "Paradise" packages and "Escape to Romance" packages which involve breakfast, champagne, and a sunset sail. Reynolds Street on the Atlantic. Toll-free: 800-228-9290, or direct: 296-3535.

The Reach (Simonton Street on the ocean, 296-5000). The Reach is somewhat brutish in design, even though it's pink. One hoped that this would be the south end of town's answer to the Pier House, but it has little of the Pier House's gracious ease. Beautifully situated on the water with a great beach, pool, and pier, it has developed a somewhat crabbed and suspicious attitude toward its guests. Taken over in 1994 by Marriott, the hotel's new management fired the pastry chef (a genius!), banalized the restaurants, tore out much of the *troppo* plantings to establish grass, and hired men in black pants, white shirts, and walkie-talkies to monitor the most cramped, difficult to negotiate parking garage in town. Every effort was made here to cram as many units as possible on the land available. The little beach is wall-to-wall chaise lounges. Jet skis, waiting to be fired up, have their own area at one end. Big Marriott-style breakfast buffet. A one-bedroom suite on the ocean is $375 in winter, $400 Christmastime, $255 otherwise. Nonocean-view $335, $350, $220. There are 149 rooms here, half of which have a glimpse of the water, which makes a big difference. All the rooms seem small.

The **Pier House** (1 Duval Street, 294-9541) is a homegrown Key West classy classic. It began it all. It was *the* place to stay in Mile Zero. The hotel is handsomely laid out—a combination of five separate structures. The rooms are tasteful, the grounds palmy. Low-key, efficient, friendly service. The beach building was recently renovated—well, it was demolished, actually—and a glorious new structure erected in its place called the **Beach Building** with 35 guest rooms and nine large, beautifully appointed suites. At the **Caribbean Spa** annex, there's

an awesome health club. The standard room here in season is
$265. A nicer room in the courtyard by the pool is $325, and one
overlooking the harbor is $385. From April 15 to December 20
these are $150, $195, and $235 respectively. Suites run from
$450 to $750 in season.

Ocean Key House (Zero Duval Street, 296-7701). The Ocean
Key House, when built, was notorious for counting Bay-bottom
acreage in their density computations. Out of scale with an
enormous parking garage at its base, which one must pass
through to attain either one's room or the pool, the exterior is
heavy-handed. But the rooms are luxuriously furnished, decorated in soft tropical shades, with large balconies and kitchens.
The showers are motel basic; you're supposed to luxuriate in
the immoderate Jacuzzi in the bedroom. Suites overlook the
street, the Gulf, and the Mallory Square parking lot. You may
come back from breakfast, open the door, and have the sensation of a cruise ship having entered your living room. Very comfortable one-bedroom suites run from $310 to $450 in season,
$60 to $100 less April to December. Two-bedroom suites,
$385–$450.

Hyatt Key West (601 Front Street, 296-9900). They call it a
boutique resort as it has only 120 rooms. The beach could be the
world's smallest, but the rooms with balconies are sited well
for sunset-watching. The lowest rate in season is $200 a night.
A suite is $450. If Fate brings you to the Rock in August, say, a
suite is yours for $250.

The **Hilton** (245 Front Street, 294-4000). Opened in 1995 (see
pages 144, 161). Immense. Dreariest lobby in the state of
Florida—you feel you're entering a bank where they don't
keep money. Complex but charmless layout with wide brick
pavilions that will soon link up with Mallory Square. Seven
thousand square feet of "flexible meeting and occasion space."
Suites and rooms. A one-bedroom suite runs $225–$475,
depending on the time of year.

The Marquessa Hotel (600 Fleming Street, 292-1919). This
old boardinghouse was refurbished in 1988 and it's charming.

In 1995 they acquired two adjacent buildings, also built in the late 1800s, and the complex now sports 27 lovely big high-ceilinged rooms with generous baths. One suite has a private balcony overlooking the street, and many of the rooms have pretty window seats that are right out of a Jesse Wilcox Smith painting. Rooms and suites $215–$325, $135–$225 in summer.

The Gardens Hotel (526 Angela Street, corner of Simonton, 294-2661). Pretty, gleaming, and serene but a far cry from the jumble of a jungle it once was when it was the private home of Miss Peggy (see page 216). A luxurious small hotel now, it's one of the prettiest, priciest retreats in Key West. Very well laid out, curvy pool, shining solarium, old brick walkways. The rooms have big beds and elaborate bathrooms, a separate little building, the Eyebrow Cottage, is particularly charming. The grounds are beautifully lit at night. Prices range from $200 to $625.

Moderates

Near the Casa and not far from the beach is the secluded **El Patio Motel** (800 Washington Street, 296-6531). This is a dis-covery—quiet, clean, and pleasant, with a garden patio, a little pool, and a terrific rooftop sundeck where you can sail your gaze over the tops of palms to the ocean. The rooms are large with little view of their own but with classic Cuban-tile floors. This is the best of the little motels in the area. Rooms are $94 in sea-son, $58 otherwise. Rooms with two double beds are $108 down to $68. You can get two rooms with a refrigerator for $122, $78 from mid-April to Christmas day.

The **Sea Shell Motel** at 718 South Street is a lighthearted, unexacting youth hostel which takes no credit cards and is $38 a night. It has a dormitory where one can sleep for $18. During Spring Break, however, the rooms are $100 a night because "the kids trash the rooms" (296-5719).

Deja Vu (611 Truman Avenue, 292-9339). You may not remem-ber you've been here before, but then again, maybe you will.

This is a resort for "naturalists," meaning clothing is optional. Clean, simple rooms, lots of greenery, nice pool and spa. Pretty little touches like birds painted on the stucco of the old motel walls. Rooms range $85–$165 January through April, $60–$130 summer and fall.

The Blue Lagoon Motel (3101 North Roosevelt, 296-1043). Actually, it's hard to know if this is moderate or not. The rates change constantly for the increasing number of festivals in town. Nonetheless, sometimes the sign goes up $49 ALL ROOMS. Though not often. An anomaly in many ways, Blue Lagoon is five well laid out coral rock buildings on filled in bay bottom right beside Roosevelt Boulevard. Jet skis come with the rooms. There are parrots. There are nippy geese. There are garish lights bathing the jet skis at night in a demented light. There are palm trees. Call for rates. In season a waterfront room is usually $140.

Key Lime Village (727 Truman Avenue, 294-6222). If you like old motor courts, *odd* old motor courts, these little pine-walled cottages are for you. Built in the 1930s and '40s by a circus juggler, the motel's most famous resident might have been Count von Cosel (see pages 226–27), who stayed here for some weeks after being bailed out of jail by the juggler himself. There is a cloudy pool and no lime trees. Guests are urged to "make friends" or stay in their little homes and enjoy their televisions and microwaves, or fool around with their cars parked at their doorstep. No place else like this in town. Rates are around $60 in summer, $110 in season.

Caribbean House (226 Petronia Street, Bahama Village, 296-1600). Tiny, colorful air-conditioned rooms. Free breakfast on the porch. $69 in winter, $49 in summer.

Downtown

La Concha (430 Duval, 296-2991). You can't be closer to the heart of things than this. Pleasant rooms done in a '20s *troppo* style, a great bar at The Top from which you can see Key West in all its improbable selfness, even a pool on one level. A room with a queen-sized bed is $160–$300 December through April. Drops $50 summer and fall. A suite is $200–$500. In March, the dreaded "Breaker" month, you might want a room *away* from the street.

The Milton Curry Mansion (511 Caroline Street, 294-5349). You can stay in the Mansion, with its Tiffany glass and lovely paneling and verandas, and not have to pay to see the place like an ordinary tourist, or you can stay in the new, more ordinary rooms surrounding the small pool in back. There's also the James House across the street. No antiques but somewhat more serene. The kitchen in the Mansion is the revered site of the first Key lime pie (an Aunt Sally did it). There's free breakfast and beach club privileges at both the Pier House and the Casa Marina. Rates in season $200–$275. Otherwise $160–$225. The phone is always ringing here, and the desk can sometimes be flustered.

Guest Houses

Guest houses abound in Key West, and some of them are very pretty, private, and friendly places, with lovely gardens and dramatic pools. (The 1990s brought an explosion of them on Truman Avenue. Every old manse on the block became one. They almost ran out of names.) Many do not accept children 16 and under, because of the cozily affectionate milieu or because patrons want to enjoy their complimentary quiche breakfasts in peace.

Some guest houses are not all that delightful, as you might imagine but hopefully not experience. Some are tiny and grumpy (the boyfriend has illusions of grandeur) or tiny and hysterical (the boyfriend has had a bad day). Some are stuffy, some too dependent on the air-conditioner. Some may promise a private, cute little upstairs porch, but too late you see that it overlooks a parking lot or a definitely unhistoric roof. The "garden" is sometimes a few deckboards around a jacketed Jacuzzi. Others could be nice if only the enthusiastic new, well-heeled owners hadn't been so "well traveled" or bought so many "curiosities" or had so much "fun" decorating eclectically. Guest houses are idiosyncratic, that's what their fans like about them. Call the **Innkeepers Association of Key West** (800-492-1911) for assistance in selection and reservations.

A pleasant place that will take families is The **Island City House** (411 William Street, 294-5702). Smack in the middle of the historic district with all its regal houses, Island City was built in the 1880s and served as a guest house as early as 1912. Another building in this small compound is the **Arch House**, which faces Eaton. Restored and renovated down to its last nail, each unit is an apartment with full kitchen. The rooms are rather dark but high-ceilinged and nicely furnished. Bromeliads bloom profusely over an old cistern. Pleasant pool, rampant garden, breakfast bar. One-bedroom suites are $165–$200. Two bedrooms $100 more. (The Island City House should not be confused with **Island House**, a men-only cruise complex on the corner of Fleming and White [294-6284] that has rooms, a pool, and a complete gym.)

Courtney's Place (between Simonton and Elizabeth on Whitmarsh Lane, 294-3480) is child-friendly. (Cat-friendly, too. At last count there were 15 individually named dishes by the little pool.) Six tiny houses have been compactly renovated here. The effect is like being in a well-designed playhouse complete with iron and coffeepot. In the heart of residential Old Town with its pretty houses and lanes. A few private rooms cost $100 or so in season. The cottages run $160–$180.

Center Court (916 Center Street, between Simonton and Duval, 296-9292). A cool, fresh, delightful minicompound with a pool, pond, and treetop sundeck. Although it shares the neighborhood with the Moped Hospital and a Laundromat, it remains hidden and elegant. Rates run $128–$148 in season. Or rent by the week. A two-story "family house" with kitchen is $1,750.

The Artist House (534 Eaton Street, 296-3977). Built in 1890, each room in this sweet old house is uniquely decorated. The large room in front has a pretty winding staircase which leads to a sleeping loft in the tower. The side rooms have claw-foot bathtubs on an enclosed porch. In one of the suites you can even bubble bathe under a chandelier. The garden is tiny and unmysterious, although it does have a lion's head sluicing water into a Jacuzzi and an obscure stone saint by the fishpond. The Artist House is formal, filled with seventeenth-century antiques, and can be noisy, particularly the rooms on the street. There is no pool.

Heron House (512 Simonton, 294-9227). One of the prettiest and best-located guest houses in Key West. Seventeen high-ceilinged, beautifully furnished rooms are available. Great attention to detail and design. Handsome yet lightly tropical. A suite for $249 overlooks an orchid garden. There are lovely touches here, from the graceful tile heron at the bottom of the pool to the stained glass windows and warm woods and tiles in the rooms. Private sunning decks, great breakfasts, lush tropical landscaping throughout. Very pleasant staff. A lot of style here. Rooms $149–$229 in winter, $99–$179 otherwise.

Merlinn (811 Simonton Street, 296-3336). The rooms here are a bit peculiar, narrow and very high, rather monkish in aspect. There are many levels to everything, as though the establishment was built on the side of a mountain. Ramps, steps, more ramps, all extremely skiddy in the rain. Good for wheelchairs, perhaps. The two-bedroom "tea house" here is wheelchair accessible. Merlinn looks a little plucked recently, as though some serious debosking had taken place. The high-ceilinged pine kitchen produces delicious breakfast. There's also an aviary, a library, and complimentary rum punch as evening falls. Rooms are $95–$105 December through April. Larger rooms with kitchens are $140. The singular "treehouse," with its private sundeck, is $160.

Key West Bed-and-Breakfast (415 William Street, 296-7274) is in a fine, three-story, hundred-year-old house just a few blocks away from the town's beloved Bight on one of the handsomest blocks in Key West. Only eight rooms; some share a bath. Everything is immaculate, fresh, and engaging. Nothing fussy here; beautiful old walls, shining floors, a porch of a very adventuresome purple. Big breakfasts, little garden, Jacuzzi. Very cool. Rooms are $80–$250 in season, $40–$150 otherwise.

The Eden House (1015 Fleming Street, 296-6868) has been around since 1924 when it operated as the Gibson Hotel. This is some ways from downtown, but in a great walking and biking neighborhood. A simple, tropical inn with fans and iron beds, it's been recently modernized with phones, air conditioners, and private baths. Just as the sprucing up was completed, Hollywood arrived and wanted to refunk the place for the movie *CrissCross*. Many coats of paint were employed to make the place look unpainted, and its engaging, slightly seedy quality was reinstated. After the filming it was all turned around again. A great old place. It seems to have interesting tenants, feeling rather like the Gramercy Park of Key West guest houses. A Conch house next door has been converted into fancier suites ($135–$250), but you can still get the old rooms with the big porches overlooking Fleming Street for $80 ($55 in summer). Other rooms with a bath down the hall are about the same. Two rooms with a shared bath run $95 each. Rockers on the porch; pool; little restaurant (**Martin's**) to the rear. Martin's serves serious German food 6–11 Tuesday through Sunday. Veal, veal, veal—enough to make a cow never want to have her calf. It may seem odd to chow down potato soup and Wiener schnitzel in the tropics, but the chef here enjoys preparing it for you. He wants to, and he does.

Simonton Court (320 Simonton Street, 294-6386). An exceptionally nice compound of little cigar-makers' cottages, an inn of rooms in an 1880 wooden cigar factory, and a Victorian manse. Four hidden and dramatic pools, one set within the crumbling brick foundation of an old house. Charmingly laid out on two acres. Quiet. The cottages have names like Iris and Heliconia. Even the rooms have soothing names: Anthurium, Periwinkles. Rooms run from $210 down to $110, according to season. All have kitchenettes. The cottages are terrific. Based on a four-person occupancy, they range from around $300 a night down to $180. Rooms in the manse (Tulip, Camelia), $175–$250 in winter down to $125–$160. Many have private decks or porches. A lovely retreat. Adults only.

The Cypress House (601 Caroline Street, 294-6939). A clean-lined inn, airy and fragrant, with handsome porches. Some of the rooms share a bath. Others have large bathrooms with glass-brick showers. There's a pool, breakfast, and a complimentary wine bar. There are only a few rooms, and prices range from $110 to $200. A two-bedroom suite is $230.

Southernmost Point Guest House (1327 Duval, 294-1715). A cigar-maker's mansion, this old Victorian is delightful. Wide porches with swings, a green garden with a resident rabbit, and a glimpse of the Atlantic. Only five rooms. Two have full kitchens, and there's a master suite which inexplicably has a bookcase of empty liquor bottles. Friendly owners, a great location. Smaller rooms are $80–$135 in season. The suite is $150. May 1 into December, everything is $50 less.

La-Te-Da (1125 Duval, 296-6706). Sixteen simple *troppo* rooms, upstairs and down, overlooking the pool and dining patio. Some rooms have Jacuzzis, all have private baths. You're close to all the lively campy entertainment that goes on here in the Treetop Bar. Divas galore. Rates are $120–$155. Lower in summer, higher for Key West's increasing number of special events.

Night-blooming cirrus at 413 William Street

Of the gay guest houses—**Big Ruby's** on Applerouth Lane has the distinction of being the oldest in the country—the **Brass Key** at 412 Francis (296-4719) is newly elegant, mature you might say, while the all-male **Lighthouse Court** at 902 Whitehead is edgier and younger—New York–style, so described. The all-male **Oasis** is on Fleming. **Colours** (410 Fleming, 294-6977) is in a lustrously restored Victorian mansion, and **Coconut Grove** at 817 Fleming (296-5107) is a sprawling, breezy white gingerbread inn with lots of balconies and porches. Rates here run between $90 and $220, in summer $60–$120. "Socializing is a requisite," and around the pools and sun-traps, "clothing optional."

WHERE TO EAT

Breakfast

Breakfast is extremely important to some people who firmly believe that a magical amount of daylong energy and luck is inherent in an eggy morning plate. These are the same people who need to be apprised practically at sunup of world news—the bombings and threats, the kidnappings and disasters, the shocking and the pathetic—and read the newspaper while they eat. An odd marriage, but one indulged in by many. There are others who desire coffee only, perhaps a bun. Still others who prefer brunch: eggs Benedict, corned beef hash, steak—practically anything, really, as long as it can be accompanied by a Bloody Mary.

Hemingway, before going fishing, would ingest simply a piece of Cuban bread, a glass of Vichy, and a glass of milk. But alas, Mrs. Rhoda's electric kitchen, where he indulged, is gone. (The shacky stylish building at 830 Fleming has gone through a number of enterprises, including, most recently, a gay bookstore called Flaming Maggie's. Oh, Papa . . .) Also gone is Shorty's on Duval, famous for their biscuits and strange French toast since 1942. Shorty's had the thinnest, palest waitresses in the Keys, and the day the joint closed was the day Truman Annex developer Pritam Singh announced that Ritz-Carlton would build a hotel on "Sunset Island." Everyone felt this said it all—the Rock was ruined. Which may be the case. The Ritz never materialized, but 110 very expensive houses did. Even Shorty Cassandras probably never envisioned the day when the Hard Rock Cafe, followed by the clonish Planet Hollywood, would tart up these strange shores.

For those who believe in breakfast, here are some possibilities:

Dennis Pharmacy (Simonton and South streets). Everyone who stays in the beach motels ends up here. Despite this, it's very Conchy. Ladies in housedresses talk about their aches and pains. Plainclothesmen can be overheard discussing cases. The intriguing thing about the Pharmacy is that although the waitress never acknowledges your order, you end up being served anyway. Great old-fashioned drugstore dining—wonderful con leche and Cuban bread beneath the antique Coppertone sign showing the little girl and her dog.

South Beach (1405 Duval, opposite the Southernmost House, 294-2727). A shambly place directly on the ocean. It's fun to start your day right on the beach, although the beach patrons at certain times can be pretty low-crust. The fruit plate's healthy but pricey. They make up for this by giving you three times more than you could possibly eat. Open until 10 P.M. with an extensive seafood and raw-bar menu. Full bar.

Little John's Beachside Restaurant (at Higgs Beach, 296-4030). This place has a perennial HELP WANTED sign on the door, and your expectation that it will be open may not always be fulfilled. Bring something to read in any case, as service might take a while. If you're not engrossed by reading, your eye might wander to the outdoor showers a distance away where the beach people are making their morning ablutions. Because it is a county beach, you may observe some peculiar maintenance work being done by county employees, such as using a leaf blower to push around the sand. Nevertheless, it's a lot more fun than having brunch at the Casa. A nice touch is linen tablecloths and napkins. They open around 8 and continue until 10. There's a full bar, the key to the restroom is on a slotted spoon as long as your arm, and the sign advertising the spaghetti and meatball special is a collector's item.

Camille's (703 Duval). Going strong. Classical music, home-made muffins, powerful espresso, and con leche. Built break-fasts (some so complicated you feel you need directions to eat them), fresh and imaginative specials. Locals love this cozy, crowded spot. Popular Sunday brunch 8–3. Open for dinner, too, Tuesday through Saturday.

Croissants de France (813 Duval). The Breton owner has expanded this tiny pastry shop where you once had to sit on the curb to eat your croissant into a pocket-sized café where you can now wait in line for a table. Somewhat elevated from the street, with a European clientele. People used to exclaim over the extensive menu here in many languages, but the word is now . . . disappointing. Worse yet, the presentation is unappe-tizing and the croissants gummy.

Blue Heaven (corner of Thomas and Petronia). A wonderful place with bright individually painted tables in a dirt yard. Everyone's favorite place, except for those who have a phobia about chickens. Roosters and hens and their little chirrupping families roam freely here, giving the place its inimitable char-acter. Wonderful pancakes, breakfast tortillas, homemade breads, towering fruit plates, shrimp, grits, and shakes. Mis-matched pretty plates, peculiarly messaged coffee cups, long lines, for everyone wants to get into Heaven. It's also open for dinner 6–10. Nice fish dishes, some vegetarian plates, even chicken (which seems a little rude). Wine and beer. Next door on Petronia is a bright, new bakery, the **Blue Heaven Bake Shop** (296-0867), practically the only one in town. They have truly delicious rolls and breads, pies and tarts, little quiches. Key lime pie is $5 a slice here, the perfect pick-me-up after a day at the beach; $18 for a whole pie. You can get your special-order birthday cake here, too.

Lunch

Lunch can be an occasion, a necessity, or just a habit. If you want to watch the street you can sit more or less *in* the street at **Mangoes** (700 Duval, see page 250). Good food, but occasional large parked delivery trucks with their motors running can make conversation difficult. Where are the drivers? Perhaps at the next table, enjoying their shrimp Caesar. Good Cuban sandwiches can be had at **5 Brothers Grocery** (corner Southard and Grinnel) or at **Sandy's** in the **M&M Laundry** walk-up at 1026 White. Best place to go in the Mallory Square area is **Rooftop Cafe** at 310 Front Street, where you can dine in the treetops. Opens at 9 in the morning and moves right past midnight. Thai cuisine is available, sensibly enough, at **Thai Cuisine** at 513 Greene Street, near the Old City Hall. Eighty-seven selections. Cold beer. Excellent. Take-out and free delivery (294-9424). Good burgers and wonderful Apalachicola oysters can be had at **Pepe's Cafe** (806 Caroline), a place of varnished walls, booths, and tiller-topped tables. An awesome ceiling fan rotates slowly, slowly overhead. There's a nice patio here with bougainvillea vines thick as trees. It's popular for dinner, too, though the wait is often endless, the rule appearing to be that *just* as you get seated, the place clears out. And the bill always comes to more than you had guessed. Pepe's is a place where tourists go happily, having been told it's not a place where tourists go. The **Half-Shell Raw Bar** across the way in Land's End Village rides rather overconfidently on its popularity. You are one of many, many served here. On windy days there is no outside seating, as the Bight would be quickly paved in flying plastic. Buy a T-shirt and enjoy the conch, which is good in all its guises. The **Margaritaville Cafe** at 500 Duval is where to go for a cheeseburger and a bracing brace of margaritas to get your afternoon going. Jimmy Buffett himself is wont to drop into his place some nights for the music—which always gives the tourist a tingle. **Bagatelle** is a pretty old house at 115 Duval, and eating on the cool verandas gives you a real sense of being on holiday. Very nice for lunch, but dinner finds the Bag in more disarray. They will possibly be careless with your meal, perhaps be annoyed by your very presence. Once, when a patron protested some fish he felt was "funny," the kitchen said, "The kitchen does not agree with you." And that was that. The long pier at the **Ocean Key House** has both a grill and a raw bar. You can linger here, watching the boats right into the sunset hour and long beyond. Remember, don't bolt as soon as the sun disappears. The real effect takes place 20 minutes later. The **Pier House** is always fun. Good raw bar, conch fritters, conch salad, fruit plates, and the best margaritas around. They have two Key lime pies available, frozen or chilled. Choose neither, for they are not very good. However, you should feel easy here, as though eating lunch is *exactly* what you should be doing. Strangely, there are often pigeons about, not on the grass, of which there is none, but on the deck, on the railings, on empty tables, eyeing you with their pigeon eyes, as though all the world were their monument. The management has had to string wire around to interrupt their flight patterns.

Dinner

Dinner is a far more serious engagement. It costs so much more and one is usually expectant, or at the very least hopeful. One might even be dressed up.

Key West restaurants are notoriously unreliable. *The* place to be one season will be empty as a weekday church the next. Proprietors have nervous breakdowns. Chefs are shot. *Dishwashers* are shot. Two Casa Marina employees got into a fight in the kitchen recently and one shot the other dead. The disagreement concerned flatware. Something about the right way and the wrong way to organize the flatware in the dishwasher. People get bored. Their minds wander to thoughts of affairs, windsurfing, or cocaine. Restaurants are as capricious as the weather, as quickly changeable as the tides. And yet the number of pretty and ambitious restaurants here is very impressive and should be investigated with enthusiasm. All the restaurants serve Key lime pie, but they have all become somewhat wary of recommending it. Really good Key lime pie is elusive, even though it's simple enough to make—just a can of sweetened condensed milk, a few eggs, and the juice of a few tart limes. The Rooftop Cafe serves a pretty good version. The bars have begun serving Key lime shooters with enthusiasm. They taste exactly like what you've been looking for but they're more fun.

Cafe des Artistes, Square One, and Michael's all present whopping bills at the end of the evening. It used to be that entering a serious restaurant in Key West was to be like Captain Kirk opening the door to an alternate reality, like Sarasota, but more and more earnest chefs are settling here, churning out the ducks, and the lamb encrusted in something, and the shrimps stuffed with crab mousse. Rich, rich fare, important fin de siècle fare. **Cafe des Artistes** prices and pretensions are particularly jarring because it stands beside Key West's last great moldering trailer park—the old curved aluminum forms are barely visible in the darkness. Inside the restaurant there is art so bad it is frequently remarked upon. Upstairs, one can dine outside, where the waiter, in the crowded quarters, might knock over your wine. Should he knock over your wine, it is unlikely that you will be given new linens to enjoy your meal. They don't need you here, you know. **Michael's** is a steak restaurant, its large kitchen vent bringing tears to vegetarians' eyes for many blocks. Sixteen-ounce steaks, 20-ounce steaks. Rib eye. Filet mignon. Meat. The a la carte spinach is sour, the a la carte potatoes oily, the bread unremarkable. People come here to eat meat and they eat it with great seriousness in the formal parlor setting inside and under the patio umbrellas outside. What is between you and the starry night? The patio umbrella. **Square One** is chic and dressy, with many tables for two lined up against a wall of mirrors. A piano player, a cozy bar, and a smooth maître d' make for a nice presentation here. Always crowded, which makes diners feel they're in the right place. Cafe des Artistes (1007 Simonton Street, 294-7100); Michael's (532 Margaret Street, 295-1300); Square One (Duval Square, 1075 Duval, 296-4300).

The pretty restaurant in the corner of the Marquessa (600 Fleming) was called Mira when it began and was so awesomely expensive that it unnerved even the rich. You could charter a boat for a week for the cost of dinner. But then they simplified themselves somewhat, moderated the prices (if only slightly), painted over most of the trompe l'oeil, and changed the name to **Cafe Marquessa**. If you need to be reassured that you can afford to dine expensively, this is the place for you. Everything's chic here. Good-looking, dressy people. In a way it could be called "Resemblances" because everyone looks vaguely "known." This is your typical haute dining experience, slightly claustrophobic. Open 6–11 (292-1244).

Louie's Back Yard (corner Vernon and Waddell off South Street, 294-1061). In a lovely old house of the palest pink on the

Atlantic is the best-known restaurant in town, and the one with
the best views. Deck dining beneath the beautiful mahoe hibiscus tree offers spectacular arboreal prospects, particularly in
summer, when silent lightning leaps across the sky. Porches,
stars, excellent service and food. Sophisticated, pricey, and
romantic, though there's a feeling in town that people are becoming a little weary of Louie's "reputation." Even so, it remains
every traveler's culinary destination. In the winter at the shuttle terminal in Miami, everybody on the telephone is calling
here, desperate for a reservation. Pleading and begging. Lying!
("We'll be out by eight, we promise.") Lunch can be less tense,
more fun.

La-Te-Da (1125 Duval, 296-6706). La-Te-Da's progenitor was
the outrageous Larry Formica, but he's gone now, along with
his long pink Cadillac convertible. Dazzlingly representing gay
lifestyle in the 1980s, it faltered, in fact collapsed, in the wicked
'90s. All the effects were auctioned off one afternoon, one by
one, from the chaises which once supported the sassiest bodies
in town to the Art Deco sofas to the mirrors, which must have
seen a great deal, to the champagne flutes to the black-mir-
rored tables to the rose-colored linens. Brunches lasted for
hours here, diners toppled into the pool, dogs had their very
own fashion show with prizes ("The Look-Alike trophy went to
Frank Cicalese and his Chihuahua Sam. They appeared as
identical, perfectly pink Easter bunnies in identical bunny
suits, slippers, and hats carrying matching Easter baskets.
Both wore sunglasses."). Proper middle-aged ladies with their

Mexican flame vine

purses firmly in hand could ascend the steps to the Crystal Cafe and be misplaced for the season. And the shrieks from the Sunday afternoon tea dance could be heard for miles.

After going through a rather charmless transition period, La-Te-Da is back, featuring the restaurant **Godfrey's.** Godfrey's is nice because it serves breakfast from 9 to 3, with eggs Blackstone a specialty. Then there's lunch, which is also served from 9 to 3, in case you've lost track a little of what you should be doing. Dinners run around $20; duck, steaks, lamb chops. A light shrimp-and-apple curry. Candlelit outdoor dining beneath the big trees is really a nice experience.

Antonia's (615 Duval, 294-6565). One of the best, most popular restaurants in town; everyone was dismayed when it burned to the ground in the Copa's fire in the summer of 1995. Quickly rebuilt, it is as elegant as ever, and the Southern Italian menu is absolutely first-class. Everything's delicious, there are a dozen specials daily. Fine wines, no bar. Upstairs there's a room for private parties. Opens at 6.

Palm Grille (1208 Simonton Street, 296-1744) used to be in a shacky little building on Frances and Southard. Then they moved. There's no getting around it. They're here now, in a building that defies a fashionable makeover, though the rooms—there are five of them—are tasteful, with the exception of one which no one ever uses, probably because of the fake rhinoceros head on the wall. There is a beautiful Victorian mahogany bar—the decor is otherwise unexceptional. The food, however, is superb; a wonderful menu, sophisticated and innovative and extensive. Gumbos, blackened fish, Cuban pork Wellington, and a marvelous selection of appetizers which doesn't try to thwart your desire to dine well economically. Numerous desserts include mango cobbler and Key lime mousse. Excellent service.

KaRUMba (1215 Duval, 296-2644). Owned by the ever-genial owner of Mangia Mangia, a pasta café at the corner of Southard and Margaret, KaRUMba is in a little building colorfully redone on upper Duval. There is a bar on each floor, and the specialties are rum cocktails, daiquiris and *mojitos,* and rum punches. The food is zesty Caribbean; a small but interesting menu. There's also grilled fish and meats with delicious sweet potato fries. The conch, however, is way too tender for dedicated conch fans—it seems to be conch for the beginner. A portion of the outside upstairs is popular for parties. There may be a group of policemen (or at least you find out later they were policemen) or newlyweds and their entourage, with the lovely bride in a breakaway gown.

Lighthouse Cafe (917 Duval, 296-7837). The owners have been saying for some time that they want to change the name here to Il Pescatore, so perhaps it will be Il Pescatore by the time you make your dinner plans. A long, narrow outdoor dining area that ends with a little fountain. The best tables are in the very back. Prettily lit, with uncomplex Italian dishes, some great vegetarian dishes, and a spicy seafood Diablo. Wine and beer. Looks uninviting during the day, but it's closed during the day.

Banana's Cafe (1211 Duval, 294-7227). A terrific tiny French restaurant in an old house open to the street. Casual but romantic. A lone remarkable waiter takes care of everything. $25 prix fixe dinners and a number of individually priced entrees. Nice wines, no cocktails. Also open for breakfast and lunch, a nice choice on this end of Duval. Sometimes closed in summer.

Cafe Sole (1029 Southard, corner of Francis, 294-0230). First there was a little Conch house, then a little Conch barbershop, then the renowned Las Palmas, followed by the renowned Palm Grille, and now there is Cafe Sole. More latticework appears with each transition and the tables get closer together, but some good ambiences never die. There's an excellent Keys bouillabaise. Wine but no bar. Open 6–10 every day but Thursday.

La Trattoria Venezia (524 Duval, 296-1075). A stylish restaurant in the heart of town with a sleek bar, gracious service, and delicious food. The charming owners, two brothers from Sicily, keep everything running smoothly. Try to get one of the two pretty tables in the window.

Seven Fish (corner Olivia and Elizabeth, 296-2777). A tiny, tiny out-of-the-way place for people who like to eat in tiny, tiny out-of-the-way places, their satisfaction increased by the fact that they're inside and the people waiting are, as yet, not. A bistro effect in what was once a grungy Mexican restaurant not far down the street from the awesome Church of the God of Prophecy, Seven has grilled grouper (no more deemed extravagantly priced at $17), a nice selection of appetizers and salads, and fare like turkey burgers and quesadillas. A cute place with its nice wines and its Whitehead Street Pottery plates. Open 6–10. Closed Tuesdays.

Mangoes (700 Duval, 292-4606). Owned and run by the chef at Antonia's, this is a popular and marvelous place to go late and spur-of-the-moment. Lots of courtyard dining and intimate nooks, plus an upstairs side porch. Extensive menu, great variety, delicious pizzas, full bar.

Keybosh (Southard at Duval, 294-2005). Crammed between a Dunkin' Donuts and a Perfumania outlet—bad feng shui indeed—Keybosh still manages to be graceful and attractive. Sponge-painted yellow walls, Billie Holiday music, rotating exhibits of art, loft dining—it's pretty and intimate. Gazpacho, cold sesame noodles, soul mama seafood soup with coconut milk. Champagne by the glass. Women love it. For the men who love women who love it, there's rib eye. Opens at 6:30.

Finnegan's Wake (293-0222). This restaurant is unfortunately located at the corner of Grinnell and James streets, near the old abandoned City Electric plant, but location doesn't matter to the roistering customers packed inside. It is extremely noisy but has good fish and chips and leek soup and is open till 4 A.M. It is named apparently after *Finnegans Wake*, Joyce's indecipherable masterpiece about (some scholars say) the fall and resurrection of mankind. The owners perhaps placed the apostrophe in the name to lighten things up.

Cafe Blue (1202 Simonton, 296-7500). The old Full Moon Saloon resided here infamously for many years, and the new owner has renovated the place (it really was a horror) completely. But the open dining seems ill-conceived in this neighborhood, opposite a bank (at least you'll know the time and temperature) and next to the **Bottle Cap Lounge**, a very basic beer and pool joint. Areca palms and pretty lighting don't conceal the noisiness of the place. Inside it's a little quieter, but the service is just as odd, a very formal tone being adopted by the waiters: "The chef is in the midst of your dinner. Would you like another cocktail?" Spanish, Moroccan, Greek, and Turkish food. You can go back several times and learn every time that they've just run out of the paella.

Jimmy's Hickory House (at the end of Maloney Avenue on Stock Island). For a journey into less *terra cognita,* Jimmy's has tasty barbecue and is open for lunch and dinner. Great old building with a working fireplace for times of random cold snaps. Steaks and flan. A guy's sort of place, with pool tables, big-screen TV, and a bar that spent its previous life as part of a Belizean rain forest.

An inexpensive restaurant fancied by the locals is **PT's** (920 Caroline Street). Pool tables, a couple of big TVs, smokey, and dim. The fare is ribs, pot roast, meat loaf, mashed potatoes and gravy. Nothing nouvelle about this cuisine. It's pretty good actually, although it all gets to taste like meat loaf. Open till 4 A.M.

Chico's Cantina, on the way out of town at the turn to Stock Island, is a pretty good Mexican restaurant, even though they do have fake cacti. Tiny, every table seems to have a view of the rest-room door. A newly opened patio area to the rear is the location to vie for. Everything's homemade; the tamales go fast. Open 11:30 A.M. to 9:30 P.M. Beer and wine. Closed Mondays (296-4714).

There are several Cuban restaurants in town. **El Siboney** (900 Catherine Street, 296-4184) boasts little decor but is reliable. ("Well, that wasn't so bad, was it?" an out-of-towner said to her husband upon emerging one evening. "No, no," the man said. He looked a little startled. "But it wasn't very good either.") But people are increasingly "discovering" this place, even sweeping up to it by pedicab. **José's Cantina** (800 White Street, 296-4366) is better. The fluorescent-light decor has been toned down some and there are even paintings on the walls. Who *is* that lady with the rhinestone glasses? Have the shredded pork, the *plantanos* (lovely soft green bananas), the *casava* (tastes a little like delicious cold cream). You can get great *ropa vieja* and palomilla steak. Fresh sangria, too. If you have a pretty place you can take takeout *to,* you're in great luck. All Cuban restaurants close early, usually at 9, and none have decent wine. But the servings are abundant and the prices low.

BARS

Ah, the bars of Key West, some more famous than the finest homes! It's said that the three hurricanes that hit town in the early 1900s blew down all the churches but left the bars standing. They change hands, clientele, and whole personalities, and some, like so many of the structures in Key West, are even moved from one block to the next, or are burned or razed. But few are ever forgotten.

The oldest bar is **Captain Tony's Saloon** on Greene Street. Names of the famous are paint-printed on the bar stools. Martha Gellhorn's name should be on one of the stools, for she was sitting in this joint when Hemingway first saw her in December of 1936. She would become the reason for his breakup with his second wife, Pauline; his third wife (people said that together they looked like Beauty and the Beast); and the reason for his move from Key West to Cuba in 1939. The bar is quaint as the dickens (a plastic shark mouths a lady mannequin and there is junk and bric-a-brac and signs hanging everywhere), and grizzled Captain Tony himself is a cutie. He doesn't own the bar anymore. He sold it after owning it for 31 years. He was once elected mayor and is now the honorary mayor of Key West. You can buy a poster of the Captain with the adage ALL YOU NEED IN LIFE IS A TREMENDOUS SEX DRIVE AND A GREAT EGO—BRAINS DON'T MEAN A SHIT.

The bar began as the Blind Pig. The Blind Pig begat Sloppy Joe's which begat the Duval Club which begat the Oldest Bar which begat the bar that bears Tony's name today. Captain Tony's, when it was Sloppy Joe's between 1933 and 1937, was Hemingway's favorite bar. It was named for a popular hangout in Cuba and was owned by Joe Russell, whom Hemingway liked to call Josie Grunts. Their friendship began when Russell cashed a Scribner's royalty check for Hemingway, something the fine old bank down the block refused to do. Russell was a rum-runner and charterboat captain, and before he bought the *Pilar,* Hemingway did all his fishing aboard Russell's *Anita.*

But *before* Sloppy Joe's was legitimately at the Greene Street location after the repeal of Prohibition, it was a speakeasy by the Naval base. It was not one of the better bars in town. Prohibition meant absolutely nothing to Key West. There were great drinking establishments everywhere—Pena's Garden of Roses, the Tropical Club, Baby's Place, Raul's, and Delmonico's. And there was the infamous Havana-Madrid Club located on Front and Duval across from the bank, only a short distance away from Big Annie's whorehouse. It had a huge dance floor of white Cuban tile and a rambling combination of indoor and outdoor rooms where music, dancing, gambling, and fistfights went on 24 hours a day.

In 1937 the rent was raised a dollar a week at Sloppy Joe's on Greene Street, so Russell bought the building across the street on Duval—it had once been a restaurant—and in the middle of one night he and "every drunk in town" moved the bar. And here it remains, almost 55 years later, still Hemingway's "favorite" bar, still pushing the *Papa Dobles* (two and a half jiggers of white rum, juice of two limes and a grapefruit half) and now offering a taco stand, a rock and roll band, and a T-shirt kiosk. You can't miss Sloppy's—it would be like going to Freeport, Maine, and not being able to locate L.L.Bean.

In the 1940s the highway down the Keys was remembered as a mangrove tunnel with birds screeching and nesting within overhanging branches that completely covered the road in shade. But in Key West there were 48 bars on and near Duval Street, plus strip joints and tattoo parlors. Where a score of gentle shops exist now, selling suntan lotions, fabrics, and postcards, were the hard-core dives—the Midget Bar, the Conch Gardens, the Wagon Wheel, and four or five saloons known commonly as the Bucket of Blood. "The town was filled with

beautiful men," an old girl remembers. "No one took anything
seriously. Life was sweet, lighthearted, and fun." There was the
Mardi Gras, where a stripper named Dixie Lee performed with
a little white muff held demurely before her. Inside the muff
was a snarling Chihuahua that would bite any sailor's hand
that ventured near. Delmonico's boasted the only trapeze stripper in show business. Her name was Alma and she swung just
above the heads of the drinkers. The very popular Tradewinds
Restaurant and Night Club at the corner of Duval and Caroline
occupied the historical Caroline Lowe House. Caroline Lowe
was the young wife of a Confederate blockade runner during
the Civil War. Martial law was in effect, yet every time Union
troops went marching down Duval, Caroline would wave a Confederate flag from the cupola on the roof. The soldiers could
never find the flag, which she would hide in a newel-post. The
Tradewinds was torched by an arsonist in the mid-1950s and
later demolished.

Gone, gone but not forgotten! Gone are the Cave Inn and the
25¢ double martinis at the Garden of Roses. Gone are the Monster, the hot gay disco on Front Street, and the Big Fleet on
Caroline, where strippers danced for the shrimpers day and
night, and the Boca-Chica Lounge, the grisly, hard-core Navy
institution on Stock Island. Most recently down (it seems but a

Captain Tony's Saloon

weird dream) is the Full Moon, the legendary bar of the 1980s. But there remains a plentitude of bars in Key West. Drinking here is almost an obligation, and close to being an art. As in Ireland, it's not the thing to drink at home.

Bull and Whistle (224 Duval). Super-loud and rowdy. Open to Duval's parade with another bar and balcony upstairs. Cover charge for live rock and roll, which can be heard for ten blocks.

Green Parrot (400 Southard). A well-known old-time funky bar with a marvelous admonition: NO SNIVELING. You have to experience the boisterous but well-run Parrot. Pool tables, darts, pinball. Great murals on the walls, professional drinks. A Key West classic. They even have poetry readings, the most famous being their Valentine's Day Poetry Slam. Reading to this mob is not for the overly sensitive, to say nothing of the overly accomplished. Parrotphiles go for the more arcane kind of metaphor—"That woman was so beautiful, she was the clean-your-snorkel kind of gorgeous." Have another margarita.

Hog's Breath Saloon (400 Front Street). On the site of the legendary Monster, a bit difficult to access now what with the expansion of the building that now houses Planet Hollywood. Sometimes they sell more T-shirts than drinks here, and they sell a great many drinks.

Schooner Wharf (at the Key West Bight Marina down William Street). This looks seedy but it's theatrically seedy. You expected Key West to be sort of like this, and here it is. All types of hip here. Dark, dark dance floor. It's always fun to watch the *Sebago* hustle away from its mooring as the *Wolf* returns to its berth after its sunset cruise. Chaos, cool heads, zippy comments. Schooner Wharf always has great music, and the T-shirt—HANG WITH THE BIG DOGS—which shows a variety of breeds, none of them exactly purebreds, enjoying their cocktails congenially at the bar—is essential for anyone's wardrobe.

Casa Marina (Reynolds Street on the Atlantic). There is the Calabash Lounge off the lobby and the Sun-Sun outside bar. Pricey, but incomparable views. As you wander about with your

Poinciana (champagne, cranberry, cassis) across the green-sward to the dimpled shore, note the sign that earnestly alerts guests to the great untoward—MARINE LIFE EXISTS BEYOND THIS POINT.

Rumrunners (200 block Duval). Has a reggae bar, a garden bar, a piano bar, a rooftop bar, and several other bars they haven't even bothered to name. Everything rough and wild. Live music goes until midnight, after which canned music plays until 4 A.M. Pizza and burgers are served until 3 A.M. Somewhere here too is a strip joint. Lap-dancing, other vile goings-on.

Pier House (1 Duval). The **Chart Room** is dark and small and is best late at night. There is an attempt to maintain the '80s perception that important people hang out here. **Havana Docks** is up a story and over the water. Dancing and live music inside. Generous decks outside. Very popular, of course, for sunset watching, though the deafening "island" music can be overwhelming. **The Wine Gallery** is low-ceilinged and musty with important wines displayed behind glass. It has a piano player. Even martinis. Excellent martinis. For old, dedicated lovers and the grandchildren.

Louie's. On the other side of the island at the corner of Vernon and Waddell, this is the quieter, classier place to be when the sun goes down. The outdoor bar on the Atlantic is called the **Afterdeck** and is simply splendid. Open until 2 A.M.

The Conch Flyer (at the airport). Used to be open 24 hours, encouraging some of the most sinister types in Key West to drop by for a 5 A.M. nightcap. Now it's open only 21 hours a day. It's a shame. The bar is barely separated from the airstrip and it has a tropical Casablanca air. Have a beer and a chili dog for break-fast and watch the little planes drop in and out of paradise. The airport is being "improved," much to everyone's dismay, par-tially in anticipation of the opening of Cuba, a 20-minute flight away.

FISHING, DIVING, AND THE
WATERS BEYOND

The personality of a fishing guide, in terms of *your* personality, is almost as important as his expertise in leading you to fish. To find your guide you have to inquire, observe, be willing to ask questions, and know what you want. In Key West the charter boats are at Garrison Bight on Charter Boat Row. There are now, in the area of Key West, 40 full-time light-tackle boats, 40 trolling boats, 20 flats boats, and a half dozen head boats (for those who want a gnarly, plebeian experience). Do you really want to go out on a boat called *No Mercy*? Well, you can. You can even go out on *Fishbuster,* ignominious for running aground on Western Sambo Reef in 1994, chewing a path 15 feet wide and 120 feet long through the corals. Or you can damn everything and go out on the 21-foot *Tailhooker* (never apologize and never explain), captained by the same Navy commander, Michael Currie (now retired), who led the battle of Peary Court and without question won it. (See Peary Court, page 210.) Gulf Stream prices are $150 per person a day, and the boats take four to six fishermen. Light-tackle guides who go into the backcountry charge around $300–$350 a day for two fishermen.

If you cruise in your car past the Bight in the slow summer months, unhired captains or their mates often beckon to you like true hookers—making an imaginary cast, reeling an imaginary reel. Go to the Bight around 4 when the boats are returning and make your arrangements there, firsthand. This is also a good place to buy your fresh fish or be given it. The Key West Fishing Tournament runs from April 15 to November 30, with lots of prizes for dead fish and even some awards for tagging and releasing live ones. Some sportsmen enjoy using extralight tackle—6- to 15-pound test line for the big ones, sailfish and marlin. Those billfish have a tournament all their own in October. "Tight lines and screaming reels to you!" the fishing interests like to say.

If you, excellent person that you are, plan to release a fish, there are some things you should do to increase its chance of survival. Use needle-nosed pliers to pry out the hook while the fish is still in the water. Wear neoprene gloves, or, if you must use a net, use a neoprene one, which will remove less of the fish's slime, the mucous layer that protects its skin from infection. Catch and release may seem a little overrefined as a sport, but fish need a break. Be radical. Find joy on the water without contributing to making it less alive.

The **Salt Water Angler** (on Simonton, 294-3248) is an excellent source for fine flats guides.

A. D. Tinkum, on his 40-foot trimaran *Restless Native,* will sail you, and fast, just about anywhere. A half a day is $50 a person, a full six hours is $70. There's a six-person maximum on *Restless Native,* and you can charter it for your own even smaller group for $60 an hour. Tinkum is also an accomplished watercolorist, this being the perfect medium for capturing the delicacy of the backcountry. Call 295-0885 or 745-5863. The boat is at Land's End Marina.

Captain Vicki Impallomeni on her 22-foot boat *Imp II* puts together wonderful day trips into the backcountry of the Great White Heron National Wildlife Refuge. These are private, personalized trips. You can fish for grouper and snapper, snorkel, beach picnic, and bird-watch. She's an animated and knowledgeable guide, and the trips are a good deal of fun. Charters are $250 for four hours, $350 for a full 9–5 day. Telephone: 294-9731.

Captain Lynda Schuh also offers smart and sensitive trips in the *Mangrove Mistress,* a boat whose design recalls the riverboats of the 1930s. These are slow and leisurely expeditions. The boat is cozy, which means small, but the experience is delightful. Three to four is the perfect, even maximum, number of adventurers on the *Mangrove Mistress,* which will probably take you through the truly beautiful tidal creeks of the Mud Keys. Lynda can even marry you (to the person you want to marry, of course) in the backcountry. $125 for two for a half day. $200 for four. Call 294-4213.

In the **Key West Bight Marina** at the end of William Street is the *Wolf,* a great-looking (even if it is a copy) topsail schooner which offers two-hour day and sunset sails ($20 and $30) and can be chartered for parties (296-9653). Free bubbly. They also do a starlight cruise for an hour and a half on Saturday nights. Here too is *Stars and Stripes,* a replica of Dennis Conner's champ catamaran. Masterfully skippered by Don Kincaid, *Stars and Stripes* glides out among the islands, and you can have a memorable day exploring reefs and beaches 10–4 for $70 (294-7877). They provide snorkeling equipment and refreshments, you bring your own lunch. Go to the Waterfront, everyone's favorite market, close by at 201 William Street and create a picnic from their deli.

Of special note is the beautiful authentic tall ship the *Western Union.* She was built and launched in Key West in 1939, the last of her kind to lay telegraph cable in the Caribbean and the Florida Straits. She was unique even in that day, the president of the Key West Maritime Society says, "because no one in his right mind was building sailing ships for work purposes." She repaired cable until 1974, then became the flagship for Vision Quest, a program for troubled teenagers. Her homecoming was an emotional one for many tall-ship buffs who worked hard for her restoration and return. Under sail, she's stunning and gives dignity to the sunset cruise routine of free beer. Day sails noon–2, $30. Sunset sails, $35. Custom charters can also be arranged: 292-1766.

There are several glass-bottom boat tours that cost around $18 for two hours. The *Fireball* and the *Discovery* both motor out to the Sand Key light. You'll often see nothing through the glass but undifferentiated turbulence. Just as often you'll get to pitch and yaw a lot.

If you're into watching others employ the waters, there's an Offshore Power Boat Week in November. Mean machines with engines of thousands of horsepower are towed through the streets and then tear around the waters. Occasionally someone crashes and dies, which may not be the point of it all, but it makes the papers. In January there's Yachting Key West Race Week, where racers from America's Cup, the Whitbread, and other challenges compete with sails.

Best of the kayak tours of the backcountry is **Adventure Charters**, based on Stock Island. The number is 296-0362. They have half-day trips that leave from MM #20 and cost $35, but the real treat is a full day on the water for $100 with a 42-

foot powered catamaran, the *Island Fantasea,* as the mother ship. A great way to explore the mystical mazeways of the Great White Heron National Wildlife Refuge, with comfortable respites and a grilled lunch on the *Fantasea.* Twelve is the maximum number of people on this expedition.

To dive the reef contact **Reef Raiders** on Duval and Front (294-3635); **Lost Reef Adventures** at Land's End (296-9737); or the **Key West Pro Dive Shop** at 1605 N. Roosevelt Boulevard (296-3823). Contact Vicki Weeks of the **Watersport People** (296-4546), who will book you on charters to your specifications. They specialize in reef trips and dive instruction. Trips usually leave at 9 or 1:30, with about two hours of in-the-water time. Base price is $35, $65 if you rent scuba gear and wet suit. For beginning snorkelers it's a good idea to wear a "float coat" so you can make adjustments to your mask without standing on the coral. They all regularly dive the Sand Key light, Eastern and Western Dry Rocks, and Cottrell Reef, which is on the Gulf side. Remember, coral is protected. Enjoy looking at it and leave it where it lives. **Sand Key** is heavily dived—it is often crowded. **Eastern Dry Rocks** and **Rock Key**, about a mile east, are noted for their wrecks and pretty stones. This area is now a Sanctuary Preservation Area, and spearfishing, tropical-fish collecting, and fishing are prohibited. The area is marked with large yellow buoys. **Western Dry Rocks** is about three miles from the light and has the clearest waters and the most caves. It also has lobsters and sharks. **Cottrell Reef** is best for beginning snorkelers.

For scuba divers, the dive shops make trips to various deep-water wrecks as well as the **Outside Reef** or **Ten Fathom Ledge**, or they can be chartered for longer trips to **The Lakes** (a series of shallow lagoons protected by islands and reefs), the **Marquesas** (the only atoll in the Atlantic, formed not by a volcano but possibly by a prehistoric meteor), or the Tortugas, where you are getting into deep, wild water with large coral formations and big turtles and fish.

It's nice to sail out to the reef from Oceanside Marina on Stock Island. The approach from here seems far less congested, and the arrival more immediate. There are a number of very pretty sloops out here for hire, all equipped with their snorkeling gear, Evian water, and granola bars.

FORT JEFFERSON AND
THE DRY TORTUGAS

Nothing will really prepare you for seeing this gigantic fort in the middle of vast waters 70 miles from Key West. Most people fly here by seaplane. Boats can take anywhere from hours to days.

Fort Jefferson is doomed and has always been luckless. Planned by Thomas Jefferson to dominate the Gulf of Mexico with walls 50 feet high and eight feet thick and with facilities for 1,500 men and 450 cannon, construction on the largest of America's coastal forts was begun in 1846 on Garden Key, enclosing a lighthouse that had been built there in 1825. Ten years later, with fantastic supply and construction problems to overcome, its hexagonal walls had risen only a few feet above the surrounding waters. Ten years after that, with almost 16 million bricks having gone into its construction, it was found to be sinking, the weight of the walls squeezing the sand out from beneath the foundation. The 16-acre key on which it was built did not consist of solid coral, as was believed, but of sand, shell, and loose coral rock. True coral lay 80 feet below the surface.

Even the lighthouses of the Dry Tortugas had problems. The original contractor for the light, a Samuel Lincoln of Boston, drowned when his ship sank as he sailed to Garden Key with materials. The first lighthouse keeper never showed up, and a succession of keepers had an awful time coping with sooty and broken glass, plugged-up wicks, and bad oil. Too, ships that approached from a certain direction, where an iron door providing access to the lantern obscured the light, ran aground on East Key. There were so many wrecks and groundings, actually, that it was necessary to build a new lighthouse on Loggerhead Key. The lovely new lighthouse was lit in 1858 and called Dry Tortugas light, while the old lighthouse was renamed Tortugas Harbor light. By 1876 hurricanes had damaged both lighthouses so severely that they had to be rebuilt. One storm was so ferocious that a lighthouse keeper said that Loggerhead Key was covered with fish scales, "blowed clean off the fishes in the ocean and scattered everywhere."

Fort Jefferson, like its smaller, trapezoidal sister, Fort Taylor, never fired a shot at an enemy and was obsolete before it was finished. Like many monuments of far more historical times, the fort was built by slaves and prisoners and overseen by craftsmen and guards. When the slaves were freed by the Emancipation Proclamation of 1863, the Army employed prison labor—the death sentences of Union deserters were often commuted to work on Fort Jefferson, the very name of which was supposed to cause hardened criminals to shudder. Prisoners were frequently forced to carry cannonballs around all day or were hung by their thumbs.

The fort's most famous prisoner was the phlegmatic Dr. Samuel Mudd, the doctor who set the broken leg of assassin John Wilkes Booth after the murder of President Lincoln. Convicted of conspiracy and sentenced to life, Dr. Mudd spent most of his time in the scorching heat making little chests and boxes of mahogany and crabwood and writing to his wife. He missed his children and the Maryland winters, writing, "I sometimes fancy I can see the dear little creatures coming in with chattering teeth and little snotty noses, shivering with cold."

He was brought, with three other conspirators—Samuel Arnold, Michael O'Laughlin, and Edward Spangler—to the fort on the gunboat *Florida*. Shortly after his arrival in 1865, Mudd attempted to escape in a departing ship, was discovered, and was confined for a time to a desolate gun room, a dungeon which can be seen today. One of his duties was to clean old bricks. "I worked hard all day," he wrote, "and came very near finishing one brick."

In 1867 a yellow fever epidemic swept through the fort; 270 people suffered from it and 38 died, among whom were small children of the officers and the fort's physician. Mudd described a burial party in a letter. The gravediggers, of course, were prisoners. "They are allowed a drink of whiskey both before and after the burying. They move quickly and in half an hour after a patient dies, he or she is put in a coffin, nailed down, carried to a boat, rowed a mile to an adjacent island, the grave dug, covered up and the party returned, in the best humor for their drinks."

Although Mudd made no discoveries in treatment or prevention (his nostrum was that sick people should be kept quiet in dark rooms), he assiduously nursed the ill, and when cooler weather came and dispelled the disease, Army officers sent a petition to President Andrew Johnson requesting the doctor's release. Johnson seemed to want to pardon Mudd, but Congress was trying to impeach him and he didn't want to annoy them further. Mudd was not pardoned until the last day of Johnson's presidency, February 8, 1869, and was not released from the fort until March 11. He had been imprisoned for three years, seven months, and 12 days. A reporter from the *New York Herald* saw him at his Maryland farm and wrote, "In his sunken, lusterless eyes, pallid lips and cold, ashy complexion, one can read the word 'Dry Tortugas' with a terrible significance."

Victims of disease and mishap were buried on a nearby key, a mortuary island bitterly called Hospital Key. The officers had fine quarters, perhaps the most comfortable and luxurious barracks in the United States, with roofs of Vermont slate, stairways of New England granite, stately verandas, and beautifully furnished rooms, but none of this splendid display protected the men from boredom, yellow fever, brackish water (the cisterns cracked and seawater fouled the fresh), crushing heat, drought, and hurricanes. The fort was abandoned in 1874, although it was briefly reactivated by the Navy in 1898 as a coaling station. The fort's bad luck was as virulent as ever. It was here where the battleship *Maine* coaled up on her way to Cuba. It is now believed that the explosion of the ship was caused not by a Spanish mine but by the spontaneous ignition of the gunpowder stored in the magazine, gunpowder which could be carried safely enough in wooden-hulled ships but exploded in the heat of steel ships powered by coal.

Hurricanes and fires have destroyed the coaling docks, the officers' quarters, and the soldiers' barracks. The vast parade ground is empty now except for the palms and trees introduced by the National Park Service, and the hot-shot ovens which once heated cannonballs so they could more effectively destroy their wooden targets. A Rodman cannon was capable of throwing a 300-pound shell three miles. But there were never any targets to destroy. And nothing attacked Fort Jefferson but Nature herself, in the inexorable guise of wind, water, and time.

.   .   .

Many people in Key West speak of going to the Tortugas, but few ever make the trip. Good weather is necessary, and money. **Seaplanes of Key West** (294-0709) takes off from the Key West Airport and costs $159 for half a day, $275 for a full day. The flight takes 35 minutes and leaves around 8 in the morning. A half day gives you two and a half hours to snorkel, picnic, explore the fort, and "walk the wall" which encloses the moat that surrounds the fort. A full day gives you more than six hours. Seaplanes also takes campers and their gear out for $299 a person round trip. **Key West Air** (292-5201) also flies to Fort Jefferson from their floating dock at Sunset Marina on Stock Island. They use hardy bush planes from Alaska. Prices are the same.

The flight to the Tortugas is astonishing. The planes fly low over the clear and multihued water, and you will see wrecked ships gleaming in the depths of reefs. You'll see living sharks and rays and the bleached bones of whales. You'll also see the macabre scrawl of hundreds of motorboat prop scars criss-crossing the seagrass beds. And then there are miles of glittering ocean dotted by the whites of waves cresting the shoals and by the gliding shadows of birds, and then the fort rises into view in all its dark improbability. A short distance away is the lighthouse of Loggerhead Key, and close to the fort is Bush Key, where thousands of noddy and sooty terns arrive to nest each March. It's their sole nesting place in the hemisphere. The terns mate in the air at night, as angels must, and when they land on the key, egg laying begins immediately, each couple staking out a two-foot homestead in the sand. A single egg per pair is laid. After August the sootys leave the Tortugas and become strictly pelagic. The Tortugas are a major rest stop for migratory birds, and in the spring, anything—warblers, hummingbirds, thrushes, tanagers, buntings, orchids, swallows—might show up and linger for a while, but it is the sheer number of the nesting terns that is so thrilling. Bush Key is off limits to people from March through September, and all the nearby keys, with the exception (ironically enough) of Loggerhead are closed May through September during the time the sea turtles lay their eggs.

You have to really want to get to Fort Jefferson, for it is far beyond Mile Zero. People who have lived in Key West for some time and still haven't gone to the Tortugas blame it on "tropical

A SAD STORY

A wretched tale has it that a group of ornithologists from Woods Hole arrived one year to observe the terns. The birds must keep their eggs covered day and night, and the breeding couple does this in four-hour shifts. This rotation is done with clockwork precision. As an "experiment" some of the ornithologists captured a male tern and took him away. When the four-hour exchange time grew near, the female became restless. When the time arrived she began to urgently call out. Shortly she was frantic, though she never left the nest. Observers noted that the entire colony seemed to gather together in "council" and selected a replacement, a bachelor bird hovering on the fringes of the flock who took to his new duties readily, settling onto the egg and swinging right into rotation duty. Meanwhile, the captured and imprisoned tern who had been taken back to Woods Hole was banded and released. He flew over 2,000 miles from Massachusetts to the Tortugas directly to his nest. His mate refused to give up her place or even acknowledge him. He'd been gone, at this point, for over two weeks. A signal was given, observers claim, and the flock as one attacked and killed him as a deserter.

creep" of the "suddenly seven years came and went" variety. But make the effort, your visit will be memorable. You can sign up as a standby passenger on board the National Park Service supply boat that goes to the Tortugas biweekly. If they have room, they'll take you. Or you can stay out there several weeks as a volunteer, an experience many rave about. Contact the National Park Service. Professional preservationist masons are sometimes working at the fort, engaged in the Sisyphean task of replacing bricks. As they replace some, others fall out. The new bricks have to be specially ordered, as brick size has changed in the last 100-plus years and they often don't line up, as the masons say, "like they're supposed to," because everything is still in the process of settling and collapsing.

The *Yankee Freedom* is a very comfortable vessel which leaves several times a week (every day but Sunday in winter; Monday, Wednesday, Friday, and Saturday in summer) from Land's End Marina at the top of Margaret Street. You board at

7:30 in the morning and are back in Key West at 7 at night. It's a three-hour voyage and costs $79. Drinks, food, and even bunk beds are available. Campers pay $94. The very good breakfast of coffee, muffins, and fruit is free. Call 294-7009. The motor catamaran **Sunny Days** (296-5556) also makes a run to the fort on Mondays and Fridays. It's a little faster but can be a lot rougher on less-than-ideal days. She leaves at 8:30 and is back at 5:30. $85 a person.

The fort is civilized enough these days. It has a pier and a helicopter pad. It has a 15-minute slide program and, like all national monuments, informative signs on a self-guided walk. (An odd tree, imported and nurtured here, is the small dense little evergreen called St. John's bread or carob tree, whose pods were perhaps the sustaining locusts of the Bible.) There are picnic tables and grills and even rest rooms. You are not going into the heart of darkness after all. There is a sandy beach and snorkeling is excellent, both around the moat walls and on the reefs of Loggerhead Key. Camping is available here for up to 20 days, but as the ranger says, you "must provide for your own existence." There is nothing here but the beach, the bricks, the constant wind, the water, and the sky, in which the magnificent frigate-birds soar.

Walt Whitman, who never visited Key West but probably would have liked it a lot, wrote a poem to the frigate, or man-o'-war bird.

Thou born to match the gale (thou art all wings),
To cope with heaven and earth and sea and hurricane,
Thou ship of air that never furl'st thy sails,
That sport'st amid the lightning flash and thunder-cloud,
What joys! what joys were thine!

Their bones are hollow, their color black, their elegant hooked wings span seven and a half feet. They are thieves and dandies, stealing fish from other birds, never getting themselves wet. They ride the currents of the air and there you are below them, far from home, almost nowhere.

INDEX

A&B Lobster House, 150
Abel's Tackle Box, 43
Adventure Charters, 259–60
Adventure Island, 69–70
African Queen, The, 10
Afterdeck, 256
Airways Building, 168
Albury House, 214
Allen, Robert Porter, 35, 36
Alligator Reef Light, 53, 54, 81, 83
Ambassador Boat Rentals, 36–37
American Diving Headquarters, 13
American Shoal Light, 81, 83
Angler's Lounge, 77
antique shops (Key West), 189–91
Antonia's, 248
Aquarium, 158–59
Arch House, 237
Arsenic Bank, 32
Artist House, 214, 237–38
Assortment, 148
Atocha, 162–64
Audubon, John James, 35, 51–52, 165–67
Audubon House, 142, 165–67
Australian pine trees, 102

"back country," ix, 32–37, 80–81
Bagatelle, 244
Bahama Houses, 218–19
Bahama Village, 181, 182–83
Bahia Honda Bridge, 89–90, 104, 133

Bargain Books, 200
Bahia Honda Key, 87–90
Ballyhoo's Seafood Grille, 24
Banana's Cafe, 249
Benjamin Baker House, 220
Bat Tower, 118–19
Benwood wreck, 17
Bibb, The, 32
Big Coppitt, 121–22
Big Pine Coffee Shop, 97
Big Pine Fishing Lodge, 97
Big Pine Key, 95, 98–104
Big Ruby's, 241
bird rookeries, 33, 166
Biscayne Bay, ix
Bishop, Elizabeth, 193–96, 222
Bishop House, 193–94
Blue Heaven, 182, 243
Blue Heron Books, 200
Blue Heaven Bake Shop, 243
Blue Hole, 101
Blue Lagoon Motel, 235
Bobo, Cuco, 27
Boca Chica Key, 121–22
Bogart, Humphrey, 9–10
Bonefish Resort, 76
Boot Key, 72
Bordello Gallery, 189
Botanical Gardens, 216
Bottle Cap Lounge, 251
Bottle Key, 35
Brass Key, 241
Breezy Palms, 45
Bud Boats, 97
Bud 'n' Mary's, 42–43, 50
Buffett, Jimmy, 244
bugs, 59
Bull and Whistle, 175, 255

Cafe Blue, 250–51
Cafe des Artistes, 245–46
Cafe Marquessa, 246
Cafe Sole, 249
Caloosa Cove, 54
Caloosa Indians, 3, 28, 103
Camille's, 243
camping, 16, 32, 58–59, 86, 266
Cannon Patch, 18
Capitana, 18
Capote, Truman, 195
Captain Hook's Marina, 71
Capt. Slate's Atlantis Dive
    Center, 12–13
Captain Tony's, 252–55
Caputo, Philip, 193
Card Sound Bridge, 8
Caribbean Club Bar, 24
Caribbean House, 235
Caroline Street, 167–72, 174
Carysford, HMS, 18
Carysfort Reef, 17–18
Carysfort Reef Lighthouse, 81,
    82
Casa Gato (Mercedes
    Hospital), 221–23
Casa Marina, 188, 231, 255–56
Castaway, 78
Celebrities, 177
Center Court, 237
Charlotte's Story (Niedhauk),
    50
Cheeca Lodge, 42, 43–44, 56
Chesapeake Motel, 40
Chico's Cantina, 251
Christ of the Deep statue, 18,
    19
Cigar Factory, The, 149
Coast Guard Headquarters,
    144
Coconut Beach Resort, 229–30
Coconut Grove, 241
Coconuts, 23
CoCo's Cantina, 113

Coffins Patch, 69
Colours, 241
Community Swimming Pool
    (Key West), 183
Conch Flyer, 256
Conch houses, 214–19
Conch Key, 64
Conch Key Cottages, 76
Conch Reef, 18, 20
Conch Republic, 152–53
Conchs, 6
Conch Train, 154–56
Content Keys, 71
Copa (Epoch), 180–81
Copper Kettle, 27
coral, 5, 7, 11–12, 17, 18, 20
Coral Grille, 42
Coral Lagoon, 70
Cottrell Reef, 260
Courtney's Place, 237
Cowpens, 28, 36
Cracked Conch Cafe, 78
Craig Key, 54–55
Crane, Hart, 193
Crane Point Hammock, 73
Crocker Wall, 31
Crocodile's, 77
crocodiles, 33
Croissants de France, 243
cruise ships, 143–44, 188
Cuba! Cuba!, 148
Cuban Consul House, 220
Cudjoe Key, 95, 113, 115–16
Curry Hammocks, 73
Milton Curry Mansion, 168,
    236
Curtis & Sons, 148
Customs House, 144
Cypress House, 170, 240

Davis Reef, 31
Delta Shoal, 71
Deja Vu, 234–35
Dennis Pharmacy, 242

Dewey House, 229
Dildo Key Bank, 32
Dillard, Annie, 193
Divers' World, 13
diving:
    on Key Largo, 12–15
    on Key West, 260
    on Lower Keys, 111–13
    on Middle Keys, 70–76, 89–90
    in Pennecamp State Park,
        13, 16–20
    on Plantation Key, 31–32
Diving Site, 70
Dolphin Research Center, 15,
    66, 68
dolphins, 14–15, 66–68
Dolphins Plus, 14–15
Donkey Milk House, 217
Drop Anchor, 37
Dry Tortugas, ix, 11, 261,
    264–66
Duane, 31–32
Duck Key, 63, 64–65, 69
Durty Harry's, 175
Duval Square, 181
Duval Street, 174–85

Eastern Dry Rocks, 260
East Martello Museum and Art
    Gallery, 147, 209, 211–13,
    227
East Turtle Shoal, 71
East Washerwoman Shoal,
    71
Eden House, 239
Edge, 150
egrets, reddish, 58
18-mile stretch, 7
Elbow, 18
El Infante, 18
Elliott Key, ix, 50
El Patio Motel, 234
El Siboney, 251–52
Epoch, 180–81

Everglades, x, xi, 8, 29–30, 32,
    102
Eyebrow House, 214

Fantasy Dan's, 120–21
Fantasy Fest, 230
Faro Blanco, 76, 77, 84
Fast Buck Freddie's, 148,
    177
Fat Albert, 95, 116
Fat Deer Key, 73
Fausto's Food Palace, 177
Fiesta Key, 56
Finnegan's Wake, 250
Fisherman's Hospital, 75
Mel Fisher's Treasure Exhibit,
    162–64
Fish House, 24
fishing:
    in Islamorada, 43
    on Key West, 257–60
    in Marathon, 78–81, 84
Flagler, Henry, ix, 4, 59, 74,
    85, 87, 133
Flagler's, 231–32
Flamingo Crossing, 181
Fletcher, 184
Florida Bay, ix, xi, 9, 29–30,
    32–34, 36
Florida East Coast Railroad,
    ix, 4–5
Florida Keys, Museum of, 73
Florida Keys Native Nursery,
    28
Florida Keys Wild Bird Rehab
    Center, 25
Fogarty House, 175–76
Nancy Forrester's Secret
    Garden, 217
Fort Jefferson, 261–66
Fort Taylor, 188, 206–9
Fowey Rocks Light, 81, 83
French Reef, 17
From the Ruins, 149

Galleon, The, 150
Gardens Hotel, 216, 234
Geiger Key Marina, 122, 181
gingerbread houses, 219–20
Gingerbread Square Gallery, 189
glass-bottom boats, 19–20, 259
golden orb spiders, 58
Grand Vin, The, 183
Grassy Key, 65, 104
Grassy Key Dairy Bar, 68
Great White Heron National Wildlife Refuge, 96, 260
Grecian Rocks, 18
Green Parrot, 175, 255
Green Turtle Inn, 46–47
Grey, Zane, 59–60
Grove Park Cafe, 46
Gulf Stream, ix, 18

Haitian Art Company, 190
Half-Shell Raw Bar, 150, 171, 244
Hall's Diving Center, 77
Hard Rock Cafe, 175
Harriet's, 23
Harrison Gallery, 189
Harry Harris County Park, 25–26
Harry's Place, 26
Hawk's Cay Resort, 64–65
Hemingway, Ernest, 10, 156, 175, 193, 200–205, 213, 220, 223, 241, 252
Hemingway, Pauline, 201, 204, 205, 220, 252
Hemingway Days, 199
Hemingway House, 192, 200–204
Hens and Chickens Reef, 32
Herbie's, 77
Heritage House Museum, 168
Heron House, 238
herons, 33

Hersey, John, 193
Hidden Harbor, 77
Hideaway, 69, 77
Hideout, 23
Higgs Memorial Beach, 188
Hilton Hotel, 144, 233
Hog's Breath Saloon, 255
Holiday Inns, 20, 177, 228
Holiday Isle, 31, 37, 40, 42, 43
Hospital, Fisherman's, 75
Hospitality House, 143, 214
hotels, 40, 69, 97–98, 106, 119
    in Islamorada, 43–46
    on Key Largo, 20–22
    on Key West, 225–41
    in Marathon, 76–77
Housman, Jacob, 51, 52
Howard Johnson, 20, 228
hurricanes, 5, 7, 38–39, 41–42
Hyatts, 150, 233

Island Arts, 173
Impallomeni, Captain Vicki, 258
Indian Key, 48, 50–53
Indigenous Park, 216
Inner Conch Reef, 31
Innerspace Dive Shop, 112
Innkeepers Association of Key West, 237
Islamorada, 5, 41–47
Islamorada Fish Company, 47
Island Arts, 189
Island Breeze Cafe, 183
Island City House, 237
Island Needlework, 148
Islander, 44–45
Island Home, 28
Island House, 237
Island Reef, 97
Italian Fisherman, 23

Jeanna's Courthouse Deli, 189
Jencks, Frederick Tingley, 35

Jimmy's Hickory House, 251
Johnson's Grocery, 182–83
Joseph's Antiques, 191
José's Cantina, 252
Jules' Undersea Lodge, 14

Karumba, 248–49
Kelly's, 168
Kelsey's, 77
Richard Kemp House, 169–70
William Kerr House, 220
Keybosh, 250
Key Colony Beach, 63, 70
Key deer, 95, 98–99, 103
Key Largo, xi, 8–47, 81, 98
  diving, 12–15
  where to eat, 22–24
  where to stay, 20–22
Key Largo, 9–10
Key Largo Dry Rocks, 18
Key Largo Hammocks State
  Botantical Site, 9
Key Largo Key, 9
Key Largo National Marine
  Sanctuary, xi–xii, 16
Key Lime Village, 235
Key Lois, 114–15
Key Vaca, 63, 71–73
Key West, xi, 4, 6, 51, 75,
  81–82, 127–266
  art and antiques on, 189–91
  bars on, 252–56
  beaches on, 186–88
  Caroline Street, 167–72, 174
  changes and confusions on,
    132–34
  Duval Street, 174–85
  Eaton Street, 217
  fishing and diving on,
    257–60
  forts, towers, museums on,
    205–13
  graveyard on, 223–25
  guest houses on, 236–41

  history of, 134–43
  map of, 128
  newspapers of, 191–92
  oldest house on, 140, 176–77
  old town, 214–23
  salt ponds on, 187
  shopping on, 147–50
  streets of, 131–32
  sunsets, 156–58, 188
  taxis, 155
  tourist town, 143–74
  where to eat, 241–52
  where to stay, 225–41
  writers on, 192–99
Key West Air, 264
Key West Aloe, 150
Key West Aquarium, 158–59
Key West Bed-and-Breakfast,
  238–39
Key West Bight, 172, 174
Key West Bight Marina, 258–59
Key West Citizen, 191, 192
Key West Hand Prints, 149
Key West Island Books, 200
Key West Literary Seminar,
  199
Key West Pro Dive Shop, 260
Key West Sculpture Garden,
  145
Key West Visitor's Bureau, 228
Key Lime Village, 211
Knight's Key, 74, 75
Kona Kai, 22
Kudu, 148

La Concha, 177, 235–36
Lady Cyana, 31
Lakes, The, 260
Lake Surprise, 8
La Mer, 229
Land's End Village, 171, 244
Largo Lodge, 22
Lash, Joseph, 193
La-Te-Da, 240, 247–48

La Trattoria Venezia, 249
Layton, 56–57
Leathermaster, 149
Lighthouse Cafe, 249
Lighthouse Court, 241
Lighthouse Military Museum,
    83, 205–6
lighthouses, 81–83
Lignumvitae Key, 48–50, 53
Lime Tree Bay Resort, 57
Little Crawl Key, 73
Little Duck Key, 85, 87
Little John's Beachside
    Restaurant, 242
Little Palm Island, 109–10
Little Torch Sandbar, 107
Little White House, 160
Loggerhead Key, 114, 264, 266
Long Key, 57–60
Long Key Recreation Area,
    57–58
Long Key Viaduct, 64
Looe Key, 95, 111–13
Looe Key Reef Resort, 98,
    112–13
Lorelei, 46
Lost Reef Adventures, 260
Louie's, 256
Louie's Back Yard, 188, 246–47
Lowe House, 215
Lower Keys, 93–126
    map of, 94
Lower Matecumbe Key, 5,
    53–54, 56–57, 81, 83, 104
Lucky Street Gallery, 189
Lurie, Allison, 193

McGuane, Tom, 193
Maine, 134, 142, 205, 263
Makiki, 190
Mallory Square, 124, 143–44,
    149, 153, 156, 157, 214
manatees, 12, 28, 33, 67
manchineel trees, 105

Mangoes, 243–44, 250
Mangrove Mama's, 97, 116
Manny and Isa's, 47
Man of War Key, 32
maps:
    Key West, 128
    Lower Keys, 94
    Middle Keys, 62
    Upper Keys, 2
Marathon, 70–72, 73, 74–81, 84
    fishing, 78–81, 84
    where to eat, 77–78
    where to stay, 76–77
Marathon Guides Association,
    43
Margaritaville Cafe, 244
Marine Hospital, U.S., 159
Marine Patrol, 12
Marker 88, 28–29
Marquesas, 260
Marquessa Hotel, The, 233–34
Marsh Sneaker, 32
Martí, José, 178
Martin's, 239
Merlinn, 238
Merrill, James, 193
Michael's, 245–46
Middle Keys, 61–91
    history of, 63–64
    map of, 62
mile markers, ix
Peggy Mills Garden, 216
missiles, 117, 122
Missouri Key, 87
Molasses Reef, 7–8, 17
monkeys, 114–15
Monroe County Library, 200
Moorings, The, 45
Mosquito Coast, 181
mosquitos, 3, 59, 101
Mrs. Mac's Kitchen, 23
Mudd, Samuel, 262–63
museums, 73, 83, 147, 168,
    205–13

Nannie MixSells, 148
National Key Deer Refuge, 97, 100–101
National Marine Sanctuary, xi–xii, 16, 111–12, 117
Native Material, 149
Naughty and Nice Gag Shop, 29
Nest Key, 32
Newfound Boat Rentals, 97
newspapers, 191–92
Niedhauk, Russel and Charlotte, 49–50
Noah's Ark, 148
No Name Key, 104–6
No Name Pub, 106

Oasis, 241
Ocean Divers, 13–14
Ocean Key House, 233, 244
Oceania Motel, 46
Oceanside Marina, 123
Oceanside Motel, 45
Ohio Key, 87
Old City Hall, 151–52
Old Town, 214–23
Old Wooden Bridge Fishing Camp, 105–6
ospreys, 95–96
Outer Conch Reef, 31
Outside Reef, 260

Palm Grille, 248
Papa Joe's, 47
Papio, Stanley, 212
Parmer's Place, 98, 106–7
Patricks, 23
George Patterson House, 169
Richard Peacon House, 217–18
Peary Court, 210–11
pelicans, 55
Pennecamp, John, 16
John Pennecamp Coral Reef State Park, 5, 10–12, 13, 15–20

pepper trees, 102
Pepe's Cafe, 244
Perkins and Son, 190
Perky, R. C., 118–19
Perrine, Henry, 52–53
Pier House, 124, 150, 232–33, 244–45, 256
Pigeon House, 168
Pigeon Key, 86
Planet Hollywood, 147
Plantation Key, 28–32
Plantation Yacht Harbor Resort, 29–30
Planter, 25
poisonwood trees, 102
Ponce de León, Juan, 3, 105
Popp's, 22
Joseph Porter House, 176
PT's, 251
punk trees, 102

Quay, The, 77–78
Quiescence, 13

Rabbit Key, 32
Rader, Dotson, 198
Raimondo's, 116
Rain Barrel, 31
Rainbow Bend Fishing Resort, 69
Ramrod Key, 111–16
Reach, 229, 232
Red Barn Theatre, 176
Reef Divers, 112–13
Reef Raiders, 260
Reef Relief, 14
Reflections Nature Tours, 104
restaurants, 26, 30, 40, 69, 97, 110, 116
  in Islamorada, 44, 46–47
  on Key Largo, 22–24
  on Key West, 143, 168, 241–52
  in Marathon, 77–78

Restless Native, 230
Rick's Cafe, 175
Riggs Wildlife Refuge, 187
Ripley's Believe It or Not
 Odditorium, 180
Robbie's, 50
George Roberts House, 220
Rock Key, 260
Rockland Key, 122–23
Rock Reef, 22
Rooftop Cafe, 143, 244
roseate spoonbills, 34, 35–36
Rumrunners, 175, 256

Saddlebunch Keys, 121
St. Paul's Church, 177
salt ponds, 187
Saltwater Angler, 149–50, 258
Sam's Treasure Chest, 190–91
San Carlos, 178–79
Sand Key, 260
Sand Key Light, 81, 82, 260
Sands Key, ix
San Jose, 19, 20
San Jose y las Animas, 18
San Pedro, 53
sapodillas, 104
Schooner Wharf, 255
scuba diving, *see* diving
Schuh, Capt. Lynda, 258
Sea Cloud Orchids, 122
Sea Dwellers, 13
Seaplanes of Key West, 264
Sea Shell Motel, 234
Seasports Dive Center, 171
Sea Store, 190
Seven Fish, 250
Seven-Mile Bridge, 75, 85–87,
 104, 133
7-Mile Grille, 78
Shark Key, 122
sharks, 90–91
Shell Key, 48
Shell Man, 12

Shell Warehouse, 149
Sheraton, 21
shrimping, 173
Shucker's, 78
Side Door Lounge, 75
Sign of Sandford, 149
Simonton Court, 239
SkyDive Key West, 121
Sloppy Joe's, 175, 201, 252–53
Smathers Beach, 187
Snake Creek Bridge, 37
snakes, 107–8
Snapper's Waterfront Saloon,
 23
Snooks, 23
Solares Hill, 191–92
Sombrero Beach, 72
Sombrero Light, 71, 81, 83
Sombrero Reef, 71, 82–83
South Beach, 184, 242
Southern Cross Hotel, 176
Southernmost House, 185, 229
Southernmost Point, 126,
 185–86
Southernmost Point Guest
 House, 240
Spanish Harbor Keys, 90
spearfishing, 70
sponges, 145–47
Square One, 181, 245, 246
Stars and Stripes, 259
Stevens, Wallace, 129, 193
Stock Island, 123–26, 216, 264
Stoneledge, 22
Strand, 179–80
Sugarloaf Club, 97–98
Sugarloaf Key, 90, 117–23
Sugarloaf Lodge, 98, 119–20
Summerland Key, 90, 113
Sunny Days, 266
sunsets, 23, 72, 156–58
Sweet Mischief, 149
Swept Away, 148
Square One, 245, 246

Tavernier, 25–27
Tavernier Hotel, 26
Tavernier Towne, 27
Ten Fathom Ledge, 260
Tennessee Reef, 57
Thai Cuisine, 244
Theater of the Sea, 39–40, 42
Thunderbolt, 71
To Have and Have Not
    (Hemingway), 204
Top, The, 177
Torch Keys, 106–10
Tortugas, *see* Dry Tortugas
Trattoria, 149
treasure, sunken, 162–64
Treasure Village, 31
trees, bad, 102, 105
tree snails, 48
Truman, Harry S., 160
Truman Annex, 159, 161–62,
    189
Turtle Kraals, 171–72
turtles, green, 47, 170–72

Underseas Inc., 112
Upper Keys, 1–60
    history of, 3–8
    map of, 2
Upper Matecumbe Key, 41–47

Valladares & Son, 175
Valhalla Beach Motel, 69
Vernon's Iron Skillet, 75
Village Art, 189–90
von Cosel, Carl, 226–27

Walkway of History, 145, 147
Waterfront market, 230
Waterfront Playhouse, 145
Watersport People, 260

Jack Watson Nature Trail,
    103
Watson's Hammock, 101, 103
Wellwood, 7–8
Western Dry Rocks, 260
Western Union, 23
West Martello Tower, 188, 213
West Summerland Key, 90
West Turtle Shoal, 71
Whale Harbor Restaurant and
    Marina, 40, 42, 43
White Banks Dry Rocks, 17
Whitehead Street Pottery, 190
White Street Pier, 188
Wilbur, Richard, 193
Wildlife Rescue of the Florida
    Keys, 216–17
Williams, Tennessee, 120, 193,
    196–99
Tennessee Williams House,
    196–99
Winchester, HMS, 5, 49
Windley Key, 37–41
Windley Key Fossil Reel State
    Geologic Site, 39
Winner-Sombrero Docks, 84
Wolf, 258
Woody's, 46
World Class Angler, 84
World Down Under, 31
World Wide Sportsman, 84
wrecks, 5, 81–83
Writers' Walk, 199
Wynken, Blynken and Nod
    Trailer Park, 21

Yankee Freedom (Ft. Jefferson
    Ferry), 171, 265

Ziggie's Conch, 46

About the Author

JOY WILLIAMS is a novelist, short-story writer, and essayist. In 1993 she received the Strauss Living Award from the American Academy of Arts and Letters.

About the Artist

ROBERT CARAWAN is a native-born Key West Conch. His etchings and serigraphs may be seen at the Gingerbread Square Gallery on Duval Street.